A Guide to Image Processing
and Picture Management

A GUIDE TO
IMAGE PROCESSING
AND
PICTURE MANAGEMENT

A. E. CAWKELL

Gower

Published by
Gower Publishing Limited
Gower House
Croft Road
Aldershot
Hampshire GU11 3HR
England

Gower
Old Post Road
Brookfield
Vermont 05036
USA

ISBN 0–566–07546–6

Typeset in Times New Roman by Evans Computers (Cheddleton) Ltd and printed in Great Britain by Cambridge University Press.

TABLE OF CONTENTS

PREFACE

This book attempts to match the astonishing progress, increasing complexity, unpleasant jargon and attraction of rapidly falling costs of electronic picture or "image" management, with the steadily increasing numbers of people trying to understand what it's all about.

At present the "market" addressed by the book mainly consists of people working in libraries, museums and art galleries. The related but vaguer "multimedia market" is much wider. The increasing use of various kinds of compact disc is bringing electronically produced pictures to a large audience.

This book assumes that the reader is "an informed layman". The minimum amount of jargon and mystique is used and a large glossary and many references are included. The rate of change in "imaging" is probably faster than in any other part of Information Technology so an effort has been made to include the very latest developments.

There is a mismatch between the ebullience of the sales media and potential users. Users seem to be visualised as computer buffs able to decide which hardware and software is required, and well able to apply it to their project. They are not. Most people intending to enter the fray would be unwise to do so without applying the *caveat emptor* rule. Indexing is one of the most important but least mentioned aspects. How can you expect to retrieve a picture from a collection of any size without it being suitably indexed? "Indexing" is not considered to be a topic likely to enhance the general bezazz of picture systems; accordingly it is discussed here at some length.

The value of convenient picture management has been appreciated for many years, although technically out of sight. In Vannevar Bush's (1945) Memex machine there would be "a translucent screen on which material could be projected for convenient reading". A user could "build a trail with items in adjacent viewing positions", and use "associative indexing... whereby any item would be caused at will to select immediately and automatically another". Bush had certainly included provision for image storage and display in the Memex. He talks about the use of microfilm and the need for compression.

The first people to implement some of Bush's ideas were the team at Xerox who demonstrated their STAR computer at Palo Alto in 1978. The STAR included WYSIWYG, ikons, laser printing and other innovations.

The leading edge cannot be visualised without a degree of technical language. In 1993 a company called Adaptive Solutions introduced its Connected Network of Adaptive Processors (CNAPS) chip. These chips can successfully move a 7 x 7 frame of pixels over every pixel in a 512 x 512 pixel picture and then perform the necessary millions of multiplications and additions to modify all the pixels in each underlying area in 9.55 milliseconds. This kind of operational speed – achievable using a microcomputer – would not have been considered possible on the most powerful mainframe available a few years ago.

But such achievements, remarkable as they are, are not described in detail. It is much more difficult to harness this power for tasks like the automatic machine-recognition of pictures in response to an appropriate question. But it is useful to possess some knowledge of the state of technology on order to avoid the purchase of equipment likely to be soon replaced by something much better and cheaper. At the same time the temptation to buy all kinds of attractive bells and whistles of no useable value must be resisted.

It is to be hoped that the style and contents will help the reader to more easily understand what the world of electronically reproduced pictures is all about.

A.E.Cawkell, Iver Heath, 1993.

CHAPTER 1

INTRODUCTION

IMAGE
>Representation or likeness of a person
>or thing.
>>Dictionary

GRAPHIC ARTS
>Any of the fine or applied visual arts based
>on drawing or the use of line.
>>Dictionary

PICTURE
>I mean by a picture a beautiful dream of
>something that never was, never will be...
>>Burne-Jones c.1870

The dictionary (Collins English Dictionary. 3rd Ed.), in the first of 17 alternative meanings, defines an image as above. Burne-Jones's romantic description of a picture is also quoted above. These definitions are how I visualise the difference between images and pictures in this book – although pictures are considered electronically rather then romantically. The distinction between Graphics and Graphic Arts is blurred; in the electronic graphics field, Graphics is particularly associated with the manipulation and display of images.

The dictionary finds it hard to put a finger on "images", and a recent comprehensive report (Clark, 1992) has the same problem with electronic images. However Clark is concerned with commercial markets for hardware and software so picture collection management – the main thrust of this book – is virtually excluded by Clark. Nor is this book concerned with "Document Image Processing" – meaning "the management of office document images of business paperwork to ease filing, storage, and retrieval problems".

I find it equally hard to decide when to use the words "image" or "picture", but I do not apologise for inconsistencies in this book. Sometimes the specificity of "picture" seems more appropriate so that's when I use it,

If all the topics covered in 1993 IT technical publications were ordered by frequency of appearance, images, preferably in colour, would probably be at the top. Imaging hardware and software are still considered to be interesting enough, or fashionable enough to feature in research proposals either on their own or as part of Multimedia, Virtual Reality, or Picture Recognition systems.

Advances in technology have made it possible to transmit, store, process, and reproduce the large amount of data contained in pictures reasonably quickly at an acceptable cost for most applications. Consequently numerous advertisements and articles are appearing in the expectation of enlarging the market.

Originally, virtually all picture indexing work was in the area of "labelling-with-words".   The notion that the automatic recognition of graphic elements might be feasible had to await the arrival of recognition software. This, in turn, has had to await the arrival of hardware with increased processing power at a lower cost.

Edwin Smura, reviewing the work done at Xerox in the seventies, noted that it was intended that records should include the provision for "captured graphic and lexical data" (Smura, 1983).   In the seventies and early eighties the question of retrieving pictures from a collection usually meant retrieving word-records stored in a computer describing the original pictures kept elsewhere because the technology of the time did not permit affordable good quality displayed electronic representations of pictures.

Picture collection databases have been around for some years but the addition to them of high quality representations of the indexed pictures is more recent.   Picture and art databases are now being used to provide convenient access to collections particularly when they are widely distributed or the originals are inaccessible.   They are also being used in the new technologies of Multimedia and Virtual Reality.

The possiblities of using computers to index visual art and artefacts prompted several projects in 1979/1980 including the Detroit Art System, the Art & Architecture Thesaurus (AAT), the Public Archives of Canada and the Yale Index to British photography.   A major objective was the standardisation of descriptive terms.   Two conferences were held at Ottawa and at the Smithsonian, Washington, in an attempt to introduce term standardisation.   The Smithsonian and the Museum of Natural History jointly developed a three-level system for indexing art collections (Fink, 1980).

In the well-known Intrex information system testbed at MIT, a CARD microfiche retrieval system made by Image Systems was used with a Tektronix storage oscilloscope for viewing the fiche, but no details are available about the indexing method used.

The problem of indexing pictures was recognised by Ohlgren (1980) who said:- "For example in a Breughel painting, does one catalog every person, every item of clothing, every action, every relation between persons in the painting, every tree, window etc?   If not, on what basis does one decide what to catalog?"   Ohlgren had identified the problem which has plagued picture indexing ever since.

In 1985 Nagy (Nagy, 1985) conducted a survey of the image database literature and concluded that "the development of image database systems represents a huge amount of thought and effort, yet few, if any, are approaching the critical size necessary for operational application".

Since 1985, and more particularly in the period 1990 to 1993, advances in technology and falling costs have encouraged the development of software packages for storing and viewing pictures on a micro-computer, but the means of finding what you have stored has received little attention until very recently.

It has been noted (Cawkell 1992b) that the people involved in "Image Processing and Recognition" – that is those interested in changing, enhancing, and recognising images – and the "Image classification and retrieval" people – that is those interested in retrieving images, usually pictures from collections – do not appear to be interested in each other's work.

The processing people often accumulate large numbers of images but they seem to be unaware that they must be indexed if they are to be found again. It is quite understandable that the sellers of commercially available software packages and the people who review them in computer journals never mention the indexing problem. Even if they have ever heard of it, indexing has a boring image incompatible with the image of a hyped-up technology and is unlikely to clinch a sale.

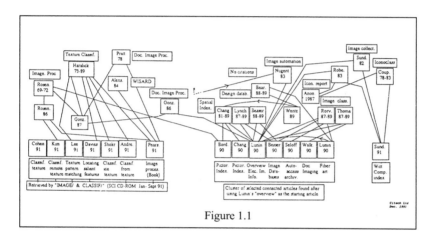

Figure 1.1

Figure 1.1 shows the result of a short investigation into the inter-citing behaviour of two groups – the image processors on the left and the information scientists on the right. Each name/date represents an article and the adjacent rectangle shows its subject. Inter-connecting lines representing a reference from the article indicated to an earlier article. There is almost no group inter-citing. A lengthier investigation would be unlikely to show much difference in the self-contained appearance of the groups.

The indexing people – librarians and information scientists do not yet seem to have realised that picture collections badly need their attention.

The references in the publication of a "Processing person" and an "Information Scientist" person, both writing about various aspects of imaging, show the differing slants accorded to the topic.

The publications which are most cited by Gonzalez (1987) are:-

Number of references to articles in each journal:-
         13 CVGIP (Computer Vision Graphics and Image Processing).
         9   IEEE Trans. Patt. Anal. & Machine Intell.
         7   Pattern Recognition.

And those cited by Lunin (1990) are:-

Number of references to articles in each journal:-
         14 Advanced Imaging (mainly news items)
         6   Proc. 9th Conf. Opt. Info. Syst. 1989
         6   Art Librarians J.
         5   Proc. Amer. Soc. Information Science

The effects of media upon pictures

There is one special case of great interest to the electronic publishing industry and that is how to deal with pictures on pages.

Documents which contain illustrations and "figures" on pages can be delivered by printing many copies (for example: journals), or by sending a photocopy, or, since about 1980, by sending a facsimile. Photocopies or fax do not handle halftones very well; special types of these machines can be used for sending rather expensive and not very good images in colour.

The scale of production operations for a journal publisher may well justify electronic composition methods where pages, including pages containing images, may exist in digitized form at some stage of production.

The constraints against composing and distributing pages in digitized form (already overcome, at least for composition, in very large scale operations such as newspaper publishing) have been the inadequate quality of digitized images, storing a very large volume of data until needed, telecommunicating it at an acceptable speed and cost, and storing and reproducing it at the receiving end.

Ultimately the printed page may become obsolete (by the year 2100?). Meanwhile "document delivery services" usually means the delivery of pages in electronic form converted to that form from the printed version.

One method of delivery is CD-ROM publishing, as with the ADONIS system. The discs have the capacity to accept a large number of articles including images (Stern 1988).

Storage and telecommunications have made enormous strides but still constrain document-with-images delivery systems. With one of the latest 18 Kbit/second error-correcting modems operating at a realistic 16 Kbits/second, and a currently achievable 5:1 compression ratio it takes about 30 seconds to send a printed page with a quarter-page half-tone illustration (4.8 Mbits or 0.6 Mbytes) over the PSTN. About 67 pages would fill a 40 Mbyte disc in 33 minutes.

When the Integrated Services Digital Network and compression devices providing ratios of 25:1 become cheap and widely available, perhaps in 5 years time, the same page would take about 1.5 seconds to send and 40 Mbytes would hold about 335 pages.

The amount of data from pages with illustrations can be greatly reduced by appropriate coding. Text is encoded (as is done when using any WP system) by generating ASCII or a similar code, and only illustrations and figures are encoded at, say, the 300 x 300 dots per inch needed to provide adequate resolution. The wasteful alternative is to code the whole page at 300 dots/inch which is actually needed only for that part of it containing an illustration.

There are three different cases of digitizing pages with illustrations – author composition of the page, digitization of an already composed page, and digitization of an already printed page.

If the author is prepared to learn the codes and nuances of standardized SGML or ODA, he or she can designate parts of the document for appropriate coding. Systems are commercially available, such as Interlink's Active Document Systems, for tagging page components, usually called Object Linking and Embedding (OLE, see glossary).

If pages are already composed and available in machine-readable form – say on the disc of a WP system or on CD-ROM – then each page may be presented on a screen so that an operator can frame and designate areas for appropriate coding.

Nagy (1991) has described a system for automatically identifying blocks of information such as title, abstract, footnote, text segment, illustration etc., in a family of journals with standardised formats (in this case IEEE journals) on CD-ROM.

When viewing a retrieved article, labelled page blocks, e.g. "abstract", for example, may be selected, expanded, and read.

Means and Ends

Image functions and operations may be conveniently divided into "Means" (the technology), top left of Figure 1.2 and "Ends" (Presentation), bottom right.

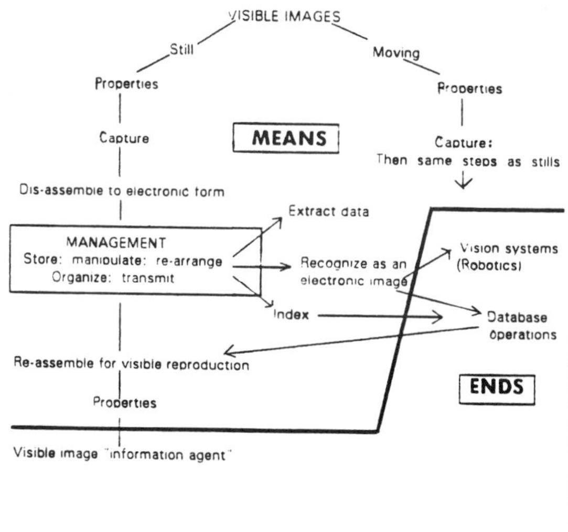

Figure 1.2 Means and Ends

An image, whether still or moving, is captured by a scanner, television camera etc., – devices designed to accommodate its properties such as resolution, brightness, colour, etc. It is then subjected to operations called "management" in the

Figure which include, store, transmit, and arrange for the required kind of presentation.

The "Ends" are the objectives set by the user of the system – that is either to   get the image appropriately presented for viewing or control purposes in a vision machine (robotics), or as a picture retrieved from a database or made visible via an agent such as videodisc, film, disc player etc., to be viewed on a display or printed.

This book is concerned with both Means and Ends.

CHAPTER 2

IMAGE SOURCES AND FORMATS

Introduction

Electronic images are derived from sources such as:-

- Broadcast television frames consisting of several hundred scanning lines.

- Television frames directly received from TV cameras or recorders.

- A device such as a laservision player, tape, CD-ROM or later CD derivative already containing stored images.

- An electronic stills camera (e.g. the Cannon Ion with PC board and software) which sends images to disc.

- A scanner which converts printed page data into electrical form.

- Drawn or "painted" images synthesised with the aid of computer software.

Electronic images are reproduced by means of:-

- Cathode Ray Tubes or other forms of display capable of changing electrical into visual representations.

- Printers able to change an electrical into a print-on-paper representation.

Images may be in "bi-level" form (composed of black-and-white elements), in half-tones (commonly known as "grey-scale" – that is in degrees of greyness from white to black) – or in colour.

They are stored and reproduced on a CRT usually as a "bit-map" - formed from pixels (picture elements), distributed along a series of closely-spaced scanning lines called a "raster", made visible by momentarily turning on the beam which is normally invisible. Printed images are reproduced as dot-structures formed by making marks on paper.

Analogue and digital data

Television is based mainly on analogue systems. Some types of TV cameras produce digital output (but not for public TV). Digital computers are mainly digital except at the display end. The data is usually digital up to the CRT connection point where it must be converted back to an analogue value to be visually acceptable when displayed.

Consequently Analogue/Digital and Digital/Analogue converters (see Glossary) are hardware devices featured in many systems. Say, for example, a smooth waveform at a level of 5.82 volts was derived from a "pale grey" image element in a picture. When applied to the display of a digital computer it would be digitized at the input by an A/D converter to change it to an 8-bit number.

After being stored in the machine and just before being applied to the CRT, it must be converted back to 5.82 volts by a D/A converter so that a pixel is displayed to produce the sensation of "pale grey" in the person who is looking at it.

Colour systems require three D/A converters in order to convert digital levels representing values of Red, Green, and Blue, to the analogue values needed to produce the sensation of a particular colour when the CRT's RGB beams strike a triad element on the screen.

Image resolution

Pixels must be very small and closely spaced so that the smallest characters or portions of graphics which are to be reproduced appear to be formed from solid lines. A sense of scale can be visualised in terms of a 4 point character which is about 1.4 mms high.

If the pixel density is 200 per square inch, the vertical part of a four point character (about the smallest normally reproduced on a printed page) would contain about 11 pixels) and would appear to be solid.

The relative effect on the smoothness of a diagonal line at different resolutions when displayed on a cathode ray tube is shown in Figure 2.1. The effect is most noticeable at certain angles and may be particularly noticeable at the edges of circular objects in pictures. Line (b) is typical of the effect on a good monitor and is barely noticeable at normal viewing distances

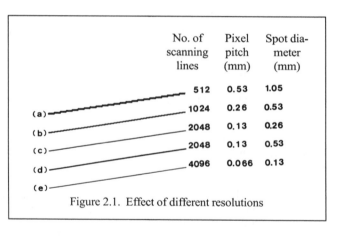

	No. of scanning lines	Pixel pitch (mm)	Spot diameter (mm)
(a)	512	0.53	1.05
(b)	1024	0.26	0.53
(c)	2048	0.13	0.26
(d)	2048	0.13	0.53
(e)	4096	0.066	0.13

Figure 2.1. Effect of different resolutions

Resolution considerations are discussed in greater detail in Chapter Three.

Compression

Compression plays an important part in reducing the enormous number of bits forming high quality images, thereby reducing excessive storage, transmission, and other requirements, as discussed in a separate chapter.

Compression developments have accelerated with the arrival of halftones, colour, and higher resolution, all of which increase the incentive to use it.

Scanners

A scanner consists of a scanning head containing a row of sensors, and the means of moving an illuminated page, relative to the head, in very small steps. The head remains over a strip of the page long enough for each sensor to generate a charge proportional to the incident light and for the electrical data from the row of sensors to be streamed out. The head then moves on to the next strip, and the process is repeated until the whole page is scanned.

A typical head is 8.5" long with sensors spaced at 300 per inch along it. A whole page is scanned in a few seconds. The electrical data is digitized at two levels for "bi-level" images and usually at 256 levels for halftone images.

Scanning systems

Inexpensive scanning systems were developed by the Japanese following the burst of Desktop Publishing system activity in 1985. For some years several companies in the United States, with Reticon the leader, have manufactured the most frequently used sensor, the Charge Coupled Device (CCD). It consists of a row of semiconductor elements within the scanner. The Japanese are the leaders for mass-produced inexpensive CCDs.

The scanning resolution depends on the size and spacing of the CCD elements. CCD maximum scanning speed depends on the maximum rate at which a charge is built up in response to incident light as each page-strip is presented, on the rate at which the charges can be read out, and on the illumination intensity.

Currently available CCDs can be read out at a frequency of 20 MHz so that with sensors arranged for 300 pixels per inch resolution, the 8.7 million black/white pixels generated from an A4 page can be handled in much less than a second. Sensor speed is not a constraint. Processing in other parts of the system is slower.

When scanners were developed for the DTP market in 1985/1986 the software provided with them performed certain basic functions considered at the time to be impressive.

For example, the software provided to run the Microtek MS-300A scanner on an Apple Macintosh controlled the scanning action and compression and decompression, enabled the user to select "line art" or "halftone" modes and to set brightness and contrast levels, and saved the scanned image file in several alternative formats compatible with different DTP software.

Many types of scanner/copiers are now available. The simplest are small hand-held devices which can be manually swept across a part of a page of up to about four inches in width. The copier is held over a strip of the page and swept slowly along it. An on-paper copy of the strip emerges as the sweep progresses.

"Flat bed" scanners embody a glass plate on which a page (or the two pages of an open book) is laid, and a sensor strip below the glass moves up the page(s). With "roller fed" scanners a fed-in page is moved across a fixed sensor strip.

More expensive high speed machines are available for dealing with high-volume document scanning, but page mechanical handling continues to be a speed constraint, particularly for bound volumes, single paper in assorted sizes, or pages with crinkled or bent edges.

To assist in the problem of scanning easily-damaged rare books, the British Library and Optronics (Cambridge, UK) collaborated to produce a commercially available CCD scanner.

The scanning CCD strip and a light source free of ultra-violet radiation are mounted behind a glass plate on the side of a V-shaped book-size box. The box is lowered just to touch the page of a book which is supported on a cradle enabling it to be opened at 80 degrees to match the V of the box. The cradle is rotatable so that the opposite page may be scanned.

Two-level and multi-level scanning; halftones

Black and white reproduction is adequate for text or line drawings, but halftones are needed for illustrations. The eye can perceive quite small changes in the "grey scale" or in "grey levels" – that is in tonal levels in the range white through to black.

For electronically reproduced images, 256 levels are considered satisfactory – the grey level of each pixel is the degree of brightness corresponding to a digitized value. Thus on a scale 1 to 255, grey level 201 would be represented as the 8-bit number 11001001.

Recent developments in scanners and scanning software are closely associated with printers and reproduction quality. For the moment I shall confine this discussion mainly to scanners, returning to the input-output inter-dependency later.

In two-level scanning, arrangements are made for each sensor to generate an impulse when the incident reflected light exceeds a fixed value, representing a "white" pixel, or no impulse when the light is below that value, representing a "black" pixel.

This method is used for pages containing text (in circumstances requiring that the text be scanned to provide a page image rather than being coded) and/or for "line art" such as diagrams or sketches.

For halftone digitization, the continuous voltage level generated by a sensor in proportion to the intensity of the incident light is quantized into a series of fixed values representing a "grey-scale" as described above.

An 8-bit 256-level system increases the number of bits required to represent a 300 pixels/inch black and white picture on a 19" screen from 16.4 to 131 Mbits, so storage requirements become 2.05 and 16.4 Mbytes respectively. See Table 3.1 in the next Chapter.

The simple method where the output from each sensor is quantized into fixed levels for digital coding, is called "fixed level thresholding". It has its limitations because it creates arbitrary edges to half-tone areas which were not present in the original.

Various techniques have been used to avoid this effect including "average thresholding", which offers some improvement. Another limitation is the creation of artefacts ("aliasing") such as moire fringes which may be reproduced in simpler systems. They may be suppressed by special electronics.

Inexpensive widely-used laser printers can print only black or white pixels of a not very small fixed size so a grey-scale cannot be directly reproduced;   software is often supplied with scanners to generate dot patterns which simulate halftones when printed as discussed in the next chapter.

Television images

Television systems provide a widely available source of electronic images.   In order to buy and use equipment for capturing TV images an understanding of TV is needed.

For the first hundred years or so of electrical communication systems, speech was conveyed along wires as an *analogue* signal – a voltage from a microphone varying in proportion to the applied sound pressure level.   The signals transmitted when the first electronic television systems arrived were also analogue.

Television camera tubes house a plate upon which are mount-ed rows of very small photo-electric elements capable of generating a voltage proportional to the incident light.   Light from the image is focused on to the plate which is scanned, row by row, by an electron beam.

The element voltages are read off in a continuous stream and the scanning action creates a pattern of closely spaced lines of voltages forming a complete "field" representing a "snapshot" of the image.   The process keeps repeating so that the camera tube outputs an analogue (continuously variable) voltage, field after field.

A video "frame" is formed from two "interlaced fields", each of several hundred lines, lines from the second field falling between lines from the first – a way of reducing both flicker and transmission channel bandwidth. Synchronising pulses are added.

At the receiver, the scanning electron beam of a cathode ray tube, running at approximately the same rate as the beam in a camera, is pulled into exact line, field, and frame synchronism by received synch-ronising impulses.   The video data (line modulation) is applied to the CRT beam to vary the brightness.

These "all analogue" principles were used in the EMI system adopted when the BBC inaugurated the first electronic public TV service in the thirties, having rejected Baird's alternative.

NTSC colour television was developed from RS170 analogue TV – a format basically as just described – in the US. A colour TV camera amounts to three cameras viewing the image through Red, Green, and Blue (RGB) filters and outputting three signals and a luminance (average brightness) signal called the "Y" signal.

The RGB signals are combined in a special way as "chrominance" signals to represent the hue and saturation values of each minute area of the image as these areas are successively scanned.

This data, with a colour-burst reference signal added for decoding at the receiver, together with Y signals, comprises a spectrum of broadcast television signals occupying, in the NTSC case, a band 4.25 MHz wide. These elaborate arrangements were implemented so that existing black and white TV sets, by ignoring the chrominance and colour burst signals, could reproduce black and white pictures.

A colour receiver decodes the composite chrominance/luminance data into the RGB components which are applied to the three electron beams of a colour CRT. The beams produce a pixel by illuminating a three-element dot on the screen. The dot is formed from three chemicals which glow red, green, or blue with an intensity in proportion to beam currents when struck by the scanning RGB beams. The combined glow produces a perceived single colour pixel.

There are three major TV systems in the world – NTSC in North America, some parts of South America, and in Japan and the Philippines, SECAM in France, Eastern Europe, and the USSR, and PAL in other countries. The differences stem from fierce politics at the time they were adopted. There are certain technical differences including differences in AC mains frequencies, and numbers of scanning lines; TV receivers are not interchangeable between systems.

The reason for the inclusion of this section is to make the point that television sets and computers both use CRTs and raster (line by line scanning) displays and produce similar looking pictures. However they are technically very different. Any device for TV/computer image handling must reconcile these differences which are mainly to do with frame formats, digitization, and field, frame. and line timing (synchronization).

NTSC interlaced fields contain analogue signals and repeat at 60 Hz. The 525 lines per frame are typically digitized at 640 x 480 pixels. PAL interlaced fields contain analogue signals and repeat at 50 Hz and the 625 lines per frame are typically digitized at 768 x 512 pixels. Consequently the line frequencies are also different.

The non-interlaced displays of digital computers have tended to be "standardized" as "EGA", "VGA" etc., containing different numbers of pixels, running at different line frequencies so an even greater range and a larger number of variables must be considered when adding an external monitor.

Care must be exercised when selecting a television "frame-grabber" board (next section) which will work properly with a particular machine and monitor.

Digital Television

Space in the frequency spectrum available for television broadcasting is at a premium and much ingenuity has gone in to cramming sufficient information into as narrow a bandwidth as possible – but still providing a decent picture on the telly. The TV picture is displayed to a public whose acceptability standards are conditioned by the movies.

The width of the frequency band to accommodate the PAL analogue TV signal is 0 to 5.5 MHz.

It is not essential to digitize TV video data for all computer imaging applications – a penalty is paid for digitizing the signal because it then occupies a much wider bandwidth. For Laserdisc optical disc players, for example, the TV analogue signals are recorded on the disc and the data is played back as if it was a conventional TV signal.

But for most applications the bandwidth disadvantage is over-ridden by the great advantage of being able to process image data on a digital computer. However at the last moment in a TV receiving system the data must be converted back to analogue before being applied to the CRT display.

An American gentleman called Harry Nyquist made the remarkable discovery as far back as 1924 (Nyquist, 1924) that all the information in a smoothly changing analogue waveform can be extracted by measuring its value twice per cycle (at least) of the highest frequency component. So if a PAL video waveform is to be digitised, the digitised data requires to be transmitted at 11 MHz, or eleven million times a second, assuming the highest frequency component is 5.5 MHz as it the case for PAL TV video signals.

The mechanism for actually performing digitization was invented by Alec Reeves in 1939 and is called Pulse Code Modulation. It could not be used for TV until much later when the electronics became fast enough.

In his 1939 British Patent 535960 (A.H. Reeves 1965) Reeves specified a method of digitizing analogue waveforms in great detail. The drafting, details, and endurance of the patent have been excelled only by the 128 patents of Alan Blumlein who worked with Schoenberg at EMI to develop the TV system for the BBC.

A smooth analogue waveform is sampled by an electronic device at fixed intervals to determine its height (Figure 2.2).

This "quantization" process changes it into a "staircase" appearance, shown superimposed on the original waveform in the top diagram.

There must be at least two samples of the highest frequency component in the waveform. In this new waveform, shown in the middle diagram, the numerical value of each step is transmitted as binary coded impulses shown on the bottom diagram. If there are, say 16 heights, each may be represented by a 4-bit code, so if the waveform is sampled 10 times per second, 40 bits per second will be transmitted.

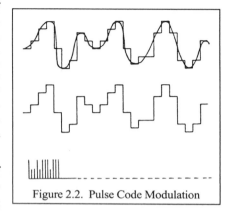

Figure 2.2. Pulse Code Modulation

The greater the number of heights the larger the number of bits per second transmitted. 256 heights (8 bits) is sufficient to make the "staircase" waveform resemble the original waveform well enough to result in good picture quality.

Once in digital format, the data can be handled like any other data to be processed by a computer. This enormous advantage is partially offset by the far lesser but still considerable disadvantage that the bandwidth required satisfactorily to "transport" the binary data impulses, now representing the data from the analogue waveform, is about ten times wider than before.

During conversion, the level of the analogue signal has to be measured with sufficient accuracy at the sampling instant by comparing its value with a staircase waveform for which the level of each step is known accurately. There have to be enough steps for the required accuracy – usually about 256. Thus if the level of the analogue waveform corresponds at the sampling instant to, say, step 102, that number must be transmitted.

In fact, 256 levels are chosen to provide good quality – so any level may be sent as an 8-bit code. When the signal is ultimately displayed the transition between steps is then imperceptible. If this has to be done 11M times per second we have a bit rate of 88 Megabits per second (Mbps) –hence the earlier remarks about the bandwidth penalty.

I should mention that the internationally agreed inter-studio bit rate for PAL digitized television signals is 216 Mbps – well above the rate of 88 Mbps suggested as being necessary above. However the BBC Research Department experimented with digital TV some time ago where the sampling rate was below Nyquist's criteria and the information per sample was 4.4 bits not 8. Data was generated at 34 Mbps. They used something called a "two field predictor" and the difference between the displayed results from this arrangement and normal TV was said to be very small.

Digitized colour TV for studio use, as opposed to what might be done within the constraints of an existing service, is done rather differently. It is specified in CCIR Recommendation 601 as "4:2:2" meaning that the signal is constructed from 4-bit luminance sampling done at 13.5 MHz, plus two 2-bit colour-difference samples each done at 6.75 MHz.

Commercial Digital Television operated within the confines of what is politically and economically feasible is a complex business and it is not easy to relate what is done in for TV purposes to what is done in computer systems.

In order not to make existing black and white receivers obsolete when colour TV was introduced, it had to be possible for a B&W receiver to provide B&W pictures from colour transmissions.   A rather complicated arrangement was devised as explained above with reference to the NTSC system, whereby "chrominance" data providing the extra information about colour for the new receivers would be included.   This data would be discarded by B&W receivers.

Chrominance data is sandwiched between "luminance" (brightness) data elements so the new transmissions occupy a transmitted frequency band no wider than before.

At various stages within the telephone and television networks today's version of PCM is widely used. The huge investment in the analogue "local loop" – the local distribution part of the Public Switched Telephone Network – and in television receivers, has been too great to be made obsolete by digitization until now. The Integrated Services Digital Network (ISDN) all-digital service is arriving very slowly, and digital television for consumers even more slowly.

Eventually all television will be totally digital including the receivers.   Sandbank (1990) suggests that the development of semiconductor memories provided a significant impetus. For example, special effects – such as showing successive positions of billiards balls after a cue stroke – were introduced. A digitized frame sequence was stored and the frames were superimposed into a single composite still picture. The picture was then converted to analogue for transmission.

The present state-of-the art is demonstrated every day on public television by the special effects, particularly in advertisements, usually produced on equipment supplied by Quantel of Newbury, UK – masters of the art of TV effects creation.

HDTV will provide the opportunity for a clean sweep to true all-digital television, but whether it will be seized on, or missed by implementing a hotch-potch of compromises for political reasons, remains to be seen. A television service could be provided by straightforward PCM encoding at a bit rate of 100 Mbps using the PAL system.

For HDTV the bit rate using similar methods would be over 2 Gbps – i.e 20 times greater than PAL bit rates – requiring a far greater channel bandwidth than is needed for the current PAL service. For digital PAL or HDTV, special coding techniques could reduce these rates substantially – perhaps down to 70 Mbps for HDTV.

The development of HDTV has been bogged down by inter-continental politics. The first major event was a proposal by the Japanese in Geneva in November 1985 for an 1125 line wide picture. The prospect of a Japanese TV takeover was unacceptable to Europeans or Americans and there have been wrangles about the systems to be adopted ever since.

Apparently Europeans are moving towards the launching of HDTV transmission in a format called HD-MAC via satellites and cable. Something called PAL plus, which will be less radical, may bring wide screen transmission to PAL terrestrial viewers from receivers with a lower cost.

The Japanese have been running a service called HIVISION Muse – a 1125 line wide screen system – since 1989. Various other alternatives have been considered and experimented with, including digital HDTV transmission.

In the United States after various proposals have been discussed, it is now proposed to jump straight to an all digital HDTV system whilst taking account of the existing needs of a very large customer base running NTSC receivers. Some kind of HDTV service is expected to start in the United States during 1996. For more information see Toth *et al* (1993).

Frame Grabbers

It was realised, probably around 1985, that several technologies had reached a point where they could be combined to provide advances in imaging. Facilities for managing the volume and speed of data representing a high quality colour image started to become available on microcomputers.

"Frame Grabbers" have received special attention. They are often supplied in the form of a plug-in board to receive and store monochrome or colour picture frames from television receivers or cameras, often with provision for "doctoring" the stored image in various ways before using it.

Television services and systems offer a ready made source of electronic images but they still, of course, provide the picture data in analogue form. A substantial new industry for the supply of plug-in cards for microcomputers sprung up. The cards capture TV frames from a conventional TV tuner and decode and convert the analogue data into a form suitable for editing into, for example, pictures overlaid with captions for incorporation into multimedia presentations.

State-of-the-art developments in microcomputers enable the bits from such sources to be processed and stored, but speed constraints in the input boards, and more especially at the display end of the micro, restricted the essential requirement of transporting a sufficient number of bits to reproduce an image with the required quality at full-screen size until very recently.

In a microcomputer fitted with a frame grabber board, the user observes a television programme from one of the sources listed above and selects a single frame, which is then stored and displayed for processing, by pressing a single key.

It will be noted from the previous section that a frame could come from a number of different sources with different characteristics so the frame grabber must ideally be able to cope with whatever range of sources the user has in mind. It must also be compatible with the micro's display or an external monitor, and should be able to output to a video tape recorder.

The important matters which the board must cope with are modifying the characteristics of the grabbed frame so that it may viewed as a stable image on the screen and on an external monitor if one is used, and to provide facilities for editing it. The most generally required edit function is to overlay captions created on the computer for viewing by the user as a composite picture recorded on tape, or possibly for viewing as print on paper.

A board such as Raster Op's 364 (Santa Clara, Ca), used in a Mac II computer, enables 30 frames/second in 24 bit colour video to run in a window on the screen. The live video continues and frames may be captured provided storage is made available. Any frame can be captured with a single keystroke, saved either in RAM storage on the board or on disc, and displayed full screen size.

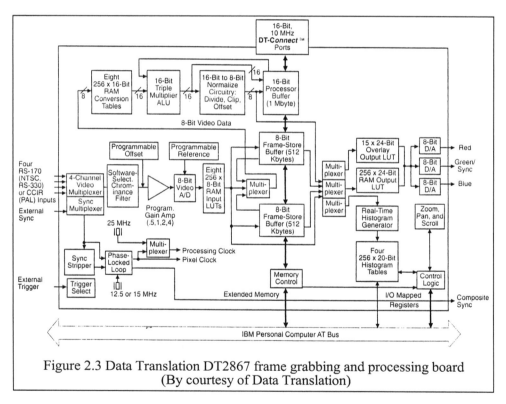

Figure 2.3 Data Translation DT2867 frame grabbing and processing board
(By courtesy of Data Translation)

A block diagram of the DT2867 frame grabber and processing plug-in board from Data Translation is shown in Figure 2.3. It contains various sections for mixing, storing, editing, overlaying and colour lookup, and delivers the three sets of pixel data required for generating 24 bit colour. 256 colours out of a possible $256^3 = 16.8M$ may be displayed. Another buffer of the same size is provided for overlaid graphics or characters. Processing facilities provided with the associated software include operations on single or groups of pixels, convolutions (operations for noise removal, edge enhancement etc), producing and controlling overlaid graphics or text, and many others.

To make processing easier, RGB may converted to HSI (Hue-Saturation-Intensity) data. Processing then usually only requires the examination of one component instead of three. See Sezan (1990) for more on the restoration of image defects.

Applications of the newer Data Translation DT3852 framegrabber have been described by Jagadeesh *et al* (1993). The board was tested when plugged into a 486DX2 66MHz computer. Jagadeesh says that Data Translation have "every reason to be proud of their board". It can accept four interlaced or non-interlaced monochrome or colour inputs.

The board was used to analyse heart movements in a micro-organism. "Many details of image acquisition, video set-up, and memory allocation are organised into well thought out, albeit complex, data structures", says Jagadeesh. The board comes with data communication facilities running at 4.5 Mbytes per second.

Digithurst (Royston, UK) also specialise in this area, and can supply a colour TV camera and plug-in card for IBM PCs. If required (and you have a special TV receiver or can get at the works of an ordinary one) you can grab a frame from a TV station. Digithurst can supply cards for quite sophisticated operations and high quality high resolution colour.

Figure 2.4 shows, by courtesy of Digithurst, the arrangement of the Digithurst Microeye PB card which includes an on-board transputer and comes with special software at £1295. It captures images and can handle up to 256 colours at one time at 640 x 480 pixels.

This particular card enables items to be compressed by zooming down into windows.

Composite pictures may be composed from a grabbed image with computer generated graphics added, using the overlay facility. Additionally graphics may be combined with live TV

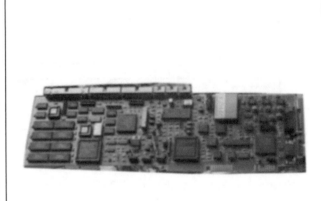

Figure 2.4. Digithurst Microeye PB card

pictures for creating, say, training course programmes.

Digithurst also supplies other boards with higher resolution and more colour. Appropriate monitors will be needed for the better performance of these boards to be appreciated.

CHAPTER 3

IMAGE REPRODUCTION SYSTEMS

Displays: introduction

Various display devices are starting to make the Cathode Ray Tube (CRT) less ubiquitous than it was, but the CRT exhibits "the sailing ship effect" – sailing ships competed for much longer against steam than was expected because of various improvements. The performance of CRTs has improved remarkably and is still improving. For picture reproduction it still reigns supreme.

Photometric considerations

Having evolved in order to perceive reflected sunlight, the eye is sensitive to light from ultraviolet to infrared within the electromagnetic radiation spectrum of wavelengths between 400 to 700 nanometres (One nm = 10^{-9} metres) centred around the wavelength of the sun's emission. This band of extremely short wavelengths corresponds to a frequency band about 700 Terahertz wide (One THz = 10^{12} Hz).

Even if the light within a band only 100 THz wide was useable, there would still be room for at least 500,000 digitized TV channels each operating at 100 Megabits per second within it. In these days of fast data transmission, the attraction of the inherent bandwidth when using fibreoptic cables with light as a data transmission medium becomes very obvious.

Light radiated from an electronic display has to be of adequate intensity, often vaguely described as its "brightness". A more scientific term is Luminance in candelas per square metre (cd/m^2).

Perception of a pattern depends crucially on Contrast. This becomes very noticeable when the controls are adjusted on a CRT display. Characters may become hard to distinguish and may be lost in the background luminance when the controls are wrongly set.

Another aspect of importance, particularly with CRT displays, is the need for an absence of flicker. An image persists in the brain for a short period after light received from it by the eye has been extinguished, but for a light source to be free of flicker under any conditions the repetition frequency needs to be 50 Hz or more.

Display methods and techniques

The CRT has endured because the mass market for monochrome and later colour television, provided the incentive for the R&D effort needed to increase the performance and size of an evacuated glass tube with some precision metalwork inside it. The CRT is a cheap, mass-producible, if non-ideal display device.

The monochrome CRTs in use today are no different in principle from those developed by Von Ardenne in the early twenties. A narrow beam of electrons hits a screen coated with a fluorescing material within an evacuated glass tube. A bright spot appears at the point of impact. In most CRT displays the spot traces out a raster produced by deflecting the electron beam with an external magnetic field applied horizontally to form a line, and with a second stepwise magnetic field applied vertically so that a succession of close spaced lines are produced.

During its rastering progress the spot may be switched on or off or varied in brightness by a voltage applied to a beam-control electrode. The completed raster frame filling the screen is rapidly repeated fifty or more times per second. If beam switch-on occurs at the same moments in each frame, apparently stationary patterns or pictures may be produced by a succession of frames.

Alternatively in Vector displays, the spot is deflected by applied magnetic fields to form lines, circles, shapes etc., which appear to be stationary because of frame repetition as with a raster display.

Resolution

For electronic processing purposes, text and images are handled as dot structures. For good quality graphics, 300 dots per inch is considered to be desirable and there is a trend toward even higher resolutions. Consequently a very large number of dots or pixels are contained on an A4 size page or "19 inch" screen as shown in Table 3.1.

Pixels/in	Pixels/mm	Pix./ Char.*	Pix./19"CRT# Hor. x Ver.	Total Mbits for 19"CRT# 1-bit	8-bit	24-bit
400 x 400	15.75 x 15.75	22	6240 x 4680	29	232	696
300 x 300	11.8 x 11.8	17	4680 x 3510	16.4	131	394
200 x 200	7.87 x 7.87	11	3120 x 2340	7.3	58	175
100 x 100	3.94 x 3.94		1560 x 1170	1.8	14.4	43.2

* Number of pixels in a 1.4mm high (4 point) character.
\# 19" CRT is assume to provide a 15.6" x 11.7" display area.

Table 3.1. Displayed bit rates

Thus, when a pixel must represent any one out of 256 different colours and there are 300 of them per square inch on a 19" screen, 131 Mbits (about 16 Mbytes) will be displayed in total.

The number of bits becomes large as the resolution is increased and larger still as the data per bit is increased for halftones or colour. The *bit rate* required when all the screen pixels are "refreshed" in order to display a steady image then becomes very high. Bit rates are a major constraint limiting the reproduction of more detail on Cathode Ray Tubes.

4 point (1.4 mm high) characters at 200 x 200 pixels/inch, contain 11 pixels – enough to make them clear. It is often argued that a resolution of 300 x 300 pixels/inch is necessary to define fine structures in images if they are to look smooth rather than slightly jagged. Opinions about better requirements tend to increase as the availability of suitable equipment increases and prices fall.

In CRT displays, for easily readable characters constructed from bright dots, a dot structure of not less than 7 (horizontal) x 9 (vertical) dots with at least one dot between characters, is needed, with one dot between character ascenders and descenders in successive rows.

The size of the fluorescing spot is the most important factor determining CRT resolution. Reduction of spot size continues to receive the attention of CRT manufacturers.

The luminance of a CRT spot varies from maximum at its centre gradually decreasing to nil at an ill-defined edge, consequently its specified size depends on the edge-point chosen. For two tubes with both spots nominally 0.5 mm diameter, the actual size will be much larger for the first if its edge is specified at the point where the luminance has decayed to 5% of its peak value compared with the second specified at the 50% point. Unfortunately not all manufacturers choose the same edge-points.

A sequence of adjacent black and white pixels, where d is the distance in millimetres between the centres of two black (or white) pixels, is formed by applying an alternating brightness waveform of wavelength d millimetres; the spatial frequency is 1/d cycles per mm. (Figure 3.1) For example for a pixel produced by a spot 0.25 mm in diameter w = 0.5 mm and 1/w = 2 cycles per mm, apparently equivalent to a CRT resolution of 4 pixels per mm.

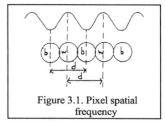

Figure 3.1. Pixel spatial frequency

In practice this relationship gives an unduly pessimistic result because of the spot's vague edge and because satisfactory contrast can be obtained without the need to modulate from full black to full white. To allow for this a correction factor of about 0.4 is applied to the spot size. In the above example the spot becomes 0.25 x 0.4 = 0.1, L = 0.2, and 1/d becomes 5 cycles per mm, equivalent to a resolution of 10 pixels/mm.

Manufacturers take account of these factors in deriving the Modulation Transfer Functions when carrying out CRT luminance measurements with a photomultiplier luminance-measuring system.

Not only is spot size treated with a certain amount of technological licence but so is resolution. Subjectively measured resolution is quoted with reference to sets of lines with different inter-line spacing on a test-card. The displayed card is viewed and the resolution is defined to be the inter-line spacing of the set of lines adjudged to be just merged.

Alternatively, in the "shrinking raster" test, the spacing

between a known number of closely spaced lines is reduced until an observer adjudges them to be just merged. The resolution is then expressed as the number of raster lines divided by the raster height. For reasons relating to the waveforms used, tests involving viewing TV-type test-card lines produce appreciably higher resolution figures than do shrinking raster tests.

Manufacturers have turned to special electronics and deflection coil design to reduce spot size. Dynamic focusing provides more uniform sharpness over the screen area and an elaborate scheme called Digital Dynamic Convergence (DDC) is sometimes used to correct for non-uniform resolution produced by production variations. The characteristics of discrete areas of the screen are corrected by data stored in Read Only Memories controlling each area.

In shadow mask colour tubes the resolution is mainly determined by the pitch of the shadow mask holes. In high quality tubes the inter-triad resolution is about 0.5 mm. However Hitachi offer a colour monitor (at a high price) with a triad pitch of 0.21 mm and 2730 x 2048 dots on the screen.

Tweaking up CRTs appears to be a black art. If high quality reproduction is required, a user should conduct tests using an image carefully selected for the purpose before selecting a monitor, and use the same image for all tests.

Reproducing a pattern on the screen

The speed of the spot is accurately controlled in CRT displays. The time interval between the moment when it crosses a point on the screen's surface and then crosses the same point again during the next frame is accurately known. Consequently a bright blob can be made to appear at the same position on the screen during each frame if the CRT beam is momentarily switched on at fixed time intervals.

Because the frame is rapidly repeated or "refreshed" the eye perceives an apparently stationary dot at that point. Under these conditions a raster is still traced out, but lines or dots do not appear because the beam is switched on only at one instant per frame.

One way of displaying a screenful of characters is to organise character cells as elements in rows with, say, one thousand elements in a row, to correspond with row by row positions of pixels on the CRT screen's surface. Each character is read into the store as a pattern of "on" pixels defined within, say, a 7 x 9 dot matrix. To display a screenful of characters the cells are scanned, row by row, in synchronism with the beam, and the "on" pixels are applied to the CRT's control electrode. The process is repeated with every frame.

Half-tones, colour, and the speed problem

On a high quality screen there may be over one thousand lines each capable of sustaining one thousand pixels, being repeated 50 times per second. The time available for switching the beam on and off may be as little as 10 nanoseconds (1 ns = 10^{-9}) or one hundredth of a millionth of a second). When switching continuously at 10 ns intervals to produce a succession of dots, the speed is one hundred million times per second, or 100 Mbits/sec.

To reproduce halftones or colour, extra data must be provided with each pixel. Thus for 16 halftones, four bits must be read out of a store increasing the on-off rate, in this case, from 100 Mbits/second, to 400 Mbits/sec – a speed which is stretching the state of the art.

Bit reduction techniques

The high bit rates and large memories required for raster scanned displays have prompted various bit-reduction techniques.

Compression or Data Reduction schemes have been in use for some years and they can be helpful in intermediate stages such as data transmission and storage. However even if half the screen of a CRT display is occupied by a uniformly grey sky, every pixel must be controlled by, say, eight bits to hold it at that particular grey level. It would seem that bit rates at the CRT itself cannot be reduced.

However instead of struggling with circuit designs of the requisite Bandwidth for conveying bits at very high speeds, memories can be organised to store data and deliver it simultaneously – the so-called "bit plane" technique discussed later in this chapter.

Compression systems are discussed in Chapter 5.

Vector Drawing

With Vector Drawing, which has come into its own for Computer Aided Design (CAD) applications, bit-reduced images are generated as a bonus. In recent years vector drawing has been introduced into microcomputer software.

Graphics created in Apple Lisa were stored as the co-ordinates of points along outlines generated automatically when the user created drawings, by assembling and manipulating outlines with the "tools" provided. Circles, lines, rectangles, polygons etc., could be modified to form drawings. In the MacIntosh, similar facilities are provided for graphics.

This type of software enables special graphic effects to be achieved economically and easily. With a microcomputer software package introduced by Adobe called *Illustrator*, capitalising on a language called *Postscript* discussed later in this chapter, extraordinary computer-aided artistic effects can be produced.

The evolution of de facto standards

80 character x 25 line displays prevailed on microcomputers for some years but eventually a plug-in board was provided to generate a 640 x 200 (128 Kpixel) display for graphics. The display on the Apple Lisa 1 showed only half an A4 page but it did so with remarkable clarity on a

screen 720 pixels wide x 364 high (262 Kpixels) considered to be "crystal clear" at the time.

The MacIntosh came out with 512 x 342 (175 Kpixels), soon topped by the Amiga's 640 x 400 (256 Kpixels). A considerably more expensive machine, the IBM 32700, became available in 1985 with a 1024 x 1024 (over 1 Mpixel) display on a separate monitor with a 19" (diagonal) tube, a very considerable improvement but still less than 100 pixels/inch.

The advent of colour is producing confusion. Suppliers of Desktop Publishing (DTP) equipment would have us believe that DTP colour is here. In practice its adoption in actual DTP has been minor. The overall costs including inputs and printing are till too high, but will gradually fall.

One problem of which it is as well to be aware, is the range of "standards" which has evolved as the technology has made increases in storage capacity and bit rates possible.

In general the total number of bits – the product of the total number of pixels and the number of bits per pixel – has been going up; each time it increases, new trade-offs for resolution against the number of displayed colours become available.

Some of the "standards" (meaning, in effect, system types which have sold in appreciable numbers) are shown in Table 3.2. Note the resolution/colour tradeoff at each advance, and how the screen resolution drops with the number of colours.

Title	Screen Resolution	On-screen colours/ Palette
CGA	640 x 200	Mono
	320 x 200	4/16
	160 x 200	16/16
EGA	640 x 350	16/64
Enhan.EGA	640 x 480	16/64
VGA (PS/2)	640 x 480	Mono
	640 x 480	16/256K
	320 x 200	256/256K

Table 3.2. CRT display types

The choice decision lies in knowing just what machine with what amount of memory will work with what monitor driven by what software.

Monitors

In TV receivers or TV-type monitors, data which are input to an "RF" (Radio Frequency) socket pass through the TV's limited bandwidth amplifier which causes picture element spreading. Text quality suffers if more than about 25 rows of text are used with 40 characters per row. In higher quality monitors, data from the computer goes direct to the monitor's video amplifier – the last electronics unit before the CRT.

The arrival of the inexpensive laser printer, capable of 300 pixels/inch, whetted resolution appetites. There is nothing like an up-market push for creating a demand which did not previously exist, but the resolution of CRT monitors still lags a long way behind such printers. A few manufacturers offer up to 200 pixels/inch in special purpose monitors, and 300 dots per inch resolution is available at a very high price.

Larger, higher, resolution monitors are desirable for the better assessment of to-be-printed pages, particularly for graphics with fine detail. Some people are prepared to pay for a high quality monitor with, say, an A4 size screen in addition to the screen provided with a microcomputer, in order to get as near to WYSIWYG – What You See Is What You Get (on the printer) – as possible. There is also a demand for high quality colour monitors.

The separate 19" monochrome monitors now being supplied with Desktop Publishing equipment come with the necessary software and/or a plug-in board for the associated microcomputer. A board may include its own processor and storage needed to handle the larger number of picture elements. These monitors typically display a total of about 1 million pixels equivalent to about 90 pixels/inch.

Microcomputers offering colour usually provide for fairly high resolution with a limited colour range. A larger range of colours, available on the screen at one time, themselves selectable from a much larger "palette" are usually displayable only at lower resolution for reasons of economy in the CRT drive circuits. In high quality CAD/CAM workstations high-quality high-resolution colour CRTs are fitted with complex electronics capable of facilities for image processing and manipulation needed for engineering design work.

The price given for the colour monitors in Table 3.3 is "list" and and likely to be negotiable. Some monitors embody only basic electronics, others are more elaborate. It is not possible in a table of this kind to include the variety of facilities included with some of the monitors.

Most CRTs have semi-rectangular screens with curved edges and both CRT manufacturers and monitor suppliers quote the size as a screen diagonal measurement. The usable display area is considerably smaller.

The monitors normally supplied with microcomputers are much better than they used to be and are quite adequate for working with text. For looking at a clearly legible complete page or at good quality illustrations in colour, something better may be needed.

The display requirements for text or diagrams in colour, and for illustrations in colour – or for that matter for text or diagrams in black and white and halftone illustrations – are rather different. In text and diagrams, resolution may be of prime importance. In illustrations, particularly "pictures" – that is artistic works – it is the colours or halftones, and their gradations and range which are usually of greater importance.

If what you are looking at is going to be printed then ideally you would like to see a good representation on the screen of what will ultimately be seen on paper. In Desktop Publishing a full size representation of a whole page under preparation is a considerable advantage. Resolution and colour will still fall well short of what can be achieved with print on paper unless a very costly monitor is used. Know-how, experience, and additional facilities are needed (see below) to relate CRT colour to printed colour.

Supplier and type	Screen size inches	Bandwidth Resolution	Scan Mhz	Video f.(KHz)	inputs	Price
Flanders Exact 8000 (**Mono**)	11.0 x 8.5	2560 x 3300	750	205	–	$3000
Chugai CPD-2040	14.2 x 10.3	1280 x 1024	120	58-70	Analogue	$3495
NEC Multisync XL	13.8 x 10.2	1024 x 768	65	21-50	Anal. TTL	$3200
Taxan Ultravision	14.0 x 10.3	1280 x 1024	?	30-72	Analogue	£2800
Hitachi HIscan 20	14.0 x 10.6	280 x 1024	?	30-64	Analogue	£2175

Table 3.3. Representative high resolution colour monitors (with one mono monitor)

The details about high quality colour monitors given in Table 3.3 include one monochrome example for comparison. A major reason for the superiority of the Flanders Exact 8000 is the size of the single-beam spot compared with the size necessary to provide a tri-beam triad spot in colour tubes. The resolution of the Exact approaches 300 pixels/inch.

Principal (Haslingden, Lancs., UK) supplies the Spectrum/24 card for an Apple Macintosh II machine using Apple's 32-bit Quickdraw software. Principal can also supply the Supermac 19" monitor which uses a Trinitron tube displaying 1024 x 768 pixels – about 72 pixels/inch on this screen. The price of the board and the monitor is £6500. No doubt the result is a good quality image in colour but it's not clear how the monitor "can add dramatic impact to desktop publishing documents" as claimed, because the documents will be viewed as print on a page.

High quality colour is just becoming available on a variety of other display devices which are gradually being introduced in competition with CRTs. So far the most successful competitor is the semiconductor screen formed from an array of active matrix supertwisted nematic Liquid Crystal Diodes (O'Mara, 1992). Such a tongue-twister really deserves its acronym – AMLCD. So far, colour AMLCDs, with advantages in size and power consumption, compete with CRTs only on portable computers.

A recent example (Smarte, 1992) is the Toshiba T4400SXC notebook computer which uses a screen containing nearly 1 million LCDs, each with its on-screen controlling transistor. It provides 256 colours at one time out of a 185,000 palette.

As costs come down, especially for larger sizes, LCDs will become more widely used, particularly in HDTV receivers where the size limit for large, heavy, CRTs is about 40" (diagonal). A 110" LCD screen has already been made. For the moment, CRTs remain supreme for the presentation of good colour at reasonable prices.

Cote et al (1992) provide a list of 24 monitors, each with their various features described, in the price range $649 – $2699. They recommend the multiscan Viewsonic Seven 17" monitor at $1399, with a dot pitch of 0.28 mm and a maximum resolution of 1280 x 1024 pixels.

Colour – principles and display electronics

Colour CRTs represent a substantial alteration in the basic CRT design. The colour tubes in use today are similar to the shadow-mask tube, introduced for colour television in the 1950s. Later a successful variation – the Trinitron tube – was introduced. The result of this competition was the development of substantially improved shadow-mask tubes.

The rate of advances in technology being what they are, we are justified in asking "Since we see the world in colour, and artists usually represent it in colour, why can't we also always see it reproduced on an electronic display or as print on paper in colour?

The answer at the moment seems to be that we are prepared to pay more to see certain images in high quality colour closely resembling the colour of the original – for example the reproduction of a Turner in a fine art book. However processing and printing for good quality colour is still relatively expensive and is becoming more expensive.

Some people will pay extra to ensure that their products are presented to the public reproduced in the best possible colour. Advertisers who want to present a food product at its most succulent have to decide, on the basis of colour realism and cost per consumer reached, whether to advertise on paper or on colour TV. A whole page advertisement in colour on coated paper in a high circulation newspaper may cost up to £42,000 in the UK.

Advertisements excepted, newspapers consist mainly of text and so the effect of enhancement of the whole publication by colour is somewhat limited. Some papers provide "colour supplements" (for which a better name would be "advertising supplements") printed on higher quality paper to provide good colour.

At the Desktop Publishing level, costs are falling rapidly but present costs are still too high for colour to be much used although the magazines covering the field would have us believe otherwise. However the demand for microcomputers with displays in colour, plug-in boards for handling images in colour, and high quality colour monitors, is such that production runs are becoming large enough to reduce costs substantially. Evidently quite a lot of people like to play with, or can benefit by information displayed in colour.

Costs will continue to drop and the know-how of colour printing will gradually become less essential as the software becomes more sophisticated and the hardware becomes better able to reproduce it. Colour will gradually spread downwards through the market.

Defining colour

Colour is specified in terms of its *hue,* which is determined by the frequency of the radiated energy, *saturation* (purity) – the amount of white light present in addition to the hue, and *luminosity* (brightness). The sensation of a particular hue may be invoked either by the radiation of a particular wavelength (specified in nanometres (nm)), $1nm = 10^{-9}$ metres) or

31

by the wavelength generated by a mixture of other colours.

For measurement purposes a given colour may be specified by matching against a colour composed of measured proportions of the primary colours red, green, and blue. Special instruments called Colorimeters are available for the purpose. Equal proportions (0.33 of red + 0.33 of green + 0.33 of blue = 1 = white).

Any other colour may be reproduced by variations of these proportions. The coefficients (proportions) are called *trichromatic units*. The tri-stimulus theory of colour was advanced by Clerk-Maxwell in 1856 and has stood the test of time; it is supposed that the retina of the eye is composed of three types of receptors sensitive to the proportions of primary colours present.

These ideas were noted by the Commission International de l'Eclairage back in the nineteen twenties who put forward the *CIE Chromaticity Diagram* shown in Figure 3.2.

This diagram has assumed particular importance for measuring and specifying colour as produced by Cathode Ray Tubes (CRTs) for colour television. The y and x axes represent the proportions of green and red (and in consequence blue since pR + pG + pB = 1) to produce the range of colours shown.

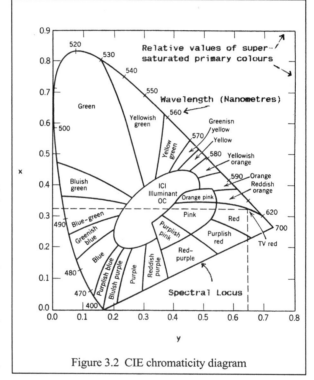

Figure 3.2 CIE chromaticity diagram

The wavelength of hues is shown round the edge of the diagram. The typical range of colours provided by a colour CRT – its "colour space" – could be shown on this diagram as a triangle with its apices some way inside the corners of the diagram (e.g. one apex at "TV red" as shown), not providing a complete colour range, but considered to be good enough for most purposes.

The above remarks apply to colour produced by radiated light. The sensation of colour generated from coloured painted or printed surfaces is produced by selective absorption of the component colours of white (ideally) light.

What we see are the components which are reflected. If the surface is viewed by reflection from a source which is not pure white the reflected components will of course be different.

Printed colour is produced by laying down the "subtractive" colours cyan (turquoise), magenta (bright pink), yellow, and black (as opposed to RGB radiation which is additive).

Some colour printers use "process" ribbons having length-wise bands in these colours. Combinations produce other colours e.g yellow + magenta = red, cyan + magenta = blue.

Reproducing colour in electronic displays

Most people will first meet "electronic colour" in their TV set. Colour television systems were designed to provide acceptable colour from a television signal transmitted along a channel of limited bandwidth, able to be decoded and reproduced on a mass produced domestic receiver.

Unquestionably the ingenious designers did a first rate job subjected as they were to these severe constraints, particularly in respect of the tube. When TV shadow-mask colour CRTs tubes first came out they represented a remarkable achievement – probably *the* peak accomplishment of the time in mass produced precision engineering.

If a person buys a micro complete with colour monitor and appropriate software, the part of it dealing with colour reproduction should not introduce difficulties.

However anyone seriously interested in colour who also wants to capture, create, or reproduce good colour graphics on his or her micro, needs to know how to ask the right questions in order to be able to buy the right equipment. For assembling a system, rather than buying a complete integrated tested outfit, the subject is a minefield (unless he/she is a computer buff who has unlimited time to fiddle about for the love of it).

Colour electronics

A great deal of data has to be managed when storing, processing, or communicating images in colour. An "image" in this context means a "bit-mapped image" – that is the representation of an image by an array of very small picture elements sometimes called pels, but usually pixels. Good quality requires that there be a sufficient number of pixels to define the fine structure of an image ("high resolution"), that tonal qualities are realistically presented, and that a good range of colours are displayed.

Shadow-mask colour tubes have three electron guns. Their focused electron beams pass through holes in a mask (grid) allowing each beam to strike the phosphor screen only at specific locations.

The screen is made up of triads of three dots which glow red, blue, and green respectively. The alignment of the mask holes with a dot of a particular colour in each triad is such that the beam from the "red" gun can only strike a red dot, the "blue" gun only a blue, and the "green" gun only a green.

Trinitron tubes embody a grid called an "aperture grille" mask which is slotted vertically, causing electrons to provide almost continuous vertical excitation, compared with the small "dead border" area present in shadow-mask tubes. In spite of improvements in the design of shadow-masks, Trinitrons are still claimed to provide slightly better quality.

The eye perceives a colour produced by the combined effect of the dots or vertical strips in each triad. Colour signals applied to each gun control the contribution of each dot. The triad pitch is about 0.5 mm in shadow-mask colour tubes. With some overlapping of displayed elements this represents a density of up to about 100 triads or pixels per inch.

The current in a gun is infinitely variable so if each is controlled by an *analogue* signal which varies according to the proportions of red, green, and blue in each pixel, colour reproduction should be excellent. This is the way it is done in television systems; the colour is as good as the whole system allows – from the TV camera, through the transmission channel and the circuits in the TV receiver to the tube.

The eye perceives the particular colour produced by the combined effect of the dots in a triad each glowing with a particular intensity. In the case of television and in some computer systems, three sets of analogue colour data are directly applied to the electron guns. In digital systems, three separate bit groups are converted into three voltages (analogue data) and are then applied to the three guns to produce the required beam intensities.

Digital computers work in bits – signals are either on or off. If the beam in a single gun CRT is switched on by one impulse or data bit for a few microseconds during its traverse across the screen it will produce one dot or pixel. A pattern of such "on" or "off" pixels, rapidly repeated, can be made to represent a "bilevel" ("black and white") image.

Colour electronics in digital systems is handled in two ways. The earliest and the simplest is quite adequate for the reproduction of text in a number of different colours. An on-off arrangement as just described is used, but with three guns instead of one. A 4-bit control signal provides 16 colours from 16 possible combinations of R, G and B, at one different overall intensity level. This arrangement has been extended to a 6-bit system providing 64 colours with R,r, G,g, and B,b, where RGB represents full intensity, and rgb represents (say) half intensity.

The controlling electronics called "TTL" (Transistor-transistor-logic) involves straight forward switching and is quite simple. However the principle becomes less attractive for a larger number of colours requiring more wires in a cable and wider bandwidth to deal with faster data.

To provide a much wider range of colour more conveniently, data is transmitted, stored, and processed in *digital* form and three sets of digital signals, specifying multiple levels of red, green, and blue intensity in bits, are fed to three digital-to-analogue converters (DACs) which translate the signals into voltage levels. The DACs connect to the three guns in the tube to control the current intensities.

Each triad in the CRT's "picture frame", typically totalling 640 x 480 = 307,200 elements, must be repeated 50 times a second or more to provide a flicker-free image, so the total *bit rate* becomes 307,200 x 50 = 15.4 Megabits per second (Mbps). The amount of additional data required to provide multi-level colour control as well raises the total to a much larger number than in the simpler methods already described.

If the colour signals applied to the guns each specify, say, 16 levels (4 bits per primary colour, 12 bits in total) the bit rate must then be 15.4 x 12 = 185 Mbps – calling for expensive wide bandwidth processing.

This difficulty is resolved in current grey-scale and colour systems by the "bit plane technique" (see Figure 3.3).

Each plane or store contains as many stored elements as there are pixels displayed on the screen; a plane is a map of the screen. There are as many planes as there are bits per pixel -in this case four. Thus the 4 bits for the 7th pixel in row 180 on the screen are held in position 187 in each of the stores.

To represent sixteen grey levels ($2^4 = 16$), four stores or planes could be arranged to hold four zeros or ones for every pixel on the screen.

Figure 3.3. Bit planes

If all four planes are read out in parallel to the CRT, the bit rate per plane is one quarter of the rate otherwise required.

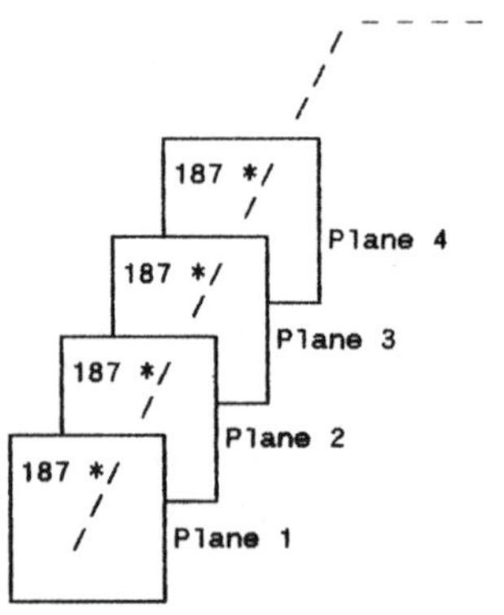

Each time the CRT beams arrive at the position correspond ing to pixel 187 all four bits are simultaneously delivered to the tube from four stores. The bit rate is therefore one quarter of the rate it would be if the bits were contained in a single store. As many bit planes as may be needed are used in systems with a very large choice of colours.

In a microcomputer with good colour there is likely to be a 24 bit system with 8 bits for each gun providing 2^8 or 256 colours at one time on the screen. However a *"palette"* is also provided, from which these colours are selected, enabling any combination of the 256 levels of each gun to be chosen. This provides any 265 colours out of 16.78M colours (256 x 256 x 256 = $2^{3(8)}$ = 2^{24} = 16.78M)

A change in the colour combination is performed by a memory called a "Colour Lookup Table" (CLUT) situated just before the DACs. The colour bits forming the word describing the colour of a pixel are input to the CLUT as an address. At that address resides another, chosen, word which has been programmed into the CLUT representing a particular colour. It may be slightly different or considerably different from the input word.

This word is output to the DACs. All pixels passing through the CLUT are input in the same way in order to output the CLUT colour word to the DACs.

Colour matching

Once the handling of a large number of colours on relatively inexpensive equipment was solved, attention was focused on exact colour selection and matching, and on the relationship between colour as perceived on a CRT and as printed on paper.

In 1989 Tektronix introduced a software package costing $50 called TekColor. It provides adjustments for colour while the user observes both CRT RGB colours and CMYK values transformed from the printer on to the screen, so that adjustments may be made in order to achieve a match between the two. Colour selection and numerical readings given during the adjustment process conform to the CIE model mentioned earlier. The system runs on a Mac and supports a number of different monitors and printers.

When you point to a colour, a small table appears on the screen showing values for the Hue, Intensity, and Saturation (HIS) of that colour. To produce that colour exactly on another occasion, the same values are set up in the table. The HIS values are transformations of RGB values as represented on the CIE diagram.

More recently Kodak has introduced a Colour Management System (CMS) which reads the colour spaces used by colour reproduction devices and converts them into a descriptive language (Blair, 1992). When a computer is connected to a particular printer and an image displayed on the CRT, the CRT is controlled to represent the image in the colours which will be reproduced by the printer.

Currently available display systems for colour and graphics

Improvements have evolved through "standards" set by Apple and IBM. When the Apple Lisa machine was introduced, its 720 x 364 pixel monochrome display was considered revolutionary. IBM started with its CGA arrangement for colour, progressing to VGA. Other suppliers have introduced enhancements. Table 3.2 on page 27 shows the titles and characteristics of some available arrangements.

At the present state of the art for reasonably priced microcomputers, resolutions up to about 640 x 480 with 256 colours are available – about 80 pixels/inch on a small 8" x 6" screen. For resolutions of 100 pixels/inch or more requiring more bits, the number of colours are often reduced in order to reduce the bit rate. For good colour with high resolution higher prices must be paid for special processing cards and special monitors. Large high resolution monitors driven by their own special plug-in cards are available at higher prices.

Graphics

The term "graphics" now seems to be used for certain operations not discussed as "picture processing" or "image processing", but describing particular images or user-controlled operations thereon, often requiring special plug-in boards.

An extraordinary effort has been put in by the chip manufacturers to develop fast high resolution colour graphic controllers to be installed on plug-in cards to be used in conjunction with special monitors. (An example is shown in Figure 3.4).

The objective seems to be to provide advanced facilities for engineering design work and Desktop Publishing with sufficient power to manipulate high resolution multi-colour images.

Figure 3.4. Graphics processor board

The facilities enable a user to create designs with special shading, surfaces, and textures, or, in less exotic applications, to create multiple windows and shift data about within them at high speed.

These "graphics co-processor" boards, many based on the Texas 34010 chip, are likely to possess more power than the micro into which they are plugged and may add several thousand dollars to its price. For example one of the earliest, the Artist T112 from Control Systems provides a resolution of 1280 x 1024 with 256 colours from a palette of 16M. An on-board 50 MHz processor is required to provide sufficient speed for special applications.

Graphics standards for "mainline computer purposes" are the outcome of work which started around 1974.

The Graphics Kernel System (GKS) standard, now an ISO standard, defines drawing element "primitives" from which a drawing may be constructed – Lines, Marks, Text, Polygons, Raster Images, and Miscellaneous. Each has "attributes" – for instance the attributes of Lines are type, scale factors and colour. A "GKS Workstation" with the appropriate software and power is necessary to run GKS.

The Computer Graphics Metafile (CGM) is associated with GKS. It provides for the encoding of GKS elements so that graphical information can be exchanged between different programs. An extension of GKS is being used called the Programmers Hierarchical Graphics System (PHIGS) for describing 3D graphics by means of data arranged in a tree structure.

The esoteric world of computer graphics design and display on high quality CRT colour workstations is moving on from flat polygonal areas filled with one colour and "wire frame structures" as used for the 3D graphics in Computer Aided Design (CAD), to special effects for greater realism.

Techniques called Gouraud Shading and the more sophisticated Phong Shading for altering individual Pixels were introduced in the eighties to produce smooth changes in shading. Further developments enable surfaces with a "textured" effect to be produced.

In late 1988, lifelike effects were introduced to provide results comparable to those produced in special photographic work, particularly in the field of business presentation graphics. A company called Pixer gained some acceptance for its "3D modelling to visual attributes" interface as a standard to make the connection between computer graphics software and visual attributes software. Pixer's photo-realistic "Renderman" software is compatible with PHIGS.

The problem of the rapid transfer of text and graphics in colour has been eased by the arrival of Graphics System Processor (GSP) co-processor chips which may be regarded as separate computers as mentioned above. A GSP consists of two separate processors – the Graphics Processor, which receives CPU commands from a special instruction set, and the Display Processor.

The Hitachi HD63484 graphics co-processor chip was announced in 1984 but the main contenders still seem to be the Texas 34010 and the Intel 82786. GSPs are associated with an important new component – a special form of buffer memory called a Video Random Access Memory (VRAM).

The results of GSP manipulation are viewed on high resolution colour CRTs from Hitachi, Cointran, and others. A GSP, given the appropriate command, can execute complex operations on large blocks of pixels and can address (typically) 128 Mbits of memory, adequate to hold a high resolution representation of a page to be displayed or printed in colour, and other data.

The Texas 34010 32 bit GSP contains over 30 32-bit registers and can be programmed in high-level languages – for instance to control animation in real time. Pixel colour control is handled by an associated chip - the 34070 Colour Palette – capable of displaying any 16 colours in one displayed frame selected from 4096 different colours.

The manufacturers have coined appropriate new hype words to convey the explosive urgency of these chips. A "Barrel-Shifter" – for use in specialised graphics applications – enables a pixel field to be rotated. "Bitblitting" (BitBlt) describes the important function of moving pixel arrays (whose size is programmable) en bloc. "Pixblitting" (PixBlt) means the moving of multiple-bit pixels containing extra bits specifying halftones or colour.

PixBlt enables one large or a number of small pixel arrays to be rapidly moved from a source area and fitted into a destination area of a different size – as, for instance, when transferring pixels between windows. The software, anticipating that "window clipping" may be required, will inhibit operations on pixels which would lie outside the new window.

Pixels from a source and destination array may be combined, thereby producing a different colour, or a pattern of designated pixels in the destination array may be made "transparent" so that when the source pixels are moved, some appear through "holes", producing various special effects. Small pixel arrays representing characters in special fonts can be fitted into new positions.

Operations of these kinds require logical mathematical operations to be carried out at high speed. With a GSP, delays in the execution of these effects are hardly noticeable. Without a GSP, delays would probably be intolerable, even with elaborate programs and additional chips.

GSPs could not work at these very high speeds if the associated memory was a conventional display RAM where the up-date of a stored representation of the screen image, and continual CRT refreshing operations, operate in turn through a single port.

In "two-port" VRAMs, up-dating and refresh proceed in parallel. The VRAM contains a "shift register" which is filled with a row of bits during the brief interval between CRT scanning lines. When the line commences the bits are clocked out to form a line of displayed pixels for refresh purposes. The effect on performance is sensational – there may be a 40 times reduction in "overhead" refresh time-wasting.

Printing and printers

Halftones and screens

Some of the printers to be described – Dot-matrix, inkjet, the thermal printer family, and laser printers – cannot print variable-size dots for reproducing halftones. Only dye-sublimation printers are the exception to this rule.

Figure 3.5. "Boats at San Francisco" dithered laser print

Halftones are displayed or printed with the aid of software to provide simulated tonal effects by variable dot clustering, enabling printers to print acceptable halftones. Very small areas are filled with a variable number of dots by "dithering" (filling with a dot pattern) in order to produce white through grey shades to black when the area is full.

The illustration of the "boats at San Francisco" (Figure 3.5) shows a dithered picture printed on a Lasermaster RX300 300 dots per inch printer, the picture having been input with a 300 dots per inch scanner. It represents typical results from relatively inexpensive equipment.

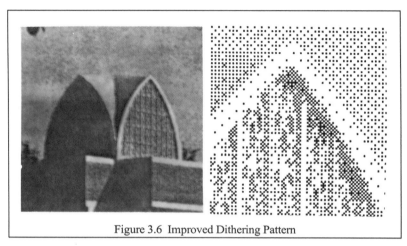

Figure 3.6 Improved Dithering Pattern

Figure 3.6 shows a more elaborate dithering dot structure. The right hand illustration is an enlargement of part of the picture shown on the left.

Figure 3.7 shows the considerable improvement in halftone reproduction obtained using a comprehensive system (Image Studio, by courtesy of Letraset) and printing on a high resolution imagesetter machine.

Larger dot-filled areas produce better halftones at the expense of a loss of detail since the small dots which would otherwise resolve fine detail are replaced by these areas which now become the smallest displayed element. But when 600 dots per inch laser printers became available the areas of clustered dots could be made smaller without reducing the number of dots enclosed in them, to restore

Figure 3.7 Half-toning using Image Studio/imagesetter

detail otherwise lost. Moreover the smaller dots enabled a method called "ordered dither" to be introduced.

Ordered dither is based on distributing and/or overlapping pixels within a very small "superpixel" area normally corresponding to a 4 x 4 pixel matrix in size. The reproduced image is divided into these superpixels filled with from zero to 16 pixels making the area appear as anything between white, through shades of grey, to black when full.

A photograph ("bromide") of a continuous tone illustration, used by printers to make a printing plate, is taken through a piece of glass with closely spaced lines ruled on it. This "screen" produces lines of variable width corresponding to grey levels on the photograph which take up ink on the plate and produce a halftone reproduction. The screen is usually rotated through an angle – often 45 degrees – to avoid interference effects associated with vertical or horizontal lines in the original.

A screen of 150 lines or dots per inch is adequate for very good quality reproduction of printer illustrations. Detail scanned in at a higher resolution will not then appear. Since the quality of reproduction of the tones in an illustration is usually of greater importance than the fine detail, attention is shifted to good reproduction of a wide range of tones, ideally at least 256, sensed during scanning.

The number of halftones that can be printed depends on the number of printed dots per inch (since the size of the smallest dot effectively dictates the tonal range) and the screen pitch, as calculated from the expression:-

Number of halftones = printed dots/inch^2 /screen pitch^2) + 1

If the printer can provide 300 dots/inch and the screen pitch is 150, the number of halftones (nH) can be nH =$(300^2/150^2)$ + 1 = 5. The "+1" is for the non-printed halftone "white". If a "high resolution" printer – such as a Linotronic 300 running at its maximum 2540 dots/inch is used, and the screen is 150, nH = $(2540^2/150^2)$ + 1 = 287 (approx), assuming of course that this amount of halftone data was input.

Dot-matrix printers

Dot-matrix printers are the least expensive. In the better quality versions 24 pattern-forming needles shoot out against an inked ribbon to impress a pattern on to paper. They can provide acceptable characters at 300 dots per inch and the more you pay the faster they print in the range 50 to 200 characters per second when printing "letter quality". When generating faster "draft quality" characters or images, the dot structure becomes obvious.

As at mid-1993 the Mannesman Tally MT360 was one of the fastest and most expensive dot-matrix printers available. It is capable of printing at 720 characters/second (draft quality).

Dot-matrix printers are not usually considered to be adequate for printing illustrations since they are rather slow and the edges in images may look rough. Colour is fair although all printer types are steadily being improved – for example the Toshiba and DEC printers.

The Toshiba "3-in-one" dot-matrix colour printer was one of the least expensive colour printers available when it was announced, selling at $949 in the US. It prints at 180 x 360 dots/inch from a 24 pin head. It provided up to seven colours from combinations available on a cyan/magenta ribbon and is said to produce remarkable results.

However the DEC LA95 colour dot-matrix printer, introduced in 1993, provides 24-pin 300 dots per inch in colour at the remarkable price of $319. It is claimed to print 240 characters per second with good quality.

Inkjet Printers

First generation Inkjet printers usually bore some resemblance to a cathode ray tube with a stream of charged particles of ink replacing the electron beam. An electric field deflected the stream either on to the paper to form characters or bent them away into a reservoir. Nearly all the newer Inkjet printers use a powered ink chamber/nozzle arrangement - the so-called "drop on demand" principle. A piezo-electric crystal, which will bend or deflect when a voltage is applied to it, is used to apply sudden pressure to a flexible ink chamber and a blob of ink squirts out.

The print-head containing a vertical column of squirters scans across the paper and matrix ink-blob characters are formed by pulsing the crystals at the right instant. Resolution is in the range 80 to 200 pixels per inch. More expensive printers are claimed to provide 300 pixels/inch. The inkjet technique lends itself to one-pass colour printing. The head contains several squirters containing inks of different colours which are controlled to squirt as necessary to produce appropriate combinations.

In 1986 the US company Howtek introduced a 240 x 240 pixels/inch 32-jet colour printer for A4 size images called the Pixelmaster. The introductory price was just under £3000. It was designed to print images derived from image scanners and was claimed to be able to reproduce 250,000 shades of colour.

In 1989 Hewlett Packard and Tektronix announced 200 dots per inch multi-nozzle ink-jet colour printers, selling in the UK for around £1000. Hewlett Packard also manufacture an inkjet colour printer which is less expensive, but has a lower resolution (180 dots/inch). Printer suppliers prefer to talk about "dots", "pixels" being reserved for CRTs and other electronic display devices.

Inkjet printers are considered to be adequate for printing illustrations in colour but they can be slow. One of the best is the Dataproducts Jolt PS which uses inks which are normally solid. The ink is heated, liquified, and projected on to the page where it rapidly solidifies. It produces high quality 300 dpi colour print rather slowly. It costs over $6000.

Current (1993) UK prices for colour inkjet printers range from £700 for the HP Deskwriter 550C to the Tektronix Phaser 3 PXI solid ink printer at around £10,000.

The speed of inkjet colour printers depends on what they are printing. Simple Postscript graphics in colour take about twice as long as the same without Postscript, while a complex coloured illustration may take twice as long again – perhaps several minutes.

Thermal Printers

Thermal printers work at up to about 200 characters per second (about 3 pages a minute) and like dot-matrix printers can be programmed for graphics. These printers have been sold in very large quantities by Seiko and Oki at $200 each. In consequence of the large demand for facsimile machines, the special paper is now much improved and fairly cheap.

The thermal printer as used in many facsimile machines prints images much faster than the machines which are primarily designed to reproduce text from microcomputer WP systems. A fast thermal printer might by now have been expected to appear as a cheap image printer in quantity production with fax Group 3 resolution of 200 x 200 pixels/inch. The reason why it has not may be due to the stability of the image. When filed, the print can deteriorate by chemical action if left in contact with certain types of surfaces.

Simple thermal printers have been overtaken by special types of thermal printer for providing high quality colour printing as described in the next sections.

Thermal wax colour printers

Originally the thermal wax process was difficult to control if the resolution was increased beyond 200 pixels/inch, but most now work at 300 dpi. Several manufacturers offer such printers including Panasonic, Seiko, QMS, and NEC.

Pages in colour of reasonable quality, printed directly by thermal colour printers can be produced for small print runs, or for the "proofing" of pages to be further processed. The first low price colour thermal printer used waxed paper on to which heated needles transferred ink by impact through a moving ink roll. The number of needles determined the resolution.

The roll contains three coloured inks (or sometimes four including black) used during three printing passes. The perceived colour, from reflected not transmitted light as in a CRT, depends on the proportions of the inks used in each pass. Tektronix was an early leader. Their 4693D included a plug-in card with several Mbytes storage – sufficient for most A4 size pages, with 256 colours, at 300 dots/inch.

Today's (1993) thermal wax colour printers transfer colour from a ribbon composed of sequences of four page-size panels coated with pigmented wax in CMYK colours. The same panel sequence repeats along the ribbon. The print head contains small dot-size printing elements which are heated to melt the wax and transfer it to the paper. The printer makes a separate pass to transfer each colour. Accurate registration is necessary.

Most thermal wax printers no longer require special paper – they will print on plain paper, usually at 300 dpi. UK prices range between £3000 and £6000. The same remarks apply about the speed depending on what is being printed, as were made above for inkjet printers. However the colour is considered to be better.

Dye Sublimation colour printers

These printers belong to the family of thermal printers but contain further refinements.

At present dye sublimation printers are used for colour printing where the best available quality is required. Since dithering is not needed they produce higher resolution printing although small text is reproduced with a slightly fuzzy appearance.

The mechanics of these printers is similar to thermal wax printers but they use dyes not inks, special paper, and the dye turns into a gas before deposition on the paper. Different colours are produced by the superimposition of primary colour dots, not by "area fill" as in dithering. Smooth continuous tone images are printed because dots tend to diffuse slightly into each other – hence the excellence for colour or halftones but the fuzziness of text.

The quality is excellent – the Kodak "thermal printer" used for printing from Photo CDs is of this type. The results are almost indistinguishable from a photograph but the Kodak XLT 7720 is expensive at £17,500 in the UK. The Tektronix Phaser IISD produces very good results at about half the price.

The same remarks about speed apply as before although the average speed for comparable items is slightly slower than the previous types of printer described.

However there has been a new arrival on the market which has had very favourable reviews – the Fargo Electronics company have produced a printer which prints with a choice of thermal wax or dye sublimation in the same machine. At $1245 the price is far less than other printers and it is far smaller and lighter. Although the machine is reviewed as having some disadvantages, its print quality is said to be only slightly lower than printers of a much higher price.

Laser printers

Laser printers usually consist of a photosensitive drum on to which the modulated beam from a laser is projected. Beam raster-scanning is produced by rotating mirrors – the way scanning was done on the earliest projection television systems. Paper is rolled against the drum surface and the charge pattern transferred from the drum is made visible on paper by heat-fused toner.

A resolution of "90,000 pixels per square inch" quoted for most laser printers sounds high. This is, of course. 300 x 300 pixels/inch. Laser printers are widely used for Desktop Publishing. The Laserwriter, H-P Laserjet and Cannon's own laser printer will print an A4 page at a resolution of 300 x 300 pixels per inch at 8 pages per minute under favourable conditions – that is when they are repeatedly printing copies of the same page containing an "average image".

It may take many minutes to print each page of a succession of different highly-detailed pages. Speeds vary enormously; Postscript printers are usually the slowest. Consumables associated with a laser printer such as toner, drum assembly etc., typically average about 4 cents per page.

Speeds depend on the printer manufacturer's hardware, the driver software which converts DTP page formats from Pagemaker, Ventura etc., into Postscript, and the interpreter program which changes Postscript into laser printer bit-map format.

Special "go-faster" hardware/software has appeared – for example the "J-Laser Quickpack" will reduce the time taken for a Laser-jet/Postscript printer to print the first copy of a simple page from 2.2 minutes to 27 seconds and from 3 minutes to 1.4 minutes for complex pages. "Postscript clone" suppliers such as Control-C Software, Beaverton, USA, claim lower prices and speeds 10 to 50 times faster. Buyers should shop around carrying their own test page.

The first laser printer was probably the Xerox 9700EPS introduced in 1978. It generated 120 high-resolution pages per minute. The first time I tried a laser printer was during a demonstration of the Xerox Star at E1 Segundo in 1981. The combination of the Star's software and the print quality was revolutionary.

Laser printers became affordable with the advent of the Canon LBP-CX laser engine which was something of a breakthrough. It enabled manufacturers to bring down the price of printers to below $3000.

The introduction of the Hewlett Packard (HP) 300 dots per inch (dpi) Laserjet printer in 1983 revolutionised lower-cost DTP reprographics. It would be more correct to say that HP and Apple between them made DTP possible. An improved version of the Laserjet was developed in 1985 priced at $2995. The most noticeable characteristics of a page of type printed on a Laserjet is that it looks far better than a typed page, and almost as good as a typeset page.

The current (1993) HP Laserjet 4M prints in 45 different "resident" selectable fonts plus the 35 fonts which come with Postscript. It prints 600 dots per inch and uses HP's resolution enhancement technology for line art but not for halftones. It is considered to be one of the best laser printers and is listed at $2199.

One of the most widely used laser printers is the Apple Laserwriter, associated with the Macintosh microcomputer which runs the controlling software. To mitigate bandwidth/memory problems the Apple printer incorporates 2 Mbytes of memory for page storage, font information, and its own 68000 processor. The current model (1993), the IIg, is priced at $2300 and provides good quality at 300 dots per inch.

The Macintosh micro contains a socket to connect to Apple's Local Area Network called Appletalk to which the printer may be connected. The printer then works as a network-connected resource for shared use. A page of information described and formed under Postscript could be sent to the printer as a bit-stream lasting about one second.

In 1993 good laser printers have become available at still lower prices. The Canon LBP4 SX, for example, prints four pages per minute at 300 dpi and is listed at $1595. It can be purchased for considerably less.

For the highest quality of illustrations a machine such as the Lasermaster Unity 1200XL will print at 1200 dots per inch providing excellent quality. It uses a 33 MHz Risc processor so it is also fast. The price is around $10,000. However fast printers have also fallen in price during 1993. The Toshiba GX400 prints at 17 pages per minute, but with a lower 300 dpi resolution. It is listed at only $4500. The QMS 1725 prints at a similar rate but at 600 dpi. The list price is $6000.

Colour laser printers are very expensive but QMS have recently produced such a printer selling for around $12,000. It produces 300 dpi colour images by making four passes, using a belt with the adherence of a toner of a different colour at each pass produced by a laser sweeping out a pattern for each of the four colours. The printer can also be used to produce black and white copies.

Its main advantage is expected to be the low cost per copy – much lower than wax or sublimation printers.

Postscript

HP's Laserjet Printer Control Language (PCL) became the *de facto* standard. The next development was the introduction of the Postscript programming/printer-command language. Like several other major developments in this field, Postscript was devised by ex-Xerox PARC (Palo Alto Research Centre) people, in this case Charles Geschke and John Warnock, who worked on the daddy of all DTP systems in the late seventies -the Xerox Star. They founded Adobe Systems in 1982.

Being a programming language, instructions in Postscript can be written to make a laser printer beam move anywhere in almost any manner to print almost anything. For most purposes, the ready-programmed printing control facilities available when Postscript software is supplied with a laser printer are sufficient, and no programming is needed.

Postscript takes a file, typically a file describing pages created using Pagemaker or Ventura DTP software, and changes the dot-structure description of text, graphics, and illustrations into a vector description. A vector is a quantity which has magnitude and direction.

A rectangle in Postscript would be described by a co-ordinate representing the position of a starting point on a page, the co-ordinates of its corners, the thickness of a line, and the instruction "move to". The printer then draws the rectangle. These instructions are coded in ASCII code. Postscript describes every item on a page in terms of its constituent lines, curves, polygons, etc.

In bit-map form, for example, a ruled line 20 dots wide and 1500 dots long requires 30,000 bits to describe it. In Postscript the description would be in the form "Start in position X and perform a 20 point line from A to B". This instruction would require perhaps 200 bits of code.

To implement Postscript operations two main processes are required. First, a file in bit-map form has to be converted into ASCII-coded vector-defining form. The ASCII code is then sent to the printer's Raster Image Processor (RIP). Secondly, the RIP changes it back into the line by line form required by a laser printer.

The benefits of this apparently cumbersome process are:-

1. The printed resolution is limited only by the printer, not by the file format. For instance if an instruction to draw a sharply curved line is issued, it may be reproduced as a series of small zig-zags on a relatively low resolution printer. However if a high resolution printer is used the same instruction would produce a smooth outline. The practical aspect of this is that while the displayed "coarse" version of a page may be good enough for checking purposes, a disc containing page data may be sent to, say, a bureau with a 1200 dpi Linotype page-setter for quantity printing. The resolution will be 1200 dpi quality.

2. Almost any shape can be designed by the user if he knows the language. Alternatively a library of ready-made designs may be purchased on disc ready to be called on to pages. The usefulness of these designs depends on the application. "Stunt-images" receive considerable attention in Postscript publicity. A user may or may not require this degree of versatility.

3. The amount of data needed to represent an image in Postscript is much less than in bit-map.

4. It is only necessary to store the description of a font in a single size. To call up the font in a different size, only a simple Postscript scaling instruction is needed.

The disadvantage is that the time taken to print a Postscript page is longer, and may be much longer than the time taken using other methods. Plug-in boards and software are available to convert a non-Postscript printer into a Postscript printer, and Postscript "go-faster" boards are also available.

With the latter, a cable from a plug-in PC board goes direct to the printer, by-passing the micro's output ports. The board contains its own processor to handle Postscript. This speeds up the time it takes to print each different page.

"Display Postscript" was first supplied with the Apple NEXT computer and is now more generally available. The conversion process needed to present a Postscript display is said to be so fast that display delay should not be a problem. CRT display quality presumably depends on the monitor's resolution.

Postscript conversion does not have to be done again for printing, so printing delay will be much reduced. Steadily increasing "chip power" is bound further to speed up processes which today are time consuming. The Adobe software package "Illustrator" greatly extends Postscript's artistic potential.

Colour printing

There is a quality gap between printing colour directly on to paper from a Desktop Publishing System using one of the several kinds of relatively inexpensive colour printer now available, and printing by overlaying from colour separation transparencies.

With a direct colour printer all that the user sees is the print in full colour emerging from the printer, the process of constructing the image from its component colours being taken care of by the machine. The results are moderate to good, and getting cheaper and better. The machine may take some minutes to produce the first print and then produces each subsequent copy rather more quickly. The method is suitable for short printing runs.

Colour separation printing involves the preparation of four transparencies – black and white films carrying data about those parts of an image containing the colours cyan, magenta, yellow and key (black) (CMYK) respectively. A colour print is produced by firstly, making four printing plates from the transparencies, and secondly performing four printing passes using inks of different colours from each accurately aligned plate. After that copies are produced at high speed.

Direct colour and colour separation printing

The perceived colour of inkjet and thermal printers which directly produce colour prints depends on the relative proportions of inks or dyes used in each pass. Postscript, the printer control language widely used with laser printers, changes bit-mapped images into plotted descriptions which are independent of printer resolution; high resolution printers produce high resolution images.

The special thermal printers previously described enable very good quality to be produced from a microcomputer – in some cases good enough for "colour proofing" – that is checking what an image will ultimately look like when printed from separations.

"Gamma correction" facilities may be included when high quality is required – "gamma" being the relationship between input data and output results. As with Cathode Ray Tubes, gamma correction is necessary in printers for the best results in order to correct for non-linearity between input and output.

Professional human printers would undoubtedly have disagreed with the idea that a thermal printer colour proof is good enough for approving material to be reproduced later along the chain. The present method of proofing is to have a "cromalin" (patented by Du Pont) proof sent back from the printing house, with colours closely resembling those to be finally printed.

It seems doubtful whether they can still justifiably disagree given the remarkable quality of dye sublimation printing.

However there still appears to be a gap between "low end" colour printing and professional colour printing. Low end means direct colour printing, or for higher volumes from software claimed to be able to produce separate files containing colour data or colour separation transparencies destined for plate making.

Some hardware/software suppliers and information technology magazine article writers would disagree with the above comments. They would say that software is available for a Mac (the Apple Macintosh nearly always seems to be the starting point) enabling transparencies or discs to be created in house and sent to a bureau for plate-making which is entirely satisfactory.

A bureau in Oxford, UK, called Typo Graphics will provide film for printing, created from customer's material, at about £115 per page according to content. They do it with a Mac II, Truvel colour scanner, and a Linotronic 300. Software called PhotoMac is used to produce colour separation files. They claim that this is a "stepping stone to high quality colour". The interesting question is what standard is demanded by people who want to get their leaflets, house journals, magazines etc., produced in colour?

These methods seem to be good enough for some but not for others. Good colour printing still needs up-market equipment and expertise. If you want to produce good-looking material in colour you can always paste in colour items on to DTP-produced pages and send them away for printing.

However it can all be done at a price which is not that exorbitant. The best-value route is probably the "Apple Mac – Quark XPress - Scitex Visionary". The minimum equipment needed is a Mac II machine with Visionary Software – price around £16,000. Visionary is a modified version of the Quark XPress DTP software which produces files of Scitex formatted data. Alternatively it will convert any Postscript file into Scitex.

You are unlikely to require this outfit for colour image output from computer-created graphics. It would be suitable for pictorial illustrations which will probably come from a photograph scanned in colour by a colour scanner; the scanner will cost a few thousand pounds.

The Visionary software generates special files for use by a bureau with Scitex equipment, in particular a "Page Geometry file" which, among other things, specifies the CMYK value of each pixel in an image. The Scitex equipment (a Scitex workstation costs £200,000) then takes over to produce the transparencies for printing. You are likely to get superb results.

   A table of "Desktop Options" was published by Neville (1989). It lists the approximate costs for systems starting with simple WP and DTP and progressing to a self contained comprehensive colour system costing £80,000, plus desirable extras of £70,000 with running costs of £800 per week. This system includes the production of film separations.

CHAPTER 4

IMAGE PROCESSING

The basis for new advances in image-query systems

When Professor Granville was asked about Professor Wile's proof of Fermat's last theorem he replied:- "it draws heavily on the Shimura-Taniama-Wei conjecture which took 15 years to formulate. I can only say it involves eliptical curves". Quite.

Following Granville's example I will only say that image processing means operations upon picture contents, often resulting in the generation of a substantially modified, if not an entirely new picture. These operations rely heavily upon matrix algebra, Fourier transformations etc., the mathematical language used to describe them. It is not easy to translate this language into English narrative. However, an attempt will be made to describe some of the basic operations upon which query-image systems depend with the minimum of mathematics.

Much of the maths and algorithms were developed some years ago and are described in textbooks such as Gonzalez (1987), Pearson (1991), Pratt (1991) and Low (1991). In the early nineteen-eighties it was of academic interest only but in the nineties the technology and algorithms have become available for applying image processing to pixel arrays.

The rate of improvement and falling costs of hardware, particularly in respect of low-cost processing speed, is encouraging more experimenters into this area of research. Progress towards content recognition has recently become sufficiently encouraging for it to become more generally usable before long.

The operations to be described cover the processing of the horizontal, vertical, and temporal dimensions of an array of pixels representing an image. The speed at which these operations can be performed is increasing all the time as a result of the introduction of parallel processing and faster chip-switching.

Gonzalez, quoting the kind of performance that was available in 1986, says that the application of a 3 x 3 pixel mask (described below) to a 512 x 512 image requires 9 multiplications and 8 additions for each pixel location, that is a total of 2.35 million multiplications and 2.097 million additions. When this was done with the Arithmetic Logic Unit (ALU) and frame buffers which were available at that time, these operations took about 0.3 seconds. Processing duration increases in proportion to the mask size. For example processing a 4 x 4 mask would take about 0.53 seconds.

Pearson says that it would take about 3 seconds to process a 3 x 3 mask on a 512 x 512 8 bit image. Assuming that Gonzalez was referring to a 1 bit image, this duration is of the same order. Pearson mentions that the speed may be increased according to the number of processors involved in the operation. Thus 3 processors would decrease the period to 1.1 seconds.

In the year when Gonzalez's book was published and 4 years before Pearson, the LSI Logic Corporation was selling a set of chips capable of performing 60 billion binary operations plus one billion (10^9) 8 bit x 8 bit multiplications per second.

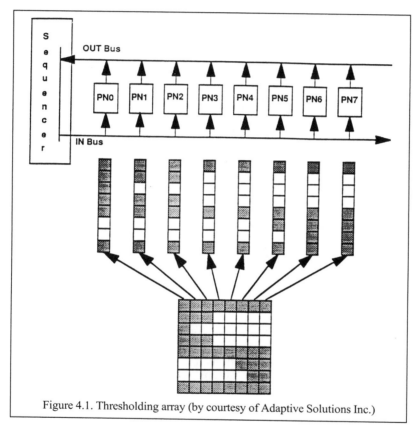

Figure 4.1. Thresholding array (by courtesy of Adaptive Solutions Inc.)

In 1993 a company called Adaptive Solutions (Beaverton, Oregon, USA) introduced its Connected Network of Adaptive Processors (CNAPS) chip. A CNAPS chip consists of 64 processors, called processing nodes (PN) in parallel. Up to 8 of these chips may themselves be connected in parallel producing a total of 512 processor nodes. The device may be used for several of the operations described elsewhere in this Chapter.

An example of thresholding an 8 x 8 array of image pixels is shown in Figure 4.1 on the previous page. It is imagined that an 8 x 8 pixel area of an image is to be thresholded with each of 8 processors being responsible for one column. When loaded, the arrangement will be as shown in the square at the bottom of the figure. The values of the pixels are then changed by an instruction passed to the processors via the common input bus.

If the arrangement is extended to a full array of 512 processors, then the change of values in a 512 x 512 pixel array would be accomplished in 308 microseconds.

The system could be used for a convolution operation where it is required to move a kernel or matrix of n x n pixel values over all the pixels in an image. For example to convolve a 7 x 7 kernel with a 512 x 512 image would take 9.55 milliseconds.

The system is also claimed to be suitable for performing JPEG compression. In this case it would carry out the operation in 4 stages - DCT transformation followed by quantisation to filter out high frequency components, run length coding to compress the result, and Huffman encoding for providing a second stage of compression. It is claimed that this operation can be carried out on a 512 x 512 pixel grey scale image in 33 milliseconds.

Note that in 1987 the time periods for carrying out processing operations were being expressed in seconds. In 1993 the times to carry out broadly similar operations are being expressed in milliseconds or microseconds. This rate of progress enables routine processing operations to be carried out today which had not been imagined six years ago.

Many different processing operations are needed in composing, querying, and retrieving operations in picture databases, particularly for query-picture questions. Some of these operations are described below.

Aliasing

A term used in various contexts to indicate the presence of imperfections in a picture introduced by processing operations – for example the effect of using an insufficient number of data points when attempting to represent a continuous function by a dot structure.

Convolution with a mask or template

A "rolling together" operation – for example, between the pixel values in a mask/template and the value of each image pixel beneath the mask. The value of each pixel in the mask is multiplied by the value of each underlying picture pixel, and the sum of these results becomes the new value, e_x, of pixel e (Figure 4.2a) in the new image.

a	b	c
d	e	f
g	h	i

a1	b1	c1
d1	e1	f1
g1	h1	i1

(a). Pixel values in a small area of the picture centred at pixel e

(b) Coefficients in a mask overlay-ing the area in (a)

Figure 4.2. Convolution with a mask

If it was required to modify the value of the centre pixel e to a new value, e_x which is the average value of the 8 pixels immediately surrounding it, the mask, as in (b), is laid over a part of a picture (a) so that e1 overlays e. A multiplying and adding operation is then executed to produce:-

$$e_x = 1/9 \ (a1 \times a + b1 \times b..........i1 \times i) \ \text{--------} \ (1)$$

In general, the values of the coefficients a1, b1, etc., may be set to the values required to produce a new picture having the required characteristics. This type of operation is widely used in image processing.

The operation is carried out for every pixel in a picture - equivalent to laying the mask successively over every pixel, each of which assumes a new value to form an entirely new image which is the result of the convolution.

Mathematically, the convolution (as in (1) above) of the Mask/Template, T (n x m) and the picture P (N x M) is expressed as:-

$$T \cdot P (N \times M) = \sum_{i=0}^{n-1} \sum_{j=0}^{m-1} T(i,j) \cdot P(N+i, M-j)$$

Edge Detection

Edge detection is applied after sharpening has been used for edge highlighting – for example by gradient edge-generation pixels. This operation can be used by comparing the levels of adjacent pixels, and where the gradient is below some arbitrary level, reducing them to black. Pixels with a gradient above that level are made white. Accordingly a white line will be generated signifying a continuity of change corresponding to an edge on the image.

However edge detection is more difficult than this for edges in textured regions and for colour pictures. See Pratt (1991). Chapter 16, for more information.

Filter

Filtering processes and filters are general terms used to describe various kinds of filtering operations, for example, after Fourier analysis – say to exclude unwanted frequencies in order to reduce aliasing.

A filtering action can also be effected by changing the value of pixels in a picture.

			0	0	0	0	0		4	6	4		
			0	1	1	1	1		6	9	6		
1	1	1	0	1	1	1	0		6	9	6		
1	1	1	0	1	1	1	0		11	14	11		
1	1	1	0	1	1	1	0		11	14	11		
			0	1	6	1	0		9	11	9		
			0	1	1	1	0						
			0	1	1	1	0						

(a)   (b)   (c)

Figure 4.3 Mask filtering

For example the 3 x 3 lowpass mask as in Figure 4.3 (a) when "moved over" all parts of the picture pixel area (b), produces the new picture (c). (After Low, 1991). The "noise" pixel, (6 in 4.3b) will disappear in the new picture.

Fourier analysis

Fourier analysis is used to convert a picture into a form which can be more easily processed, filtered, etc., using suitable algorithms for manipulating its contents, particularly when including Filters.

A rectangular single impulse of length t seconds will become rounded off when passed through a channel of finite bandwidth. The reason is that the pulse is composed of a range of sinusoidal waveforms and the faithful transmission of its edges requires that the channel will pass the very high frequencies of which they are composed.

The component frequencies occur regularly at f, 2f, 3f, 4f etc., where f = 1/t. Thus if the pulse length is 100 milliseconds = 0.1 seconds, f = 1/0.1 = 10 Hz, 2f = 20 Hz, etc. The amplitude of these harmonically-related frequencies steadily decreases making them easier to filter with a low-pass filter. The determination of these components is known as Fourier Analysis.

A similar principle holds for recurring data, although there are some different consequential effects. The process of sampling the amplitude of a continuous waveform at appropriate intervals so that it may be represented in a "discrete" form is known as the Discrete Fourier Transform. If a waveform band-limited to a frequency f is sampled to determine the amplitude at intervals spaced 1/2f seconds apart, the waveform will be completely defined by these samples.

An associated operation called the Fast Fourier Transform is based on the speed advantage obtained by a method for reducing the number of multiplications and additions required when "discretising" a continuous series.

Gradients

A gradient is the value difference between adjacent pixels. The gradient will be large when there is a large difference between adjacent pixels

Figure 4.4
"Shrink wrapping"

– as at edges in pictures. A gradient image of an edge can be computer-generated based on a continuity of large gradients.

Histograms

A diagram in which the height of a column or the length of a row represents the number of occurrences of a value, such as intensity. The examination of a histogram of the intensity or grey levels in an image may be indicative of the value at which to set the threshold or transition level from black to white.

Masks

A "mask" or template is an array of pixel values arranged in a grid-like box of 2 x 2, 3 x 3, or n x m size. It is stepped across the grid formed by a corresponding number of pixels in an image. At each step the values of the image pixels are changed – a process known as convolution – in order to modify, enhance, or otherwise process the picture. See also Convolution.

Perspective Transformation

The modification of an image in order to simulate a different viewpoint. It requires operations based on a camera model.

Figure 4.5. Example of erasing procedure

Quadtree processing

A method of splitting regions of an image to isolate individual within-scene objects. The method involves splitting the image into smaller and smaller quandrant-shaped regions and then merging different regions according to certain rules. Object areas and perimeters may be expressed in terms of bit quad counts.

To produce a quadtree, a black and white image is split into four quadrants. Each quadrant is in turn split into four and so on. The entire image can then be represented by a quadcode representing the position of any sub-quadrant in the hierarchy. A number of sub-quadrants will contain all white, or all black pixels. Information need be saved only about the smaller of these two classes, the existence of the majority type being implied. By omitting the implied class, a substantial degree of compression may be obtained.

The idea is most effective when a picture contains large areas containing all black or all white pixels. Dash (1993) shows that it is equally effective for coloured pictures and for those with a rectangular format. He suggests that quadtrees may be useful for other applications such as "spatial analysis in desktop mapping, geographic information systems, pattern recognition, and CAD applications".

Segment Labelling, Boundary Matching, Bug Following and Curve Fitting

Methods of identifying and specifying the closed contour of image segments. For example a bug follower describes the path of a spot which crosses and re-crosses boundaries, turning left or right according to certain rules and producing a somewhat ragged outline of an enclosed area.

Scaling, Rotation, and Warping

These effects are produced by mathematical operations using a set of moments which are invariant to rotation and scale changes. Warping is a method of changing the shape of an image using mathematical operations to produce effects as if the image was printed on a flexible rubber sheet.

Shrink wrapping

A term used to describe the close-contouring of an object with an edge-following outline using a special algorithm after it has been roughly outlined by a user.

Sobel operator

A mask or template with values which accentuate edges.

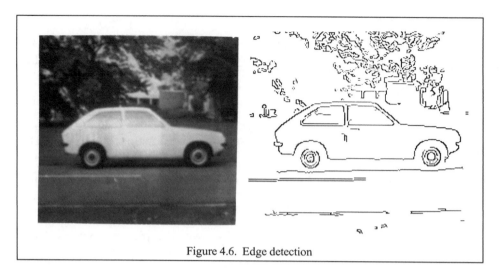

Figure 4.6. Edge detection

Template

See Mask.

Template Matching

A method of comparing a query object of interest with all the objects in a database. The query object of interest is sequentially scanned and compared for similarity with all the objects in the database which have been similarly scanned.

The usual procedure is to generate a difference measure between the query object and the unknown objects. The database objects showing the smallest difference are considered to be the best matches. The method is computer intensive since an enormous number of unknown objects may need to be compared against the query object.

Thresholding

A method of changing a grey-level picture into a bi-level picture. All the grey levels below a certain value are set to zero brightness or all the levels above a certain level are set to maximum brightness. An example of executing this operation is shown elsewhere in this chapter.

Outlining

Work continues on improving on processing methods, or a combination of methods, which are component parts of the work of object identification. Daneels (1993) devotes a paper solely to the subject of interactive outlining. Object outlining is provided as a part of many software processing packages. The user outlines an object with a few points, perhaps three or four, or whatever minimum number is needed to make it clear which object is of interest.

The machine then accurately traces the border of the object which was crudely indicated by the user. Figure 4.4 shows a bird roughly outlined by the user using "point to point" lines, and the same picture after being automatically "shrink wrapped" by the software. The illustrations, by courtesy of IBM, are taken from Daneels *et al.*, who used a two-stage method based on Kass's (Kass, 1988) "snakes" algorithm.

Samadani and Han (1993) review several procedures which are available for finding boundaries. In Haddon and Boyce's (1993) method for edge-based segmentation each pixel is paired with its nearest neighbours and examined to discover whether it forms part of a boundary.

Examples of image processing

Some examples are provided in Figures 4.5 and 4.6. The horizontal line traversing the first picture in Figure 4.5 is the result of scratching the negative when unloading the film from the camera. The same picture after line erasure is shown in the second picture.

The erasure procedure was carried out by controlling the movement of a "rubber" on the displayed picture, using Photoshop software on an Apple Cuadra 700. The picture was printed on a Kodak Ektatherm printer as used with the Kodak Photo-CD equipment. When erasing the erased area is automatically filled with pixels matching the local surrounding area.

Figure 4.6 shows an "edge" picture on the right derived from the photograph on the left using edge-detecting software. Several of the techniques described in this chapter have been used in the systems described in Chapter 7 about indexing in the section covering indexing by query-pictures. A modified version of the "Snakes" algorithm is used, for example in the Niblak system for picture-query matching.

CHAPTER 5

IMAGE COMPRESSION

Introduction

It is strange that a topic able to confer such great benefits has received so little exposure until recently. If a message is compressed one hundred times it may be transmitted in one hundredth of the time, or transmitted at the same speed through a channel of one hundredth the bandwidth. It may be stored in a store one hundred times smaller.

Although these comments are not strictly correct – there is a compression/decompression overhead of around 5% – the benefits and cost savings are huge and in some cases make certain operations feasible which could not be considered at all until recently.

The relevance of C.E.Shannon's work to information technology has been discusssed by Cawkell (1990a). The English language contains a great deal of redundant information and Shannon appreciated the potential for compressing it. He showed subjects a portion of text and they were then asked to guess the remainder (Shannon, 1951 – see Figure 5.1). They often got the next symbol right at the first guess.

---

56   THE BELL SYSTEM TECHNICAL JOURNAL, JANUARY 1951

first line is the original text and the numbers in the second line indicate the guess at which the correct letter was obtained.

(1) T H E R E I S N O R E V E R S E O N A M O T O R C Y C L E A
(2) 1 1 1 5 1 1 2 11 2 11 15 1 17 1 1 1 21 3 21 22 7 1 1 1 1 4 1 1 1 1 1 3 1
(1) F R I E N D O F M I N E F O U N D T H I S O U T
(2) 8 6 1 3 1 1 1 1 1 1 1 1 1 1 6 2 1 1 1 1 1 1 2 1 1 1 1 1 1
(1) R A T H E R D R A M A T I C A L L Y T H E O T H E R D A Y
(2) 4 1 1 1 1 1 1 11 5 1 1 1 1 1 1 1 1 1 1 1 6 1 1 1 1 1 1 1 1 1 1 1 1 1   (9)

Out of 102 symbols the subject guessed right on the first guess 79 times, on the second guess 8 times, on the third guess 3 times, the fourth and fifth guesses 2 each and only eight times required more than five guesses. Results of this order are typical of prediction by a good subject with ordinary literary English. Newspaper writing, scientific work and poetry generally lead to somewhat poorer scores.

Figure 5.1. Shannon's measurements of redundancy in language

Methods based on the exploitation of *redundancy* in language and data were the first to be used. The second method, a variation of the same principle, was the *transformation* of data into another form containing fewer data elements, to be described later.

Falling storage costs and faster processing are enabling larger volumes of data to be rapidly compressed/de-compressed. Progress in this area is remarkable but such are the incentives to handle very large data volumes that this rate of progress is not enough. Completely new methods, made feasible by enabling technology, have been developed in the last few years.

Redundancy reduction 1. Some examples

Simple methods of compressing large databases have been used for some years (Alsberg 1975). For example in a personnel record a Fixed-Length one bit code in a "gender" field to replace the 8-bit characters M or F for Male of Female immediately provides an 8:1 compression.

In the IBM HASP (Hessonite Automatic Spooling Priority) scheme used in 360 computers, data was divided into strings of duplicate and non-duplicate characters preceded by a control byte indicating the string type and length. For a string of duplicate characters, the control byte denoted, say, "23 0", meaning that 23 zeros would follow.

Variable frequency of data occurrence provides the opportunity to use a variable-length code. Huffman codes – an extension of a principle first used in the Morse code – have been discussed by Cawkell (1990).

In Huffman codes (Huffman 1952), the letters of the alphabet are arranged in order of probability of occurrence and are allocated variable length codewords. Thus E is 101 and Q 0111001101. The net effect is that the total number of bits used to represent a passage of text will be much less than would be the case if a fixed length code was used.

A simple example of "coarse" Huffman-type encoding is provided by a book database for indicating the name of the publisher against each book. The database contains, say, 2000 different publishers, each normally denoted by an 11-bit code.

However the distribution will almost certainly be of the Bradford type – for instance 6 organisations publish, say, 20% of the books, 25 a further 20%, 100 the next 20%, and so on. A compression/decompression publisher code table containing a 3-bit code for the first six, a 5-bit code for the next 20, a 7-bit code for the next 100 publishers, etc., would occupy much less space than the 11-bit code otherwise needed for each of the 2000 publishers.

Research into methods of data compression has been in progress since the early days of data processing. Calvin Mooers devised a scheme (Mooers 1960) called Zatocoding for punching holes in edge-notched selector cards, each representing a document in a collection.

The Zatocode design required an answer to the question "If the list of subjects to be indexed requires that a code using p holes be used, and the average number of subjects per card is q, how large must be the field of holes available for punching in order to limit false drops to an acceptable number?"

The scheme is an exercise in data compression because "random superimposed coding" is used – several overlapping codes may be punched in a field with a limited number of holes without excessive false drops if the design is right, permitting more subjects to be punched into small cards.

Systems transmitting information in a succession of frames, as in a television system, present compression opportunities because "Information" is imparted by a change – an unchanging situation generates no new information.

In PAL TV systems, used in the UK and elsewhere, each complete TV frame, consisting of two interlaced parts each transmitted 50 times per second, is transmitted 25 times per second. This is adequate to cope with the fastest rates of change commonly encountered such as the motion of a racehorse, motion in athletic events, etc., but most of the time each frame is almost a replica of its predecessor.

Thus when an unchanging detailed landscape surmounted by a uniformly blue sky is transmitted for, say, five seconds of viewing time, data is continuously transmitted. But only one frame, not 125, is necessary to convey the essential information. A TV set with a one-frame store would enable a system data reduction factor to $1/125^{th}$ of its former volume in this case.

Note that this is redundancy reduction without an impossibly difficult pattern prediction process. All it requires is a "no change" detection scheme.

This solution suffices to illustrate general principles – when there is no change, send a code to tell the system to send no new data until a change occurs. For more practical solutions see the section below about run length coding.

Sperling (1980) has described a rather interesting experiment which was not a matter of reducing data for transmission through a channel of limited bandwidth, but rather of finding out at what point the error rate became unacceptable as the channel bandwidth – an expensive commodity – was reduced.

In television programmes for the deaf, presenters use sign language, but the signs are still visible if a channel of much narrower bandwidth than a TV channel is used. Even when the bandwidth is decreased to about 20 KHz there is only a small loss of information.

This puts communication with deaf people using the telephone network for video communication almost within reach, and well within reach with special lines or with the Integrated Services Digital Network (ISDN).

Another interesting idea has been described by Yeh (1989) for "image browsing" – in other words getting some idea about the content of an image sent down a line of limited bandwidth, e.g. a telephone line. The user cuts off the transmission as soon as the detail is sufficient to show that the image is unwanted.

The image is crudely digitized into a relatively small number of bits which may rapidly be sent down the line in a short period of time. The transmission is then repeated with improved digitization taking a longer period of time so that it may be accommodated within the channel's bandwidth, and so on. The user stops the transmission when he has seen enough to decide that the image is of no interest, or allows it to continue to the point where the reproduced detail is sufficient for the purpose. For a good general review of earlier data compression methods see Lelewer (1987).

Redundancy reduction 2. Run length coding

To apply redundancy reduction the characteristics of the data must be known and predictable. One principle that is often used in practice is "run length coding" – the replacement of long runs of unchanging data by the shortest possible code.

For example if the "grey levels" of an image are quantized into 16 levels in order to be digitized, the level "off-white" will always be quantized as, say, "level 2". A strip of the image consisting, when scanned, of, say, 289 off-white elements, may then be represented as a long string of twos amenable to compression as a code which says, in effect, "289 twos, signifying off-white, follow".

As another example, when we have digital television – an expected development during the next decade – uniformly blue sky occupying one third of a frame normally requiring around 2 Mbits of data, could instead be transmitted as a short code "2000000 83769878" requiring a relatively small number of bits. This means "the next two million bits will be blue". The code bits would be "decompressed" just before display at the receiving end and blue pixels would be reproduced in the sky area.

Much work has been done on compressing facsimile data to enable detailed images to be transmitted quickly. Stand-alone scanning machines have inherited the methods used – they have been found to be good working compromises – providing effective compression with reasonable compression and decompression processing times (Mussman 1977, Bodson 1983).

In fax, run length coding is used in which a row of data is stored and runs of black or white bits are identified. Codewords for numbers of bits have been previously stored in lookup tables for black and white bits. The machine looks up the codeword less than but nearest to the number of bits in the run and then inserts the difference in binary code.

For instance if the number of black bits to be compressed is 865, and short codes are given in the black lookup table for 850 and 900 bits, the machine selects the code for 850 and follows it with the number 15 in binary. A similar, but inverse process takes place before image reproduction.

The time taken to compress and decompress, and the compression ratio achieved, vary according to page contents, the compression algorithms (rules) used, the power of the processor, and whether or not special chips are used for the purpose.

It may take under a second or more than a minute. For a short business letter consisting of lines of text with much white space the compression ratio will be 20 to 40, while for a page consisting of halftone illustrations there may be no compression at all.

Redundancy reduction 3. Edge detection

Quite a different approach has been researched for some years based on information redundancy. An edge or boundary following a sequence of identical pixels is a change of information requiring the handling of high frequency data. If edges can be satisfactorily detected the potential for compression exists provided that fewer bits are used in the implementation of the scheme than are used in conventional reproduction.

Current work on this approach has been described by Lee (1989). Low frequency parts of the image are filtered out and coded by transform coding (see below). Changes are detected by taking every pixel and checking its edges by examining the pixels above, below, and on both sides of it. A scheme for encoding the changes is described. The coded data from which the image may be reconstructed consists of a combination of the low frequency and the edge data. Compression ratios of 23:1 are claimed.

Redundancy reduction 4. Speech compression

Speech was one of the earliest data types to be studied because not so long ago telecommunications *was* speech telecommunication. Speech continues to receive attention particularly in the context of cellular radio and synthetic speech. For multimedia digitised speech, compression is almost essential otherwise storage requirements become excessively large.

Some remarkable results were obtained in the early work on Vocoders. In a vocoder, speech is analysed in terms of the vocal tract parameters which created it and is reproduced by using a pulsed sound source modified by vocal tract parameter data. The information needed to provide very artificial but understandable speech created in this manner was achieved with a transmission rate as low as 0.1 to 0.4 bits per sample.

Considerable compression development work (Jain 1981, Haskell 1981) followed the adoption of digitisation – implemented because the handling of data in digital form provides substantial advantages over analogue. This advantage is partially offset by the greater bandwidth occupancy of the digital form. Digitisation of analogue audio or video signals requires that the varying level of the analogue waveform be "sampled". The value of levels are transmitted as a code.

A code describing the amplitude of a sample of a smooth waveform is required once per cycle (Hz) for complete reconstruction of the waveform at the receiving end. In the case of a complex waveform containing many components of different frequencies, numerous samples are required. When represented as a continuous graph the quantised waveform assumes a step-like appearance.

Speech compression is the art of ingenious methods of bit reduction. A crude way of doing it, which results in a steady reduction in quality and the introduction of quantisation noise, is to simply reduce the number of samples taken.

Most of the work has revolved round improving Pulse Code Modulation (PCM) – the basic method of waveform quantisation – and the transmission of coded levels. The rate still widely used and considered necessary for good quality speech is 8-bit sampling 8000 times per second, producing a bit-rate of 64 kbps, requiring a transmission channel of a relatively wide bandwidth.

The variations and improvements on PCM include Adaptive Differential PCM (ADPCM) using 4 bits per sample. Continuously Variable Slope Delta Modulation (CVSDM) with only 1 bit per sample 32,000 times per second, and a relatively new method dependent on chip processing power called Codebook Excited Linear Predictive coding (CELP) have been introduced.

CELP analyses the speech pattern during a short interval of time and consults a "speech pattern reference table", compiled from speech pattern statistics, which shows what kind of pattern is most likely to follow a given pattern. It then applies the difference data between the two patterns to the first pattern and sends it as the second pattern. The result is a very low bit rate of under 5 Kbps.

Redundancy reduction 5. Recurring images

In television and other similar types of display, a CRT screen is filled with a frame of data representing an image, to be immediately followed by another, usually very similar frame. A succession of frames are displayed at a rate of at least 25 per second to provide a flicker-free apparently continuous picture. Motion is conveyed by small frame-to-frame changes – motion may appear to be jerky if it is fast enough for the part of the image in motion to move an appreciable distance from frame to frame.

The development of fast cheap processing devices enables a frame to frame examination to be carried out to detect areas within which motion or a change of scene is occurring, and to supply a stream of data only about those areas.

This area has been the subject of intense activity for many years, one of the pioneers being Professor Cherry working at Imperial College (Cherry 1953). A company called Cawkell Research & Electronics, adopting some of Cherry's ideas, conducted some work (prematurely) to send TV pictures along a telephone line (Cawkell 1964).

Activity has been further stepped up in view of the expected advent of High Definition Television which requires a very wide bandwidth. Current work has been reviewed by Tonge (1989) who starts by pointing out that the bandwidth required for HDTV is at least five times that of current TV.

The most popular method for the compression of HDTV signals, used in the Japanese MUSE and in the European HD-MAC systems is called "sub-sampling" – that is the TV signal is sampled for coding purposes at a rate lower than that required to completely re-construct the waveform (Nyquist criterion). A 40% reduction in the required bandwidth can be obtained by this method. This is done with little deterioration in picture quality by using a new type of digital comb filter designed to deal with distortion in the frequency spectrum which would otherwise occur.

Recent developments 1. Compression software for microcomputers

In 1990 a number of compression packages for PCs were reviewed in *PC User* magazine (Price 1990). They were said to achieve compression partly by compacting DOS files which are allocated more space in the DOS file-cluster arrangement than they really need, and partly by using algorithms for variable length coding, Huffman encoding, or the Lempel-Ziv algorithm (as used in the latest modems) in which short codes are substituted for high-frequency strings which are automatically selected and stored.

The main applications seemed to be for compressing files during disc backups. The compression ratios obtained are not large but worth having. They provide from 25% to about 50% file compression, nearly always performing better on text files than on programme files.

Prices range from £8 to £150. Some include compression software among several other "utilities" which usually accounts for the higher price.

Recent developments 2. H.261 Codec.

The H.261 Codec was developed under an EC programme and has been recently ratified under CCITT aegis. Its purpose is to provide compression in videoconferencing schemes. It compresses a 352 x 288 line image in what is known as the Common Intermediate Format (CIF) running at 30 frames/sec into a bit rate of 64 Kbps for transmission, for instance, via the ISDN.

Recent developments 3: the CDI and DVI schemes

The compression scheme developed by the Philips/Sony team and used in the Compact Disc Interactive system has been described by Preston (1988). CD-I was developed from Compact Disc Digital Audio – CD-DA – the CD you buy in your record shop. Sales of CDs, launched in 1982, are now approaching 800M in total, with add-on CD players costing about £100 in the UK.

A CD delivers data at 170.2 Kbytes/second and has a total capacity of 650 Mbytes. Such a disc could store about 650 PAL colour TV frames, each containing 1 Mbyte of data. If played back at TV rates it would provide a programme lasting about 30 seconds, but at the CD rate of 170.2

Kbytes/second the programme would be in slow motion and would last a bit longer. However CD-I is organised to process data in a different way – quite different from the usual method of delivering data in a linear fashion, line by line and frame by frame.

A CD-I player contains a store for holding a screenful of data – say a picture of a bunker on a golf course. The store is filled once with data from the disc and this fixed amount of unchanging data is repeatedly scanned and presented on a CRT for as long as may be necessary. This system is very like the "no change detection" scheme sugested on page 62.

The organisation of CD-I includes various facilities to enable a variety of programmes to be presented without the "refill rate" -far slower than the bit rate in conventional TV – from affecting the picture including:-

- Reduction of the colour data in images by a special coding scheme.

- Provision for the coding of text and graphic images using a colour lookup table and run length coding.

- Provision of the means for up-dating small areas of the screen at a rate acceptable to the eye – normally at 10 to 15 frames per second.

- Provision of 4 separate stores ("image planes") with a total capacity of 1 Mbyte capable of storing four sets of data which may be scanned out in parallel to present four sets of data on the screen.

- Provision for using the planes as overlaid "matte" images. A "front" image may be partially transparent allowing parts of a "back" image to be displayed, or a solid small front image may have a transparent surround to reveal a background image.

- Provision for moving one image over another to provide full screen animation requiring far less data than is required for a full-motion picture.

In a CDI scheme in which a golf-ball alights in a bunker, the disc delivers a small amount of data once, representing the flight and finally the appearance of the ball. Thereafter this data is stored and displayed by repetitively scanning it. For an image such as this which is displayed for seconds, or perhaps tens of seconds, the disc is only required to deliver up-dating data. CD-I programme content must be of a kind able to provide entertainment without the store refill rate exceeding 170.2 Kbytes/second.

The associated software provides the necessary control such as that required for "interactive play" routines. Thus a user with a control device such as a "joystick" may operate the figure of a golfer to play a shot towards what appears to be, say, the 18th hole at St. Andrews, or possibly towards any hole on that course or on any other course of his choice.

For the similar Digital Video Interactive (DVI) scheme elaborate compression methods have been developed by General Electric/RCA to enable data for one hour's motion video playing time to be stored on a DVI disk – the same size as a CD-ROM disk. A compression ratio of up to 100 to one is obtained by a combination of several techniques.

Having started in 1983 at RCA's David Sarnoff research centre, DVI work continues there under the control of GE who took it over in 1985, and from 1988 when it was acquired by Intel.

To produce the disk the data is compressed using a mainframe computer but in the DVI player decompression will be carried out by two Very Large Scale Integration (VLSI) chips. One runs the decompression algorithm at 12.5 million instructions per second (mips) and the other deals with the display format.

A VLSI chip contains 100,000 or more transistors. The DVI VLSI chips were developed at the Sarnoff Research Centre, but Intel has acquired the technology and expects to manufacture them.

The compression of a rapid succession of slightly different images enables different data between successive images to be coded and signalled. When a succession of very similar images are handled in this manner huge compression ratios may result.

A DVI disc can provide up to 72 minutes of full screen motion video at 30 frames per second. Alternatively it can provide up to 40,000 still pictures, 40 hours of audio, 650,000 pages of text or some pro rata combination.

Intel has announced several products – a plug in board for PC AT computers for capturing and storing data in local storage, and a playback and decompression board at a total price of about £4000. A complete DVI playback PC with monitor and CD-ROM drive is expected to sell for £7000. IBM is expected to announce a DVI workstation soon.

Recent developments: 4. Transform coding.

When data strings may assume a very wide range of possible values – like the number of possible patterns in a high quality illustration – alternative transform coding methods may be more suitable.

The number of possible patterns in even a very small image, of which only a small, virtually impossible to compute, fraction will form meaningful images, can be $10^{6^{14}}$. The enormity of this number is evident when compared with the 1.3×10^{26} molecules in a gallon of water - (Jain 1981).

This problem is tackled using transform coding in which an image, or sections of it when it is processed as a mosaic, is represented in terms of characteristics which are representable by a comparatively small number of samples (see below).

The mathematical process known as the Discrete Cosine Transform (DCT) is a classic example of the elegant use of the compact processing power currently available to perform the elaborate operations in real time needed to substantially compress data "on the fly".

In the version of DCT incorporated in the Joint Photographic Experts Group (JPEG) standard – worked out by ISO and CCITT groups - a digitised image is coded by processing blocks of 8 x 8 pixels in sequence from the top to the bottom of the picture.

Each block is scanned in order to generate information about the rate of change between the pixels present. A checker-board pattern in a block would produce a stream of high frequency data elements, an all-white or all-black block would represent a low frequency change. The "information" in the block is confined to the high frequency elements which are Huffman encoded – a highly economic code. Decompression goes through the same processes in reverse.

The Inmos A121 chip was developed during 1989 to handle this type of operation. It runs at 320M operations/second, taking 3.2 microseconds to carry out an 8 x 8 DCT process and taking 15 milliseconds to handle a 625 x 625 pixel image.

In April 1990 the 27 MHz C-Cube Micro-system type CL550 chip designed to perform according to the JPEG standard, was announced. The price is $155 in quantity. It will compress an 8 Mbit video frame by 10 times in 0.033 seconds for 30 frames per second video. Alternatively it will compress a 200 Mbit high resolution full colour still picture to 8 Mbits in 1 second.

A 1992 advertisement for the Leadview board and software, says that the system will provide compression ratios between 2 and 225 times, with compression times of 8 to 10 seconds. "We are so sure you'll be impressed" says the advert, "that we include a 30-day money back guarantee".

The speed needed by the user depends on the application. When an image is scanned in colour, later to be reproduced, using, say, a desktop publishing system, it depends on the user's patience. When motion video is involved, say in a games application, compression/decompression systems must be very sophisticated and very fast.

Practical implementation of compression chips (Apiki 1991) arrived with the impending Standardisation of JPEG algorithms, to be arranged by ANSI and ISO. A chip conforming to a modified Standard for motion video is manufactured by C-Cube Microsystems.

Current discussion centres on whether it is better to use one chip – a "fixed performance general solution" – or to implement the standard with several chips and software. The standard provides for several variations, so the second approach enables a "custom-built for the application" system to be provided (Cavigioli, 1991). Cavigioli also describes the way the JPEG effort developed and gives a description of its features.

Numerous devices now incorporate chip-implemented compression schemes to the Standard which provides for "lossless" 2:1 compression -that is the compressed picture is virtually perfect – up to a compression ratio of about 30:1 where degradation starts to become noticeable. Leonard (1991) provides a set of pictures including one showing just acceptable 32:1 compression; at 300:1 the picture is still just recognisable but fine detail is lost and edges are very ragged.

JPEG compression works by compressing the halftone or colour bits which are applied to the beam or beams as voltages to change the intensity level of a displayed pixel. Because of the importance of the maximum bit rates that can be delivered by different media – for example CD-ROMs, Video Recorders, etc., an important objective is to compress pictures to the bit rate which a particular media can deliver. The delivered data is converted to real time data by the de-compression software running on the associated machine.

Instead of ratios, compressions are therefore often expressed as "bits per pixel". Cavigioli (1991) provides a subjective assessment of JPEG compression ratios from original 16-bit per pixel pictures as follows:-

8 bits/pixel	(2:1) compression	"Lossless".
1.5 ..	(11:1) ..	"Indistinguishable from original".
0.75 ..	(22:1) ..	"Excellent quality".
0.25 ..	(64:1) ..	"Useful image".
0.10 ..	(160:1) ..	"Recognizable image".

Whether others would agree with these assessments is another matter.

For motion video, the delivered bits, after decompression, must run at the designed rate for the application. For example for 30 US television frames per second to be delivered to a US television receiver or computer screen and to provide normal-looking pictures, the data rate is about 28 Mbytes or 224 Mbits per second. Applications of motion video compression are discussed under " multimedia" in the next chapter.

A variation of JPEG called Motion-JPEG is JPEG speeded up to enable motion video to be compressed and decompressed in real time. However attention is now moving on to the Moving Picture Experts Group (MPEG) Standard where bit rates become particularly important (Le Gall 1991). A major objective is to compress TV bit rates down to 1 to 1.5 Mbps or lower.

Several companies have announced compression products – UVC Corporation supplies a card providing up to 500:1 compression for multimedia applications, Intel a JPEG i750 DVI motion video processor, and NEXT Computer includes compression with its newer machines.

SGS-Thomson has also developed a JPEG processor – the STI140 which will compress/decompress colour still pictures at a rate of 30 frames per second providing compression ratios of up to 30:1. It sells at $200 in lots of 1000.

In June 1991, Philips announced that a C-cube chip will be used in up-rated CD-I players. It will enable about one hour of video plus audio to be accommodated on a 650 Mbyte CD-I. Compression will enable the data rate to be slowed down to less than 1.5 Mbits/second.

Recent developments 5: Fractals

The 1989 OED defines "Fractal" as "A mathematically conceived curve such that any small part of it, enlarged, has the same statistical character as the original". Until about 1990 fractal compression methods excited some interest in academe but a wider interest was soon aroused with the arrival of commercially available high-compression ratio software.

Fractal geometry is about "scale invariance", a property of natural objects first observed by Renoit Mandelbrot around 1961. It is based on the fact that small portions of an object often resemble larger parts.

Mandelbrot noticed that the coastline of Britain looked much the same when viewed from different distances. The collection of inlets and peninsulars visible at 5 Km, looks similar to the larger collection visible at 30 Km of which the smaller collection has become a part.

Michael Barnsley, working at the Georgia Institute of Techno- logy, Atlanta (Barnsley 1988), devised computer algorithms which take portions of complex images and performs transformation operations on them called Iterated Function Systems (IFS) – from which a set of points may be plotted providing a coarse image of salient features called Fractal Transform (FT) codes; the information necessary about the spatial relationship between points is preserved in the codes, enabling the original image to be re-constructed by an iterative scaling-up process.

The reduction process amounts to the elimination of redundant geometric information. The Compression ratio between the original and the reduced image and the time taken to generate the latter depends on the complexity of the shapes present in the original. Some parts may exhibit great redundancy, in others there may be very little.

In 1987 Barnsley demonstrated the reduction of a 780 x 1024 pixel image which took 100 hours but achieved a compression ratio of 1000:1. Barnsley claims ratios of up to 10,000:1 or more, and at the 1990 Birkbeck College, London, Conference on Chaos and Fractals, demonstrated 45 seconds of 30 frames per second motion video on a PC containing two special boards, retrieved from a 1.2 Mbyte Floppy disc.

Normally over 700,000 bytes (5 Mbits) per frame are necessary for motion video, but this demonstration represents about 1037 bytes per frame -a compression ratio of about 670:1.

A high quality compression board for plugging in to a 386

MSDOS micro-computer with 640K memory and hard disk, is sold by the company for £6000 with software for around £2000. It will accept 24-bit colour input files in various formats.

A system user could compress a file, to, say, 10 Kbytes and send it on disk or transmit it very cheaply to another location and load it into any suitable micro which contains the decompression software – for instance a 286 or higher machine with 640K and a VGA display. The resident decompression software is licensed at £95 per user for up to 100 users, reducing for larger numbers. No special hardware is necessary for decompression.

The results obtained by these new compression systems are open to different interpretations and it seems necessary to proceed with caution.

Beaumont (1991) has described the principles of fractal compression in some detail using a number of illustrations to show effects in working systems. He describes a scheme which compresses an 8-bit per pixel halftone picture into a picture requiring only 0.8 bits per pixel- that is a 10:1 compression- "without introducing artefacts obvious to the untrained eye. Compression down to 0.5 (16:1) produces visible artefacts but the picture quality is still reasonable". The accompanying pictures (Figure 5.2 by permission of Iterated Systems) lack their original colour and probably suffer a little from being re-reproduced. The pictures demonstrate resolution independence and mathematical zoom-in. In conventional zoom- in both the size of the image and the size of the pixels change.

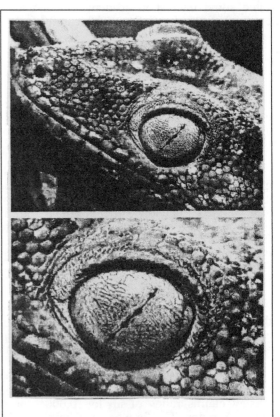

Figure 5.2. Fractal compression.

The upper image shows a zoom-in, still at a resolution of 1280 x 600 pixels, although it is only one quarter of a 1280 x 600 image scanned into the system. It was printed after decompression from a 10 Kbyte compressed file. The lower picture, also printed from a 10 Kbyte compressed file, is zoomed in to provide a picture of 5120 x 3200. The printer used is a Mitsubishi 600 dots/inch printer. An effective compression ratio of nearly 5000:1 is claimed. The picture quality does not seem to have suffered much from this enormous ratio.

The time taken to compress and decompress presumably depend to some extent on the power of the machines being used. It could be 10 minutes for compression but only a few seconds for decompression. Using this system a very large database containing high quality pre-compressed pictures could be easily stored in megabyte instead of gigabyte capacity. A few seconds for the decompression of a retrieved picture would be acceptable.

This dramatic performance is as claimed by Iterated Systems. I have had long conversations with two different users – one at a large research establishment and another at a commercial organisation. The research user says that the obtainable compression ratios and quality as obtained on a range of images are no better than those obtained with alternative proprietary systems and they will not be using it; the appearance of compressed pictures depends very much on their content. The commercial user finds it acceptable for use at very high compression ratios.

CHAPTER 6

MULTIMEDIA, HYPERTEXT, COMPACT DISCS, AND PICTURES

"When I use a word" Humpty-Dumpty said in rather a scornful tone "it means just what I choose it to mean – neither more nor less". "The question is" said Alice "whether you can make multimedia mean so many different things". "The question is" said Humpty-Dumpty "which is to be master -that's all"

(With apologies to Lewis Carroll)

Multimedia philosophy

If the meaning of a word may be discovered from its usage, then "Multimedia" means "The processing of information derived from or presented in several different media". "Hypermedia" appears to be a synonym for "Multimedia", but since "Hyper – " means "over or excessive" perhaps it should be avoided.

Successful multimedia applications listed by Feldman (1991) include videodiscs and interactive video for training and education, videoconferencing, interactive videodiscs for marketing, and CD-ROMs in libraries. Feldman discusses a far larger number of applications in the "tentative toe-in-the-water" stage. Various future scenarios, future prospects, what might happen when the ISDN and other wideband channels become available etc., are also discussed.

Wilson (1991) divides the applications market into Education, Training, Simulation, Internal and External Business Communications, Retail Product Information, Museums, and Domestic (Home). Wilson says, after stressing the importance of the £2000 barrier, that "Education is a growing issue and in the UK the combination of performance and cost looks as though it is earning Acorn the Government endorsement".

Case examples of many of these applications are discussed in Chapter 8.

The presentation of text with graphics, derived from several different "media" such as WORMS, CD-ROMs, scanners etc., may be labelled "multimedia". But this Chapter is not about systems of this kind which have been available for some years: it is mainly about the presentation of information with sound, animation, pictures, and motion video as well as with text and graphics.

The bones of the multimedia idea can be seen in the object-oriented scheme incorporated in the Star machine devised by the people at Xerox's Palo Alto research labs in the late seventies.

If a user is able to invoke the behaviour of an object on the screen which embodies certain properties of data, then the system may legitimately be called "object-oriented". The system interacts in a familiar, real world manner with the user instead of imposing the mechanics of its hardware and software upon him.

Unfortunately the Lewis Carroll misquotation above would be

equally apt if "object-oriented" was substituted for "multimedia". The phrase "object-oriented" is applied to all kinds of systems regardless of their qualities.

In multimedia, extra dimensions of information are added to object-orientation so that the user employs all his or her senses (excluding, for the time being, smell) in the exchange of information with the machine. The situation is made to seem quite like the familiar real world environment.

It now seems as if multimedia has got beyond the flash-in-the-pan stage when it was hyped up by manufacturers to join VCR's, Camcorders, Desktop Publishing, DAT, and other gadgets with which we can apparently no longer do without, but which are running out of steam.

Perhaps McLuhan's vision is on the way to fulfilment. In one of his earlier books, *Gutenberg Galaxy* (1962), McLuhan suggested that communications media determine the nature of social organisation. New media provide humans with new psychological-structural equipment. Will a $24 billion market, predicted by one Nostradamus for 1994, come true?

Lewis Mumford (1963) thought that:- "by centring attention on the printed word, people lost that balance between the sensuous and intellectual, between the concrete and the abstract... to exist was to exist in print: the rest of the world became more shadowy". Mumford also thought that McLuhan was pressing forward in the interests of the military and commerce. A later author imagines a scenario where the "sole vestige of the world of concrete forms and ordered experience will be the sounds and images on the constantly present television screen or such abstract derivative information as can be transferred to the computer" (Carey, 1981).

Be that as it may, it is obvious that the boundaries between Information, Entertainment, Education and Commerce are becoming even fuzzier. Will, for example, multimedia online databases greatly enhanced by graphics and sound, appear with "a controlled pictorial index language whose terms are the descriptors of the significant structure in digital images" as confidently claimed by Bordogna et al (1990)? It is already being claimed that "Multimedia databases will radically change the way you look at and work with information" (Shetler, 1990).

Shetler's Binary Large Objects (BLOB) database may "present you with any combination of data fields, images, and text objects" and may contain "spreadsheets, graphs, fax, object-code modules, satellite data, voice patterns, or any digitized data... it could be very large – up to 2 giga-bytes" ("Satellite data" is much the same as any other data but it sounds impressive). For online access you will have to await the arrival of SONET (optical) telecoms otherwise it will take a week for the stuff to arrive.

Why shouldn't the presentation of information about, say, houses for sale, be accompanied by the sights and smells of the neighbourhood? The enterprising Estate Agent who sends you an entertaining disc may be stealing a competitive advantage. Why shouldn't shareholders receive clips on videotape showing the products of their company in use, with the report (which would be much more interesting if its sections came up via hypertext links) which they receive annually from the chairman?

Indeed, why in the home of the late nineties shouldn't "the multimedia machine be a computerised entertainment centre combining the functions of today's audio and video systems, television set, games machine, and home computer?" (Cookson, 1990).

All these things may happen – in a review of *Macromind Director* in the October 1990 issue of *Byte* the writer says "The Overview Module (shown in Figure 6.7) allows business people to create excellent presentations easily". For others, however, "easily" is not the right word at all. In the very next issue of that journal, the potential user – an experienced computer person – of a multimedia board, advertised as being for "reasonably knowledgeable people who aren't computer experts" found that "there was not one single sentence in the instruction manual that she understood".

A related subject was discussed in a UK national newspaper (Virgo, 1990):- "Organisations buying computer systems generally ignore the largest costs... the cost of disruption and training is commonly up to double the cost of developing and testing the software which is itself double the cost of the hardware".

To cover the cost of the technical effort and expertise needed to acquire and use appropriate multimedia hardware and software, together with the time and the artistic and creative effort of providing a presentation, you should probably double the number again.

On the other hand liberation is at hand to offset some of these constraints. Multimedia processing, particularly motion video processing, is much less constrained than it was. Extra power, storage, and run-time is much improved. Demands have arisen for real time graphics processing requiring about 20 Mips, and fast rendering to produce photographic realism which requires 300 Mips.

Graphics processing, which incorporates a dedicated computer within a computer, is advancing rapidly. IBM lapses into hype-language when enthusing about its PS/2 90 and 95 machines which "thanks to dazzling XGA (Extended Graphics Array)... (provide) a new standard in high resolution quality, conjured up in the blink of any eye".

The other liberating factor is compression (See Chapter 5). Compression joined the ranks of over-hyped multimedia-related topics comparatively recently. CCITT standard H.261 has been agreed and a Codec enabling videoconferencing to be carried on at bit rates of from 64 Kbps to 2 Mbps is already used by British Telecom. This is a proven application, not a pious hope.

Digital Television speeds for high quality colour picture reproduction are normally over 200 Mbps, but British Telecom say that at the 2 Mbps rate used for teleconferencing with the codec "it requires a keen eye to spot the difference between a compressed and a broadcast picture". This kind of compression must soon become available for multimedia purposes and its effects will be – and I must use the word – sensational.

A colour TV frame may be typically represented by about 1 Mbyte (8 Mbits) of data. At 30 frames per second, a run time of one second requires 30 Mbytes of storage. Techniques are available to extend the run time by compressing motion video by a large ratio. (Sandbank, 1990 is the standard work on Digital Television)

The Multimedia "end-product" at the present time is usually a "multimedia show" controlled by an experienced presenter, or a publication stored on a CD. Multimedia enhancements seem to add real value in education and training, and it is in these areas where applications are appearing.

Boring old, plain vanilla, business or information product providers have not yet acquired the gizmos needed to add the necessary multimedia bezaz (to use some foreign but explicit words). But you don't try and justify the cost of intangibles like your new multimedia fun-image – it's an act of faith.

Gale (1990) is prepared to be more definite about the future, although less expansionist than the forecasts mentioned earlier. In 1994 he foresees 18 multimedia applications, 22 "market segments", and 14 "end user platforms". These precise estimates are offset by an appropriate degree of segment broadness – for instance "documentation" as an application, "consumer" as a market segment, and "computerised entertainment/information systems" as an end user platform.

The major markets in 1994 (in current millions of dollars) will be Consumer 4337, Heavy Manufacturing 2211, Other 2103, Government 2055, Motion Pictures 1239, Education and Libraries 850, Computer and Information Services 450, and Retail Trades 352. Total $13,597 Million. If this be true I should obviously interrupt the completion of this book and rapidly get into the multimedia business.

A major effort is in progress to introduce Standards by the CCITT, ISO, and the Industry. The composition of multimedia Standards is a highly necessary but very difficult topic emphasising the standard Standards problems – how to fix the Standard on a particular date in the face of rapid advances, intense competition, the setting of *de facto* standards by fleet-of-foot entrepreneurial organisations, and the un-desirable consequences of being quickly overtaken by events because the Standard is set too early. The likely result may be the setting of a Standard with so many alternatives and options that it is ineffective.

A number of multimedia Standards are briefly described in the Glossary. For further information a recent issue of *Information Services & Use* (IOS Press, Amsterdam), notably the articles by Bryan (1993), Soares (1993), Fromont (1993), Froment & Creff (1993), and Pring (1993), summarise current progress.

Mainly about hardware

Figure 6.1 shows a multimedia system conceived in 1977, although the word had not yet been conceived, or perhaps it was an early attempt at Virtual Reality.

78

It was called a Spatial Data Management System (SDMS) and was used for research and experiments at the Massachusetts Institute for Technology (Bolt, 1977).

The user sat in a special chair and used joysticks to control a back-projected picture, listening through multiple loudspeakers. Many years later an increasing number of CD-ROM disks began to appear on the market. A recent innovation is that they are designed to run on multimedia PCs.

A multimedia PC is an ordinary 386/486 PC with a high resolution colour display, a sound board, a CD-ROM drive, and a sufficiently large amount of RAM and hard disk memory.

The first addition to convert a PC into a multi-media PC is a sound card. There are quite a few different types on the market today, but the most widely used, compatible with most CD-ROM multimedia disks, is the Sound Blaster from Crea-tive Labs. This card will enable the system to generate high quality music and sound effects, as well as offering a digitised voice channel and a text-to-speech synthesiser. Output is of FM quality with up to 11 voices. Output power of 4 watts per channel is sufficient to run loudspeakers.

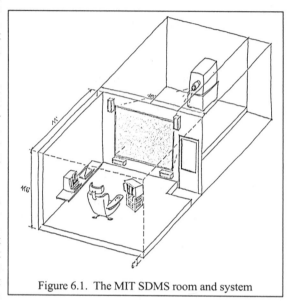

Figure 6.1. The MIT SDMS room and system

The next requirement in a multimedia system is a suitable user interface programme. Here the choice is simple since the most suitable product if you have a PC is Windows 3.1. This version is a considerable advance on version 3.0 and includes support for both CD-ROM drives, and sound cards. It is also an interface which is compatible with a lot of the products from CD-ROM disc publishers.

A good example of the capabilities of multimedia is provided by a multimedia PC composed of all the necessary units, together with Windows 3.1, loaded with the Multimedia Beethoven disk produced by Microsoft.

The Apple Macintosh microcomputer, introduced in 1984, was noted mainly for its high resolution 512 x 384 pixel screen and excellent graphic user interface. It had an 8 MHz processor, 16/24 bit data path/bus, 400K floppy drive and 128K memory. But its integrated design and lack of slots for cards provided no scope for third party developers.

The Mac II, which came out in 1987, became the leading machine for multimedia applications. In 1990 Apple introduced the Mac IIfx with a 40 Mhz 68030 processor and 68882 co-processor, cache memory, and 3 auxiliary processors. This made the machine up to four times faster than the improved Mac II (the Mac IIx). The US Mac IIfx price was originally $12,000 - about £7500. An equivalent Apple machine today costs about one third of that.

Apple also introduced the 20 Million Instructions Per Second (MIPS) 8/24 GC display card, with a 30 MHz RISC processor on board, providing 8 bit colour at 640 x 480 pixels, or 8 bit (256 level) grey scale at 1152 x 870 pixels. The price was about $2000.

A major reason why the Mac II became the multimedia leader was the slots which opened it up to third party suppliers. A huge range of add-on hardware and software became available. Another reason was, as someone said in regard to multimedia applications, the "Mac is doing what it does best – providing a consistent user interface, seamless data exchange, and gorgeous 24-bit colour graphics".

The main features of the Mac II are:-

- 15.7 MHz 68020 processor with six NuBus slots for 96-pin cards and 68881 co-processor (4 to 40 times faster than the Mac Plus).
- 32 bit data path/bus.
- 1 to 8 Mbyte memory and up to 80 Mbyte internal hard disc.
- Video output card with colour lookup table. 32 bit colour. The Apple video card limits the potential to 8 bit pixels providing 256 colours from a 16.7 million colour palette on a 640 x 480 pixel screen. Third party suppliers can provide cards giving a much larger choice of colours.
- Screen stretchable to spread over up to 6 monitors.
- Stereo sound with 4 synthesizers available.
- Two Serial ports, several bus connectors and an SCSI interface with pseudo-DMA or triple rate data transfer.

In September 1990 the company announced a low priced machine – the Classic – and by 1992 it had re-organised its range to consist of the Classic, Powerbook, the powerful Quadro, and the improved Macintosh II models. At the top of the range is the Quadro 900 which runs on a 25 MHz MC68040 chip. It includes SCSI and Nubus ports, an Ethernet adaptor, and a video system incorporating a VRAM. It uses dedicated I/O processors and provides mono and stereo output. It includes 4 Mbyte RAM expandable up to 64 Mbytes, and a 160 Mbyte hard disk drive.

In 1992 Apple deleted a number of their older models, including their portable, but retained the 3 Powerbook models. Powerbooks are notebook computers using the 68000 processor operating at 15.66 MHz. Powerbooks use a 640 x 400 pixel display with a super twisted nematic LCD, backlit with a cold cathode tube. Apple launched their Newton pen-based machine in mid-1992.

The Commodore Amiga microcomputer was noted for its colour before the Mac. It could also display video images from an external source synchronised to on-screen effects produced by its user ("Genlocking"). However for several years it has been eclipsed by Apple. But in 1990

Commodore made a very strong bid to catch up with a new machine – the Amiga 3000 – having a performance nearly matching the Mac II at half the price at the time (£3160 with 2 Mbyte memory, 40 Mbyte drive, £3610 with 100 Mbyte drive).

The 3000 is a 32 bit machine with the same processors as the Mac IIfx – 68030 and 68881 co-processor – running at up to 25 MHz. The machine includes an enhancement of the Amiga special set of three controller chips which provides much of its multimedia capabilities. The "Agnus" chip is a graphics processor providing functions like fast drawing, filling, and moving blocks of pixels; "Denise" deals with computer and video resolution and scanning; "Paula" handles sound.

Memory is from 1 to 16 Mbytes, with an internal hard disc of up to 100 Mbytes. The screen displays 4 bit per pixel colour out of 4096 colours at 640 x 400 pixels. Four expansion card sockets are provided. A 200 pin socket is also fitted ready to accept a next generation 68040 processor. Ports are similar to the Apple II. In addition to its new Amiga version 2.0 operating system, the 3000 will also run Unix.

In August 1990 Commodore introduced what was arguably the first complete purpose-designed multimedia system, anticipating the systems reviewed below. The CDTV interactive graphics CD-ROM player/microcomputer was demonstrated at the November Computagraphics show at Alexandra Palace, London. CDTV disc preparation is much less expensive than preparing CD-I discs. Commodore expected 100 disc titles with CD-I-like presentations before the end of the year, intending to make its mark well before CD-I got going.

The price with software (and VAT) was a low £699 at that time. The CDTV is a CD-ROM player and integral Amiga computer with a 68000 processor and a set of ports including RS232 serial and parallel, external drive, stereo out, video out, composite video out, MIDI interface for music, and the usual ports for desktop peripherals.

CDTV "user authoring" will be developed, and professional authoring was well under way in 1990, with suppliers of ready to use entertainment discs, using conventional mastering processes, coming to the market. The machine includes a 64 Kbyte card memory slot, but no floppy disc drive. The CDTV may have been premature and wrongly priced because not much was heard about it after the launching ceremony.

The equipment needed to provide a fully fledged multimedia show is untidy and could be expensive. For example it might include a Mac ll with additional boards, CD-ROM player, videodisc player, videotape player, external sound amplifier, and loudspeakers, with assorted software, interconnecting cables, and the space to accommodate it all. This is the penalty for using a cobbled-together rather than a purpose-designed solution, although most of the units are mass-produced in a competitive market.

This situation is changing with the emergence of purpose-designed equipment in anticipation of a much large demand. Quite recently the industry seems to have become convinced that the multimedia market is now large enough to warrant the manufacture of both "up-grade" kits to convert a micro into a Multimedia PC (MPC), and also purpose-designed multimedia systems.

Both types of system have been reviewed by Loveria (1993) who concluded that the up-grade kit from Creative Labs provided the best value, and that the NCR 3331 MLS was the best value complete system. The Creative Labs system includes a Sound Blaster audio Pro 16 board, a Panasonic CD-ROM drive and other accessories. The price is $800. The NCR 3331 MLS includes a 33 MHz DX micro, 8 Mbytes RAM, 240 MByte hard drive, Toshiba Photo CD/XDA compatible CD-ROM drive, sound card, and comes with a super VGA chip-set and DVI adaptor. It costs $3805.

Up-grades and complete systems come with a range of software, authorware, and sounds library, and also several CD-ROM titles such as Grolier's Encyclopedia, Microsoft Bookshelf, Sherlock Holmes, etc., included in the price.

Current activities by IBM and Apple, major players in the multimedia business, indicate that multimedia is now regarded as a major field, if not *the* major field.

IBM introduced a range of PS/2 based multimedia systems in 1992 covering a price range of $3355 to the top of the range Ultimedia M77 486DX2 model. The software is called Multimedia Presentation Manager (MMPM/2), an extension of IBM's OS/2 operating system. All models include 8 Mbytes of RAM, an SSCI 212 Mbyte hard-drive, microchannel architecture, and a Kodak Photo-CD/XA CD-ROM drive.

Considerable attention is paid to sound quality – CD 32-bit over-sampling running at over 80 KHz is used (see below under CD-DA). Action-Media II DVI boards using the i750 chip-set are available for Ultimedia models. They will play 30 frame per second 640 x 480 pixel motion video pictures in a 4" x 5" window.

An IBM PS/2 Ultimedia machine includes audio adaptor and microphone, internal speaker, CD-ROM/XA drive will CDs, tools, and application samples. Over 30 Ultimedia/tools will become available from a number of associated companies such as Macromedia, Vision Imaging and others. The tools offer authoring, creation, capture and editing facilities for providing video, audio, animation, music etc.

IBM has also developed a number of Ultimedia units and software for the AS/400 series of machines. For example the system/400 package enables application programmes to control video devices and windows.

In May 1993 IBM launched its PS/1 low cost multimedia PC called the PS/1 Multimedia System. It includes a 386 processor, 85 Mbyte disc, Philips CD-ROM drive, and audio adaptor. It is suitable for playing family and educational CD-ROM discs, and will read Kodak Photo-CD images.

Apple are moving towards all-purpose machines, placing less emphasis (according to Thompson and Smith, 1993) on that hackneyed word "multimedia" and more on a new phrase "digital media" or "audiovisual" – almost as hackneyed as "multimedia".

It is hard not to be impressed by the Apple Mac Quadra 840AV although it "only" contains a 68040 40 MHz processor. It will support 16 bit colour on a 21 inch 1152 x 870 pixel monitor. This machine has reduced the gap between "standard" and "special" hardware for managing still television pictures and motion TV. The Quadra will accept PAL or NTSC signals from, say, a video camera. The machine comes with system 7.0 and Quicktime software and live video can be dragged to a re-sizable window anywhere on the screen. A video clip to be captured and run as a Quicktime movie provides a window of about 4" x 3" at 320 x 240 pixels in colour.

Figure 6.2. Apple Quadra 840 AV system

The resident arrangement, just described, will record at about 1.5 Mbytes per second, and may be stored on the 500 or 1000 Mbyte disc provided with the system. This will eat up storage at an alarming rate.

In order to run and record a significant length of 24-bit colour motion video in PAL format, full screen, some extras are still needed – an extra plug in board and a faster disc with improved compression software. The disc will be a disc-array with JPEG compression software providing storage, under these conditions, at about 100 Mbytes per minute. Thus a 1 Gbyte disc system will provide storage for 10 minutes of video, said to be "as good as VHS reproduction" although the JPEG compression ratio must be fairly high. A special card and SCSI/2 interface will be needed. A user may require other peripheral units to handle inputs and outputs to make the most of its performance.

The Quadra AV (Figure 6.2) integrates telephone, modem and fax into a single desktop system. It also includes Apple's new speech recognition system known as Casper. The system requires to be trained and includes a 60,000 word dictionary. The recognition software has been compiled with reference to a large number of speakers with various regional accents from all parts of the United States. Appropriate dictionaries will be needed for foreign countries which will require a similar compilation effort. Text-to-speech software for translating text into synthesised speech is included.

The effectiveness of speech software is notoriously difficult to assess. Its applications range from the management of routine commands to conversational dictation. This system will operate somewhere between these extremes requiring subjective judgement on whether it will handle, reasonably effortlessly, the application the user has in mind.

This machine is one of the most advanced available is not cheap relative to other offerings, although, once again, both the price and performance would have seemed impossible a few years ago. Approximate U.K. costs are £3,800 for the Quadra 840AV plus a 21" (say) colour monitor at £2,500 and £145 for a keyboard. As an example, a Canon colour laser printer/copier/scanner will cost about £5,500 including software. The special disc array for motion video and the interface will cost about £3,000. Application software to mount multimedia presentations may well cost another £1,500.

Software

A large amount of multimedia software of two kinds, is available that which comes with "ready to play" media, and that which is available for loading into a machine to assist in low-cost "authoring", that is for the creation of multimedia presentations.

Quicktime is a substantial advance in multimedia techniques. It is a system extension to the Apple 7.0 operating system used on Apple Mac microcomputers, introduced to handle animation and video including motion video, with sound. It enables a picture or motion video to be displayed in a window on any Mac with a 68020 or later processor running system 7, preferably with at least 4 Mbytes of memory.

Quicktime is widely used and has 4 major components – system software, file formats, compression, and interface. Its design is such that it will support many different kinds of data and soon after it was introduced in 1991 a number of suppliers advertised cards for Macs running Quicktime. For example a board may be used to capture live video and convert it into Quicktime format, enabling a "movie" to be edited and merged. A board of this type from VideoSpigot will continuously process NTSC or PAL motion video into 24 bit-colour digital data.

A "Movie" file may contain sound, video, or animation in any combination, and parts of it can be cut and pasted in the same manner as a graphic.

Quicktime will support a number of different types of compression software, notably the JPEG algorithm. The compression system will handle 24 bit colour movies running at 25 or 30 frames per second in a small window – the first time this was achieved on a microcomputer. In some cases a compression ratio of 25:1 is possible.

CD, DVI, and other disc systems

Some remarks about CD and DVI systems in regard to their Compression systems arrangements were made in Chapter 5.

CD-DA

CD-DA (Compact Disc – Digital Audio), usually known as CD, is a magnetic disc medium which has now taken over from vinyl recordings. Sales of CDs, launched in 1982, are now OVER 700M, with add-on CD players costing less than £100 in the UK. CD-DA is of passing interest here because it introduced the concept of CDs in all its forms.

The system was originally developed for sound recording to a Philips/Sony specification. When recording, marks are made on the disc by a laser corresponding to the digits of digitised sound. They are read back by a lower-powered laser. Elaborate error correcting arrangements are included in the system.

The first player – the Sony CDP-101 – appeared in 1984. Players connect to amplifiers or hi-fi equipment. Certain aspects of CD technology have become the forerunners for the variations next described.

It seems not to be widely known that Compact Disc players do not necessarily reproduce the potentially excellent sound quality available from a CD. To digitize sound for recording purposes, 8-bit samples are generated by sampling the analogue waveform at 44 KHz. However the process results in the acquisition of harmonic data which sounds unpleasant.

To get rid of it a technique called "oversampling and filtering" is used in CD and CD-ROM players. The scientific basis for it is doubtful, but the improvement is undoubted. Bit rates are increased and if the discerning purchaser knows how to ask the right questions and the vendor knows the answers, he or she will hear about "8 x 2", "16 x 4" etc players. The first number denotes the number of bits per sample, and the second the pseudo-sampling ("oversampling") rate.

The best CD players, such as the Cambridge Audio CD3, embody "16 x 16" which means "16 bits with 16 times oversampling". Oversampling is also used in the Amiga CDTV. Considerable attention is being paid by Amiga, IBM, and others to sound quality. CD-ROM sound technology is the same as CD technology.

In January 1993 Nimbus announced that they could play 2 hours of video from a special disc run on a compact disc player. An ordinary CD player could be used for full motion video because the laser track used by Nimbus is only 1.2 microns wide and track read speed is reduced. The net result is a doubling of the data density.

A black box developed by Nimbus and C-Cube connected between the output of the player and a TV receiver contains a C-Cube chip which decodes the MPEG algorithms as they come off the disc. A double density 12 centimeter CD can contain over 2 hours of full colour motion digital video with sound.

CD-ROM

A Compact Disc – Read Only Memory is a Constant Linear Velocity (CLV) 4.7" disc containing data recorded in a CD-like digital format. Evidently the coded content of the signal does not demand "oversampling" to improve visual results although oversampling may be used to improve sound quality. A CD ROM drive comes in a separate box for connection to a microcomputer or as a unit which will slide into the drive aperture provided on the front of a microcomputer. There is a trend to connect a CD-ROM to the controlling micro through the Small Computer Standard Interface (SCSI) to increase data transfer rates.

Standardisation and drive problems are quite different from CDs where disc format was standardised from the start and compatible players followed thanks to the domination of two manufacturers, Philips and Sony, and their specifications in the "Yellow Book".

CD-ROM software formats must include uniform ways of describing and locating on a disc information about a single Volume (a CD-ROM disc), a Volume Set or collection of discs, and a file. A file is any named collection of data.

Each set of several sets of files could be a self-contained information product and a user could be allowed access to one or more products on the same disc. Alternatively the product might be so large that the file set for that product occupied a Volume Set comprising several volumes. There are other aspects of importance such as automatic error correction and file directory arrangements.

CD-ROMs were read-only discs until very recently; there is scope for an optimum directory arrangements (achieved, perhaps, by a hashing algorithm) to minimise seek time which is inherently slow.

In the event, software formats were initiated by the High Sierra (HS) group – formed from a number of manufacturers in the US and including Philips and Sony. Successive attempts at finalisation before the end of 1986 were unsuccessful, but agreement was eventually reached and HS became a *de facto* standard with the intention of getting it through as an ISO standard to add universality and respectability.

This idea was fine in principle and it enabled the industry to develop. The process was remarkably quick since it had been pushed by a relatively small number of organisations. It duly became the basis for ISO 9660, independent of machines/operating systems, approved, again remarkably quickly, by late 1987.

The "standard standards" problem then began – how to develop and implement bug-free software conforming to ISO 9660. HS was not widely replaced by ISO 9660 because the former had been adopted and it worked. Suppliers either would not wait for the ISO software or would not use it because their customers did not have version 2.0 of MS-DOS extended memory called for by ISO. However ISO 9660 is now being adopted following a special plea on behalf of users who want hassle-free choices which work on any system.

Although "making CD-ROM discs/players work" is relatively easy for the user, "relatively" means compared with the other frightful hassles accompanying your average IT system. This means that many people will not find that installation is easy. The difficulties to be expected have been discussed. They are sufficient to call for articles telling you how to get out of them. One particular problem was "easily" tackled by *Byte* contributor Pournelle but Pournelle is a computer buff with very wide experience. Just how easy is it may be assessed from Pournelle's comments:-

"Of course the solution was obvious, Access to CD-ROM drives requires two actions. First you have to load the CD-ROM driver with CONFIG.SYS. Then you have to execute the MSCDEX.EXE program which loads Microsoft DOS extensions that allow DOS to recognise disc drives large than 33 Mbytes. Then use LOADH1 to install the Amtek Laserdek driver with CONFIG.SYS and when I wanted to access the CD-ROM drive, open a window and execute MSCDEX.EXE command inside the window". Easy for a computer buff, but for others?

Although CD-ROMs were not as successful as was expected by the ebullient forecasters, they have lately become successful enough to be well established in the "information world", competing mainly against online searching. The capacity of a CD-ROM at around 550 Mbytes, is sufficient to store quite a large textual database. No telecommunication charges or delays are incurred when using one.

The fact that colour, graphics, illustrations etc., can also be stored on a CD-ROM is an added bonus, although such additions eat up storage space. One of the highly effective methods of data compression is likely to be adopted to reduce this problem.

CD-ROMs cannot be as easily and cheaply up-dated as online databases, so if there is a need for frequent up-dates, a CD-ROM may be unsuitable for the application. However the price/up-date frequency difficulty does not disqualify CD-ROMs from medium-term up-dating or from being suitable for many different kinds of application.

A number of organisations will undertake to prepare a master disc from a customer's database and produce copies from it. A special tape must be prepared together with the directory structure, ready for making the "pre-mastering" tape which will include synchronization bits, headers, error correction etc., to the "Yellow Book" standard. From this a master disc is prepared to produce copies – the CD-ROMs for customers.

A specialized software house will prepare the pre-mastering tape and the price for preparing a master disc from that tape will average about £2000, with the price of copies ranging from about £50 each for a small quantity, reducing to £3 each for large numbers (Philips prices).

CD-ROMs may now also be produced at a price appropriate to non-professional producers. The Philips CDD521 drive is sold with an Adaptek 1542 SCSI-2 adaptor, Advanced SCSI Programming Interface (ASPI) driver, software MSCDEX.EXE, and DOS utilities called CD-Write. CD recording depends critically on an uninterrupted stream of data, particularly when – as with the CDD521 – the drive runs at twice the normal CD play speed, requiring a sustained transfer rate of better than 300 KBps.

The work space where you assemble the material written to the CD is a hard disk. CD-Write converts on the fly from the hard disk's DOS file system to the CD's ISO 9660 file system. It can also redirect the ISO 9660 images that it creates to a hard disk and can write such a preformatted image to the CD.

The system can be used for publishing because the CD can be written on – it carries a groove covered by a layer of organic die and a reflective layer. The laser fuses the die to the substrate to create pits which can be read by normal CD-ROM readers.

With regard to "transportability", most CD-ROM discs are readable using different microcomputers controlled by different operating systems. The micro is loaded with a driver program providing for all discs that will be used if they have a standardised logical file structure. If that structure is known to the programmer who writes the driver, an appropriate driver will enable files to be opened and data to be interpreted.

Not only that, only if the arrangement of data in the files is standardised will the user's application program be able to search the files and obtain results meaningful to the user each time he places a disc from a different information provider on his drive.

A new type of drive called "multispin" is now being developed and the first to appear on the market is the NEC InterSect CDR-74 - available in both Macintosh and PC versions. The drive speed is doubled and transfer times and search times are speeded up.

The speeds of current CD-ROM drives are set to make CD audio play at the right speed for audio reproduction. Manufacturers have solved this problem in the new drives by adding controllers that play back the audio tracks correctly.

There are several CD-ROM points of interest in the Commodore CDTV described in the previous section. A proprietary compression system of unspecified performance was adopted pending agreement on compression standards. The importance of effective compression can hardly be over estimated. The capacity of CD-ROMs for the CDTV may be increased by using the six spare 8-bit control channels for graphics.

Semi-standardised CD-ROM players are now reaching the critical mass needed to encourage the supply of a wide range of products for similar applications – for instance for bibliographic database distribution.

CD-ROM drives come as internal units for a micro or they may be purchased in external separate boxes. NEC, Hitachi, and Panasonic are the major manufacturers. Storage capacities are either 630 or 560 Mbytes.

Next Technology, Cambridge, England has developed a jukebox to hold 270 CD-ROM discs – a storage capacity totalling 175 Gbytes (1400 Gbits). It contains 8 drives, so more than one CD-ROM is accessible at one time. The jukebox is controlled by a PC and it takes 5 seconds to transport a disc on to a drive. The cost is £22,000.

The Perform 600 machine may be bought with a fast internal CD drive, the Apple CD 300i. The 300i provides a serious price and performance improvement over Apple's external CD-ROM drive, the Apple CD 150. It also has full-blown support for Kodak's Photo-CD system, and there is a direct sound connection from the drive to the Perform's internal speaker.

From about 1985 onwards, CD-ROM versions of well known databases such as *ERIC, MEDLINE, SCIENCE CITATION INDEX,* etc., have become a viable complement, if not a replacement, for printed or online-searchable versions. At least two other major applications are of interest – selected data distribution (for example the supply of census data to be selectively transferred to hard disc for specialised use), and "Smart Discs" (where included software enables retrieved information to be further processed).

CD-ROMs have also expanded into areas beyond bibliographic databases. As early as 1987 the financial CD-ROM *Lotus One Source*, sold 19,000 copies, followed by Microsoft's *Bookshelf* with 10,000.

In Armstrong's 1990 directory, 19 titles are selected for comprehensive evaluation. Of these, 10 are bibliographic databases, 6 are directories, dictionaries, or encyclopaedias, 1 includes full text abstracts, and 1 is a numeric database. Libraries probably still form the main market, but business applications are now showing the fastest growth.

In a recent article, Hollis (1993) says that a UK survey reveals that more people still use online information services than CD-ROM but the gap is narrowing. A major advantage of CD-ROMs is "end-user empowerment" – in other words end-user searching is often carried out directly, while online searching is usually done by an intermediary. Moreover most libraries may not charge for a CD-ROM search, but they may charge for online.

Stoneman (1993) from the CD-ROM publisher Silver Platter reports trends in CD-ROM publishing. The number of CD-ROM/Multimedia titles has increased from 48 in 1987 to nearly 3,600 in 1993. In a recent report it is claimed that over 1100 new titles were published in the first six months of 1993 alone.

There are now (1993) over 2,800 CD-ROM/multimedia companies, although the rate of formation of new companies has slowed down considerably. The fastest rate of increase in CD-ROM/Multimedia publications by price has been in the range $100 or less. "Acquiring data rights for electronic media will continue in importance but it is a huge task to convert existing print resources into electronic form. Safeguarding data rights during distribution will be a growing concern" says Stoneman.

CD-ROM XA (Extended Architecture)

CD-ROM XA, announced by Philips, Sony, and Microsoft in September 1988, is a disc format providing some of the functions available on CD-I without departing much from established CD-ROM techniques. It conforms to the ISO 9660 standard.

The main advance towards multimedia with XA is a new standard text/graphics format for microcomputers independent of operating systems, and a coding system for sound as specified for CD-I, but with discs playable on both CD-ROM and CD-I players.

A fully compatible XA drive incorporates Adaptive Differential Pulse Code Modulation (ADPCM) decoding and decompression for separating interleaved audio channels. One objective in using CD-ROM XA is that Kodak Photo-CD discs may be run on it. A CD-ROM XA drive should also be able to cope with multi-session Photo-CD discs where the disc contains several different batches of pictures.

CD-I (Compact Disc Interactive)

CD-I was developed from CD; a CD delivers data at 170.2 Kbytes/second and has a total capacity of 650 Mbytes. Such a disc could store about 650 PAL colour TV frames, each containing 1 Mbyte of data. To play the data at TV frame-repetition rates, data delivery would need to be at a rate of at least 25 Mbytes per second and the disc would play for 24 seconds or less. At the CD rate of 170.2 Kbytes/second the programme would be in slow motion and would last a bit longer.

A US NTSC television frame is often digitized at 512 x 480 pixels but for CD-I, because the eye is relatively insensitive to colour variations, a reduced-rate alternate line coding scheme is used for colour component signals (chrominance) called DYUV producing 360 x 240 pixels – one third of NTSC, i.e. a 3:1 compression ratio. With 8-bit colour, a frame then consists of 360 x 240 x 8 = 691 Kbits = 86,400 Kbytes.

In a CD-I system the CRT is refreshed 15 times per second (half the TV rate), and the CD playback bit-rate is 170 Kbytes/sec. Therefore there are only 170/15 = 11,330 bytes available 15 times per second for the screen. A full screen requires 86,400 bytes 15 times per second but what it gets is 11,330 bytes so only 86,400/11,330 = 13% of its pixels can be up-dated each second.

However CD-I is organised to process data in a different way -quite different from the usual method of delivering data in a linear fashion, line by line and frame by frame.

Since a CD-I actually delivers data at 170 Kbytes per second, special measures must be taken for displaying it. A store in the player holds 1 frame of data which is scanned at TV rates, but new data is fed into it only when there is a *change* of information – quite unlike normal TV practice where the system always runs at the equivalent of about 25 Mbytes per second whether there is a change of information or not. In CD-I a number of other coding and display techniques are used to overcome the data rate problem.

The data stored on the CD is likely to be audio, graphics, text, motion video etc., which are loaded in and out from the micro's disc as needed. The picture on the screen usually consists of overlaid separately-controlled areas with *part* of each one sometimes containing motion video, all parts controlled by the software which also selects which data to shift from the hard disc. Applications include interactive games, interaction with encyclopaedias, interactive learning systems etc.

CD-I includes various facilities to enable a variety of programmes to be presented without problems arising because of the slow bit delivery rate from the disc, as explained in Chapter 5 about compression.

1993 CD-Is should include full-screen motion video. Most players contain a slot for a motion-video decoder scheduled for late 1992. There were about 50 titles at the start of the year. Combined sales estimates for CDTV and CD-I of about 400,000 units have been forecast for 1994.

The biggest question is over the home market, says one observer. Can CD-I achieve all that Philips hopes for it or have they missed the boat as some critics believe? "Rumours of a DVI unit targeted at the home cannot be dismissed, although software for it will be a crucial issue, and what impact will CDTV have?... Corporate communications, depending as they do on networking, will move with systems which support this need".

CD-I was launched in the US at the end of 1991 with 100 disc titles, and players with interactive control software. One title is "a guide to photography" where a user adjusts his camera settings to photograph a subject, take the shot, and then looks at a "print" to check the results. Another title displays "pages from a colouring book" and a child can fill in the colours.

DVI

Intel introduced a Digital Video Interactive (DVI) development system for CD media called Pro750 ADP in 1989 to be followed by a product called ActionMedia using a DVI CD-ROM in 1990.

The major difference between CD-I and DV-I is that DV-I incorporates more efficient MPEG compression using inter-frame content comparisons so that only new data is supplied to a frame. No data flows into unchanged parts. The net data rate reduction enables one hour of full-screen motion video to be stored and delivered from a CD-ROM, should that be needed.

Rash (1992), under the heading "Real products for real users" says that the "IBM/Intel *ActionMedia II* supports high quality full-motion video at 30 frames per second, VGA and XGA images, and digital audio. It conforms to a series of de facto multimedia Standards that ensure interoperability... Instead of the usual still images, IBM and Intel used full-motion footage... more important, *ActionMedia II* stores the video images and digital sound on a standard Netware file server hard drive instead of on a slower CD-ROM drive".

Referring to another product, *Curtain Call*, Rash says "Imagine how powerful your presentation would be at the next meeting if you could mix your slides with photographs and recorded sound. Imagine presentation text and drawings other than the usual Times Roman, Helvetica, and black line art that you usually see... full-motion animation and video will be coming shortly".

I agree – such a presentation would be most enjoyable. I can also imagine the cost of gaining authoring experience, preparational time, artistic design ability, source material acquisition, synchronisation, continuity editing etc., required for such a presentation.

DV-I is not in the "CD hierarchy" – it is currently an Intel product. However it builds on CD disc technology – a DV-I disc is basically a high capacity CD-ROM disc running on a standard CD drive. Until recently, motion video had to be recorded on a DV-I disc via a mainframe computer to compress it to 5 Kbytes per frame. The disc will then play 72 minutes of full-screen colour motion digital video (VCR quality 256 x 240 pixels). Alternatively it will store and play 40,000 medium resolution or 10,000 high resolution (512 x 580 pixels, 750 Kbytes uncompressed per frame) still pictures, 40 hours of audio, 650,000 pages of text, or some pro rata combination.

Decompression is carried out by a 12 MIPS VLSI (Very Large Scale Integration) chip and a second chip handles the display.

However, astonishing advances in compression techniques discussed in Chapter 5 enabled Intel to announce in November 1990 the availability of plug-in boards for microcomputers with 80386 processors, containing chips with on-chip proprietary microcode capable of "mainframe" online compression rates. The microcode can be replaced so that DV-I compression/decompression algorithms can be made to comply with expected standards in due course. A DV-I player with a 30386 PC, keyboard, joystick, audio amplifier and loudspeaker sells for about £5000.

One consequence of this development is that with an Intel TV-rate frame-grabber board installed in the micro, motion video from a camera or a broadcast TV signal can be compressed and captured on hard disc in real time, the disc removed, and the TV programme played back on someone else's micro. Most discs have insufficient capacity so the most convenient removable "disc" could be the removable cartridge on a Bernouilli drive external to the PC.

Motion video

Space in the frequency spectrum available for television broadcasting is at a premium and much ingenuity has gone in to cramming sufficient information into as narrow a bandwidth as possible – given that a consumer-acceptable picture is required. That picture is displayed to a public whose picture acceptability standards are conditioned by the movies. The width of the frequency band currently available for PAL analogue TV is 0 to 5.5 MHz.

It is not essential to digitize TV video data for all computer imaging applications – you pay a penalty because after digitization the signal occupies a much wider bandwidth. The Laserdisc optical disc players, for example, simply record TV analogue signals which are handled like conventional TV signals.

But for many applications the bandwidth disadvantage is over-ridden by the great advantage of being able to process image data on a digital computer. However at the last moment in a TV receiving system the data must be converted back to analogue before being applied to the CRT display.

During the last year the bandwidth disadvantage is being shrugged aside in the growing belief that transmitted motion-video – in the form of compressed multimedia material for domestic services – may become feasible because of de-regulatory, technical, and inter-connecting activities in cable TV, telephone system, and networks.

The Plain Old Switched Telephone System (POTS) is by far the most universally available communication channel into homes and businesses. The frequency band of POTS is just about wide enough to transport data at up to about 140 Kilobits over second (Kbps) – the speed specified for the

ISDN primary data rate. However it seems unlikely that the ISDN will be the telecommunications media for multimedia data exchange. It is too slow. Even its much faster proposed successor, the B-ISDN, may be a non-starter, nor will telephone system fibreoptic cable into homes be arriving for a while.

It seems that a combination of cable TV, network (for example Internet) and possibly ADSL – a relatively new technique for data transmission at 2 Megabits per second or more for over 90% of the "local loop" in the UK – may arrive sooner than expected.

The cable TV operator Telecommunications Inc., Denver, alone has 10 million subscribers out of an estimated US total of over 50 million. Internet is believed to have at least 7 million users. In Europe about 30 million homes are connected to cable but connections are patchy. Germany has about 13 million subscribers. It is not clear whether these figures refer to "homes passed" by cable, households actually connected, or the total number of viewers in connected households. In the UK, additional franchises have increased the total of homes passed to at least 9 million although only about 600,000 households are actually connected. However there were 50,000 new connections in the last two months of 1993 so growth is rapid. Continental customer bases of viable proportions exist.

A number of companies seem to believe that multimedia transmission will soon be feasible. Presslink's library of 120,000 photos, may be searched online. Springer Verlag and AT&T will be offering patent graphics. Access to dial-up picture libraries is being considered by Kodak Picture Exchange, Time/Warner, Continuum, and Picture Network International. The Interaxx TV Network will provide you with a box to sit on top of the telly "to make every TV set in America fully interactive now!", via their network. User's response will be via an included 9600 baud modem along a telephone line.

Microcomputer systems are now capable of running full-screen motion-video. Recent developments enable a standard PAL motion-video TV programme to be displayed full screen on a microcomputer when the TV programme is being delivered from a CD.

In mid 1993, Videologic demonstrated a CD driving a full screen motion video system on a microcomputer. Two boards are plugged in to a 486 PC (it would also work on a 386) – the DVA-4000 which will accept RGB computer input and PAL or NTSC colour television signals from a video cassette recorder, laserdisc player, or TV tuner, and the MediaSpace board for compression/decompression which incorporates a C-Cube CL-550 chip and an Inmos T400 transputer.

It would appear that (appearances are deceptive as later discussed) the DVA-4000 board converts incoming PAL colour TV data by sampling it "on the fly" at 13.5 MHz, releasing digital data at 13.5 x 8-bit or 108 Mbps in real time. This data may be mixed with graphics to provide a composite TV/user's own graphics synchronised display. Analogue VGA output is provided for a monitor - that is 8-bit colour at 640 x 480 pixels.

The MediaSpace board provides variable compression using motion JPEG format. Summarising the details provided in Chapter 7, C-Cube is the company which pioneered the technology of compression chips to the proposed Standard emerging from the Joint Photographic Experts Group (JPEG). This standard graduated from methods of compressing still pictures to compressing motion pictures as well. It will become an ISO standard and a CCITT recommendation. More recently motion is being accommodated in the MPEG standard using inter-frame comparison methods.

Summarising again details from Chapter 5, the basic principle is to use Discrete Cosine Transform (DCT) coding of the levels of each pixel in 8 x 8 blocks. The amount of "information" in a block depends on what is happening. If the picture content is changing rapidly there may be a difference between each pixel, but in areas of little change – for instance in a picture of blue sky – each pixel, and runs of 8 x 8 pixel blocks, may all be at the same level. DCT processing produces far less data in this situation since there is no change in information, so there is substantial data reduction (otherwise known as compression).

The degree of compression may be adjusted when a MediaSpace board is fitted, and the chosen amount depends on subjective judgement. The current status of video compression has been reviewed by Waltrich (1993).

Other necessary facilities are a Philips CDD 521 CD Writer, a Pioneer DRM604X variable-speed CD Player with an SCSI card and software, and a hard disk of sufficient capacity to record your motion-video. The Card is a Small Computer Systems Interface (SCSI) and the software deals with formats and controls the data in and out of buffer storage between hard disc and CD.

The procedure is to record TV on to the hard disc via the micro containing the Videologic cards in order to compress it, shift this data on to the Philips Writer and record it on a CD. Subsequently the CD is put on the Pioneer, and the disc is played into the micro in order to decompress and display it. The big question is how long will the TV programme last when a CD-full of motion-video data is recorded and played back in this manner?

The maximum bit-delivery rate for the Pioneer is four times the normal CD player rate – 612 K/Bytes per second. The capacity of the CD is 600 Mbytes so if it was set at the right speed for that data to be delivered over a period of 30 minutes it would be delivering it at about 330 Kbytes/second, or 2.64 Mbits/sec. To get a TV signal producing 88 Mbits/sec (as described earlier) on to the disc to provide a programme of 30 minutes it would need to be compressed about 33 times.

These figures are only of about the right order because the operative words used in the above explanation are "It appears that....". The Videologic system chips have their own way of doing it so the compression rate needed in practice is probably not 33 times. Picture quality after a compression of 33 times would be unacceptable to most people. As demonstrated at a recent exhibition the quality was good – almost certainly the compression ratio was less than 10:1

The fact is that the CD played on the Pioneer with the rest of the gear as described and did provide 30 minutes TV full-screen. That is quite an achievement. It may be compared with the performance of the Apple Quadra 840 AV, discussed earlier.

The total cost of the gear required to do the job including the Pioneer, Philips Writer, 486 micro with large capacity hard disc and other accessories would be about £11,000. If you wanted to get copies from the "master" CD produced on the CD Writer, Philips would do the job within 2 days at £1995 plus £2.75 per disc up to a total quantity of 500, or within 10 days at £1125 plus £2 per disc. We still have some way to go for programmes to become widely available on CD drives of this type which you can run with your own inexpensive equipment.

Creating multimedia presentations

Authoring is a major problem for multimedia programme developers and a number of authoring tools have become available. They usually include a means of controlling programme flow and timing and handle animation, voice, motion and still video, graphics, text and audio. They have been developed for running on PCs and Macintoshes. Once a production has been prepared the data has to be changed into a form suitable for a presentation media – for instance to conform with ISO 9660 for a CD-ROM.

A multimedia development system really needs to include a powerful microcomputer with a good monitor, a CD-ROM drive, a large hard disc – say 600 Mbytes – stereo loudspeakers, a microphone, and mouse. Suitable input devices would be a video recorder or video disc drive. Sound may consist of 16 bit stereo with a high sampling rate – at least 44 KHz, and a MIDI interface. Adaptor cards may be needed for compression, MIDI interface and video.

An attempt is being made by a company called the Microelectronics and Computer Technology Corporation (MCC) to bring a degree of standardisation to multimedia interfaces. They have formed a Consortium of industry members including companies like Apple, Bellcore, Kodak, Philips etc.

A major multimedia problem awaiting a solution is Copyright Management. A company called 3DO in San Mateo, California, is making available a very large database containing music, sound effects, and thousands of photographs, footage and clip art, available to licencees without copyright restrictions. By March 1993 nearly 100 publishers had become licencees.

The book by Burger (1993), which includes a Chapter on producing multimedia presentations, may be highly recommended as an introduction to Multimedia. It provides background information on computer, video, and audio technology and is written in an easily-readable style. The word "Bible" in its title is apt.

The production Chapter introduces the layman to show-biz production language and practices covering planning and pre-production considerations, scripts and storyboards, budgets, legal issues and aesthetics.

Hypertext

Apple-based multimedia, controlled by Hypercard hypertext software is very popular. An explanation of some basic aspects of sound and video follows and some of the more interesting items of equipment and software and the way they are used will be described.

Hypercard, or one of its more recent alternatives such as Supercard or Hyperdoc, may be used as a convenient multi-media program to control a presentation of text, sound, music, voice, graphics, pictures, animation or motion video.

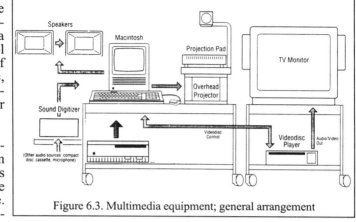

Figure 6.3. Multimedia equipment; general arrangement

A complete description of Hypercard is outside the scope of this article. Equipment arrangements may be as shown in Figure 6.3. Suffice it to say that Hypercard is a programming system for use by non-programmers.

Fields, Cards (a Mac "screen-full" with a border looking like a card), and Stacks, roughly correspond to Fields, Records, and Files in a database. A statement called a script in the Hypertalk language (words in English) is associated with each Object on a Card.

Since a Button is one of the most important Objects, it is convenient to use it as an example of how the system works. When the cursor is placed over a Button, normally captioned, and the mouse is clicked, a Message is sent to a Script for it to be executed to perform some kind of action.

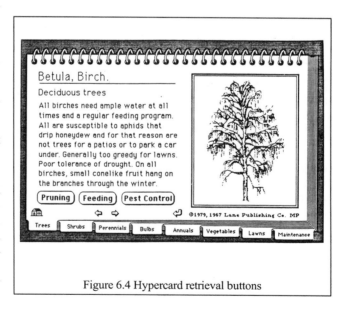

Figure 6.4 Hypercard retrieval buttons

For instance the action might be to activate a link to another card in the same, or a different, stack to retrieve the other card. Thus in Figure 6.4, the buttons "Pruning", "Feeding" and "Pest Control" retrieve cards containing that information. For simpler arrangements non-programmers may create their own Hypercard system using the wide range of ready-made facilities provided.

Writing Hypertalk Scripts, which consist of standardised English phrases or words used in order to create a command protocol, requires a longer learning commitment but is still relatively easy.

Multimedia interest in Hypercard centres on access to third party software. A Command is a Message containing a keyword which will cause the script for an object containing that keyword to be executed. A Function is some kind of instruction. External Commands (XCMD) cause a "resource", or code module, written in Pascal or Assembly language, to be executed by a command message. An XCMD may be used to control Driver interoperable software associated with an external device such as a videodisc player.

A resource has to be written by a programmer but when Hypercard-compatible devices, and software or special purpose software are used this is not necessary because the software includes ready-made resource code and driver, and the XCMD can be installed in a Hypercard stack. The user may then create a button, labelled appropriately, to execute a script containing the XCMD.

Adding Voice and Music

The Mac II contains a small loudspeaker and a stereo output socket for connection to an external amplifier and loudspeakers. Sound quality and cost considerations are then the same as those applying to domestic hi-fi equipment.

One way of adding sound to visual material is to use an Apple CD-SC drive, which plays CDs or the audio tracks from CD-ROMs, in conjunction with Apple Hypercard CD Audio Toolkit. The toolkit provides XCMDs for a stack to control the player by accurately selecting passages of speech or music from the disc.

This is not only convenient but it provides the great advantage that the stored music consumes no microcomputer memory or disc storage. The CD-Audio Stack from Voyager (Santa Monica, USA), will select tracks and automatically generate buttons for selection purposes.

Musical instruments and synthesizers are another source of music; connection to computers has been standardised in the Musical Instrument Digital Interface (MIDI). Apple make a MIDI connector interface which plugs into a Mac serial port and also provide the driver and software to manage incoming sound.

If sound is digitized, sound passages of any length may be represented on the screen as if the sound was frozen, and all kinds of control and editing functions become possible. However the real, playable, sound, behind the screen representation of it, eats up computer storage space. To digitize it, the value (level) of the amplitude of the sound waveform is periodically sampled. A 4 bit sample, providing 16 different values, would provide poor quality since there is insufficient data to properly reconstruct the waveform; 16 bits are needed to provide good quality.

If the sampling rate is too low, data between samples which needs to be digitized will be lost and the high frequency response will suffer.

Sampling 22,000 times per second with 8 bit (256 levels) per sample produces digitized sound of reasonably good quality. The sound playback duration for different digitizing conditions is shown in Figure 6.5.

If the sound amplifier and speakers are of high quality, and the user wants to reproduce a piece of music with the highest quality, an increase of the rate to 44K 8-bit samples per second may be needed, requiring 1 Mbyte of storage for a 22.7 second recording.

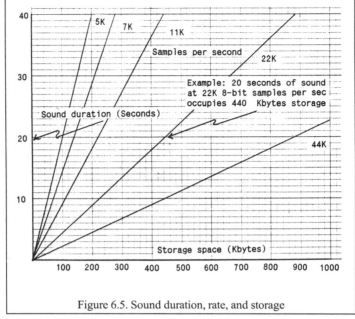

Figure 6.5. Sound duration, rate, and storage

It is important to know about the const-raints of storing digitized sound in RAM memory or on disk. The uninterrupted duration of a passage of sound stored in memory is proportional to memory size. If the memory is too small and must be filled from disc during the passage, there will be a break in the sound unless special measures are taken.

The "special measures" are to add processing power with appropriate software to reload memory almost instantaneously. This will require an extra card for the Mac with its own digital processor. One of the best known sound packages is the Farallon (Emeryville, Ca, USA) MacRecorder Sound System 2.0 outfit. A small electronic digitizing box plugs into the serial port of a Mac for voice, sound effects, or music input.

Farallon's Hypersound software creates a stack requiring XCMD Commands to record or play sound.

Sound Edit is an associated software package which provides a range of facilities including compression options, cut and paste sounds represented as waveforms on the screen, mix sound channels, alter quality, and so on. Figure 6.6 on the next page shows the appearance of the screen when different sound channels are being mixed into a single channel.

Controlling and using pictures and Video

The major sources of still graphics or full colour illustrations are scanned items, computer-generated graphics, and art of various kinds, either user-created or imported from other software.

98

A Hypercard can contain graphics and illustrations in colour up to a size of 18" x 18", 1280 x 1280 pixels. If parts cannot be seen because the screen is too small, those parts may be scrolled on to the screen.

Animation – meaning usually relatively unsophisticated motion - may be created without excessive cost or effort. Greater realism requires more expense and professionalism. One way of making animation sequences is to create a picture, copy it on to second card, alter it slightly using Apple Paint, copy the altered picture on to a third card, and so on.

Studio One software from Electronic Arts provides animation control from Hypercard stacks with XCMD driver control for loading and playing sequences. It includes the automatic creation of intermediate stages of smooth animation between two different scenes – which will save an enormous amount of time.

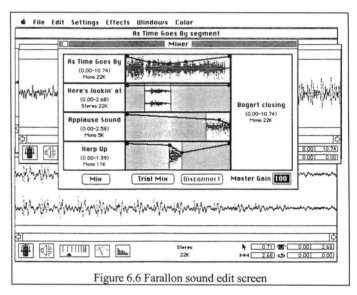

Figure 6.6 Farallon sound edit screen

Special details and technical background for capturing, processing, and outputting full-screen real-time motion video on a microcomputer were discussed on pages 92-94. An explanation of less costly alternatives for showing motion video on part of the screen – which may be adequate for many purposes – follows.

Motion video, usually in either NTSC or European PAL analogue form, may be imported from TV receivers, cameras, videotape or videodiscs. Data is displayed on a TV CRT by smooth pixel-to-pixel changes of brightness and colour in direct proportion to the light reflected from the original objects. The NTSC system uses 525 scanning lines per frame repeating 30 times per second. PAL uses 625 lines repeating 25 times per second. Both systems use interlaced scanning in which the frame is divided into a field of odd-numbered lines followed by a field of even – numbered lines, providing 60 and 50 fields per second respectively, reducing the flicker which would otherwise be noticeable.

In computer systems, images are represented as an array of picture elements (pixels). Until they are translated for display on the CRT, colours are represented by bit codes. The consequences of these substantial differences between TV and computer representations of pictures are fourfold.

Firstly, incoming data must be digitized if it is to be processed by the computer user.

Second, if not digitized and not processed, it must be synchronised so that, combined with any internally generated data, it may be viewed as a stable display.

Third, considerable processing power must be available to move very large numbers of bits if image changes produced by the user's processing and editing commands are to be viewed without delay.

Fourth, a monitor with appropriate resolution, scanning rate, and colour capabilities must be used for viewing the work. The presentation may be edited and recorded for repeat performances.

The main motion video functions which can be handled using a Mac II with 4-8 Mbytes of RAM, at least 80 Mbytes of disc, a colour monitor, and a variety of third party plug-in boards and software are :-

• Import TV-standard NTSC or PAL motion video from a Hypercard-controlled videodisc player or a camera, and display it in real time in a window on the Mac's screen or on a separate monitor. The system is not fast enough to allow full-screen colour at TV resolution.

• Connect the monitor directly to the video source, such as a videodisc player, for the direct full-screen colour TV resolution display of motion video, and control the videodisc from Hypercards, while presenting associated material on the Mac's screen.

• Overlay and synchronise ("Genlock") Mac text and graphics non-interlaced picture data, with the imported interlaced composite TV signals (which contain all the synchronising and picture data within the signal). Record the composited pictures in NTSC or PAL format on VHS, or better S-VHS videotape for presentations elsewhere.

• Use the tape for mastering videodiscs for interactive presentations. The random access seek time for Level 3 Laservision-type Constant Angular Velocity (CAV) videodisc players with Hypercard control via an RS232 connector, ranges from 3 seconds, to 0.5 seconds for more expensive models.

• Replace video data in a given colour (the "key" colour) with a different set of video data if you want to add special effects.

• Capture and digitize video frame-by-frame with a "frame-grabber", and output frames with added animation frame-by-frame under Hypercard control.

Figure 6.7 on the next page shows progress in preparing a presentation using the Overview window in the original version of Macromind Director (Macromind Inc., San Francisco, by courtesy of the Que Corporation (See Bove, 1990)) – a software presentation program enabling most of the functions described above to be implemented. Event sequences including text, graphics, sound, transition effects, and animation are being controlled with the aid of selection ikons and a display of the complete sequence.

Macromind Director is one of the most widely used multimedia software packages used on the Macintosh. In 1992 a new version, Director 3.1, was introduced capable of controlling Quicktime movies. Director files may be saved as Quicktime movies.

A separate good quality monitor is desirable for these operations and essential for some of them. Monitors, or more particularly the CRT's inside them, continue to improve. The currently most popular are probably the 14" and 17" (screen diagonal) 640 x 480 pixel (IBM VGA resolution) monitors. The colour tube alone costs about $300. By the time LCD display panels get to this stage, CRTs will probably have improved to 1000 x 1000 pixels and will cost $100, so the CRT will be around for some years yet.

The line scanning speed of Mac II's normal 640 x 480 display is fixed but third party video adaptors offer alternatives, such as rates between 800 x 560 for the 37" Mitsubishi monitor (at £6000), up to 1365 x 1024 pixels. Scanning speeds and frame rates are likely to be different in the various adaptors available.

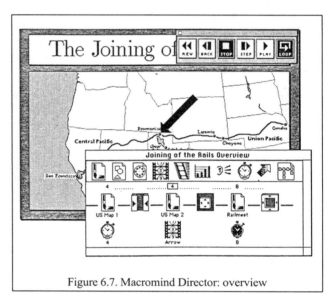

An auto-tracking monitor where the scanning rate automatically synchronises, is the best choice.

Figure 6.7. Macromind Director: overview

Typical ranges are 30-57 KHz horizontal and 40-75 Hz vertical. Another desirable feature in monitors is to be capable of running from NTSC or PAL composite video signals, RGB analog, or RGB TTL. With these alternatives the monitor should cope with almost any requirement.

Medical applications

After some information about flames over marshy ground, a will-o'-the-wisp is defined in the third edition (Makins 1991) of the *Collins English Dictionary* – a lexicographical *tour de force* which I can recommend -as a "person or thing that is elusive or allures and misleads". That is exactly what multimedia is.

There is a particular technique which I have seen referred to as multimedia only once. It includes all the necessary ingredients for that label – CCD cameras, image capture and enhancement on workstations, associated text, voice, data compression, drawing tools, pattern matching, high resolution displays and high-speed networks. Everything is ready to be seized upon by the multimedia generalists as an example of an application which has taken hold to the extent that a complete issue of a journal has been devoted to it.

Although singled out for special mention in the Ovum report mentioned below, the reason for its obscurity until recently is that it comes within the orbit of medicine, not information technology. I first came across it in a piece by Cowen (1989) about its use at Leeds University, and later, in full strength, as described by numerous authors in *Computerized Medical Imaging and Graphics* 15(3), pages 147-203, 1991. I am referring to Picture Archiving and Communication Systems or PACS. PACS systems embody new developments which are of interest to anyone involved in multimedia.

The objectives of PACS are to digitize, display, and if necessary enhance, images captured by computed tomography, magnetic resonance, computed radiography and other techniques, and bring order and accessibility via wideband networks to the files of film in which they are stored.

PACS was called (uniquely to my knowledge) multimedia by Karmouch *et al* (1991) in a French journal. This is a useful short review of PACS by some researchers from the Telecoms Research Institute of Ottawa.

PACS includes many interesting database, communications and application activities. One aspect of multimedia which is steadily attracting more interest is how to deal with the immense amount of data required to represent high quality pictures . This is a major issue in PACS systems. A computed radiography image contains 2000 x 2000 x 10-bit = 40 Mbits of data. Wide bandwidths are needed for the networks which transport the data.

The Ultranet network with Sun Sparcservers type 490 connected to it is used to satisfy the general PACS yardstick of 4 Megabytes/32 Mbits per second (Stewart 1991) data rates. The total data rate in the Ultranet hub required to manage five client-server exchanges of data is nearly 14 Megabytes/112 Megabits second. At these speeds optical fibre with the FDDI standard will be appropriate.

Since indexing images in a collection is a problem area, the piece by Taira (1991) in the above journal about databases is of some interest. But there is no mention of any consequence about indexing or its problems in this or any of the articles in this journal.

The prototype of a new type of PACS system, described by Badaoui *et al* (1993), is being used in France to handle 180,000 images. There are three parts to the system – the interface, a part which translates a user's query into a form understood by the system, and a dictionary containing the structure of the image data.

In the French system a special relational database is used to retrieve images, associated descriptive data, and related documents such as reports.

Futures and conclusions

The business market for multimedia software and systems in the US and Europe will grow from £500m in 1991 to £9bn in 1997, according to one forecast. In 1991 there were only two significant uses for multimedia in business – interactive computer-based training systems and point-of-information/point-of-sale kiosks.

But by 1994 a survey – based on detailed case studies of 25 systems suppliers, software developers and users – reckons that there will be four main products operating system extensions that support multimedia, multimedia enhancements to spreadsheets and wp packages; business presentation packages, and information access packages that include publications, databases and tools.

By 1997 the survey adds two new categories which will extend the market still further – multimedia-enhanced electronic mail packages and groupware, including videoconferencing facilities.

An organisation called First Cities intends to create a significant marketplace for networked multimedia information and entertainment products and services by accelerating developments of a national infrastructure for entertainment, distance learning, health care, and electronic commerce.

According to Craig Fields, MCC chair and CEO, "Our ultimate goal is the creation of a seamless environment for the spontaneous use of integrated interactive multimedia services in the home, the community, or on the move". MCC will provide:-

- Software that will enable individuals to connect their homes to the interactive multimedia services networks.
- Software to enable communication delivery organizations to provide a gateway through which customers can connect.
- Applications servers that will enable distribution of a wide range of services through the gateway and into individual homes.

The companies joining MCC in the initial phase of a national multimedia testbed are Apple Computer, Bell Communications Research (Bellcore) Bieber-Taki Associates, Corning, Eastman Kodak, Kaleida Labs, North American Philips, South-Western Bell Technology Resources, Sutter Bay Associates, Tandem Computers, and US West. Discussions are under way with additional companies whose services include cable television, satellite, telephony, entertainment programming and publishing.

Some more opinions about multimedia are included in a Frost & Sullivan report (Clark, 1992).

According to this publication, in 1991 Multimedia was worth about $7000M and £2178M in the US and Europe respectively. The expected expansion in the US is enormous – an increase to over $25,000M by 1995, but the European expansion rate is much slower – to $3066M by 1996. In the US, Multimedia is said to have "attracted much attention and generated great excitement throughout diversified sections of business, industry, government and academe". Apple had 40% of the US "Multimedia basic systems" market in 1990, but in Europe it was dominant (1991) with 58.5% of the "Multimedia market", the next contender being Acorn with 4.1%.

Major manufacturers now consider it worth while to market "multimedia systems". These are really powerful microcomputers with extensions, integrated to be more easily managed (we must assume, since I haven't tried one) than a micro plus some add-ons. This idea occurred to Commodore/Amiga back in August 1990 when they launched their "CDTV" in the UK at around £700. It has not been much in the news since.

A new generation called MPCs (Multimedia Personal Computers) by the Multimedia Council, is supposed to include at least a PC, CD-ROM drive, audio adapter, Windows with multimedia extensions, and speakers or phones. Loveria (1993) likes the Creative System's MPC upgrade for "add-ons" and NCR's 3331 MLS complete system based on a 486DX 33 MHz micro at $4294 including large-screen monitor.

F&S's figures seem to give the lie to the idea that Multimedia is still often said to be an idea looking for applications. If any confirmation that this notion should now be dropped is needed it is provided by the 5th issue of *ITEM* (April 1993) – a directory of current and evolving image databases and multimedia systems. *ITEM* is edited by Isobel Pring and is published by the International Visual Arts Information Network, the Library, Suffolk College, Rope Walk, Ipswich 1P4 lLT, U.K.

139 projects in 16 different countries are listed in this publication. They are classified in various ways. Their titles include *"The Art Loss Register"*, *"Canal Builder"*, *"Journeys through London"*, *"Geology Information Programme"*, *"National Museum of Denmark Image Database"*, *"Uffizi Project"*, *"Interactive Multimedia Project for Diffusion of Energy Concepts"* – to give you a few examples of project diversity. Many more projects are listed in Chapter 8.

"Journeys through London", for instance, being prepared for CD-I using information from the Museum of London, will comprise journeys made from Roman times onwards, during which the "traveller" may explore topography, architecture, society, and occupations.

Many of these 139 projects describe multimedia systems used within museums and art galleries but 40 of them have resulted or will result in published multimedia titles for wider use. 62.5% of these are on videodisc, 12.5% on CD-I, 7.5% are on Macintoshes and the remainder on CD-ROM XA, CDTV, and PCs.

As Isobel Pring says in her Introduction, this situation reflects multimedia's brief history where videodisc was for a time the only option. A videodisc will store about 54,000 NTSC analogue TV pictures providing an hour-long TV programme if used for that purpose. This emphasises the only major disadvantage when changing to digital systems – the much greater bandwidth required for a digital picture system.

It appears as if other advantages of CD technology, advances in compression techniques, the rapid drop in price of players, and the versatility of systems such as Photo-CD will encourage publishers to go for these media at the expense of videodisc.

In a conference which took place in July 1993 in the Sainsbury wing of the National Gallery entitled "Electronic Imaging and the Visual Arts" (EVA), digital systems were used exclusively in those papers where a particular media was mentioned. No new projects were described using videodiscs.

A speaker from the Getty Conservation Institute (Marina del Rey, California) believes that Photo-CDs have "a great deal to offer conservation".

Photo-CDs created from ordinary 35 mm film shots can be obtained with images at five different resolutions. The appropriate resolution may be selected for conservation records. A point here is that there are several options. The Kodak Photo-CD maximum resolution is 2000 x 3000 pixels with 24 bit colour – a total of 96 Mbits (12 Mbytes) of data. Compression without much loss reduces this to 4.4 Mbytes. Accordingly compressed high resolution or an alternative lower resolution picture may be chosen as required.

Marcus et al (1991), discussing the evolution of modern Graphical User Interfaces (GUI), say that they have been made possible by developments in dedicated computers, bitmap graphics and the mouse. Further advances will include Gesture recognition for character and command input, real-time 3-dimensional animation, sound and speech with combined modalities - for instance, visual and acoustic cues to improve comprehension and retention.

According to Alan Kay and Raj Reddy, leaders in the art, say Marcus et al, workstations will execute 1 Giga-instruction per second, have 1 Gigabyte of memory and a Gigabyte Bus, and will cost less than $10,000. They will support real-time dimensional graphics with transformation and smooth shaded rendering at about 1 million triangles per second.

A gesture translation, for example, will change 2 dimensional mouse movements into 3-dimensions. For instance if a user adds a propeller to a computer model of an aircraft, the object will be projected into screen space and the axes compared to the vector formed by the cursor's start and end positions. Translations will automatically display a 2 dimensional shadow in 3 perpendicular planes on to a "stage" setting, including the newly added propeller, in order to aid spacial perception.

The problem of authoring for multiple media, they continue, is far greater than the sum of the authoring problems in the individual media because it is necessary to coordinate and synchronise the media into a coherent presentation.

Video and sound materials are especially demanding, since few users have experience in video editing. Skilled interdisciplinary teams of cognitive psychologists, user-interface designers, graphic designers, and content-area specialists will be required to produce user interfaces that help users do useful work and produce material of lasting value.

"It will become possible to direct a design assistant", for instance, "to alter the shape of the corners on the dinner plates designed last week so that they fit production methods for Rosenthal china and meet hotel restaurant durability requirements".

Note that some parts of this directive can be expressed by natural language, some by pointing, some by sketching, and that feedback in the form of a realistic pictorial display is essential. Some of these technologies are within our grasp but fully general natural-language understanding will take considerably more time.

To conclude, a good deal of truth lies behind some light-hearted comments made by Nightingale (1991), an engineer at BT's research laboratories at Martlesham.

"Image processing specialists sometimes wonder if more money could not be made by submitting some of the by-products of their work to avant-garde art galleries. Meaningless rubbish could be passed off as un-fathomable profundity by the writing of an appropriate pretentious covering note", Nightingale suggests.

He is not very complimentary to his own profession. for instance, he says that very important decisions have been taken about standardising coding schemes without any properly conducted subjective testing. Engineers have an emotional preference for figures to subjective opinion. Why worry about some fool of a layman even if he is the customer when the coding method can be shown to be better mathematically?

Nightingale points out that a user of a mail-order company's 500-page illustrated catalogue can look through twenty pictures of lawn-mowers in a few seconds. Our very well developed capability for taking in *what is important to us* at a glance means that to compete successfully with such a catalogue a very efficient system indeed would be needed.

In a photographic videotex mail-order system, twenty 576 x 720 16 – bit pictures would take about 35 minutes to receive over a 64 Kbit line.

He does not look forward to video-telephone. "Few of us have total control over our appearance. We may be less attracted to the idea of a videophone since with an audio-only system we may cloak our advancing decay in the mystery of the disembodied voice".

CHAPTER 7

INDEXING PICTURE COLLECTIONS

> A perfect picture, I say; for he yieldeth to the
> powers of the mind an image of that whereof the
> philosopher bestoweth only a wordish description
> which doth neither strike, pierce, nor possess
> the sight of the soul so much as the other doth.
>
> Sir Philip Sidney (c. 1575)

> The intolerable wrestle with words and meanings.
>
> T.S. Eliot

> If you know what you are looking for why are you looking, and
> if you do not know what you are looking for how can you find it?
>
> Old Russian proverb

A note on Document Image Processing

Many publications have appeared about the processing of images and graphics in offices known as Document Image Processing (DIP) systems, as used in organisations like the US Patent Office, Prudential, TSB, etc.

Office and business documents are digitized for easier storage and processing (Cawkell, 1991). The space-accommodation arithmetic providing the incentive for DIP is suggested by Helms (1990). "Today only 5 out of 100 items are stored in a computer. Each of the remaining 95 pieces takes about 10 times as much space per piece because of its non-coded nature. Thus it takes about 200 times as much space to store that 95% as the original 5%".

The indexing method used for DIP systems is discussed by Hales and Jeffcoate (1990):- "Index information usually consists of the document identifier, a description of its content, and a number of keywords. Such information is held in a database... and is entered by the operator after the document has been captured and before it can be moved into permanent storage... a well designed indexed database is crucial to the success of the operation".

In this chapter a different set of problems are discussed − the indexing of pictures in large collections in electronic format.

Indexing basics

Any information system may be considered in terms of its cost, effectiveness, and benefits. If the performance of one system is to be assessed and compared with the performance of another, some method of measurement needs to be devised. The assessment of the potential and actual value of a research project which may precede system development when several different options are being considered is equally important.

Failure analysis is a related aspect which also needs attention. Unless this matter is considered when a system starts to be used, we will never know why items known to be in the collection are not retrieved, what might be done to improve performance, and what mistakes may be avoided in future systems.

Although there is increasing activity in compiling picture databases, for instance covering pictures, sculptures, photograph and slide collections, museum objects, architectural drawings, illustrated manuscripts and maps, etc., indexing methods are often ignored. Recently there has been a further increase as detailed by Pring (1993) and Hemsley (1993), but with one exception (Cawkell 1993b), indexing continues to receive virtually no mention.

This is surprising because when pictures are indexed today, this is done with descriptive words introducing all the well-known problems of meaning and ambiguity associated with text-indexing. There is some evidence to show that the imaging fraternity probably do not talk to librarians/information scientists (Cawkell, 1992b) as discussed in Chapter 1. Moreover the need for the discriminating power of indexes has not yet been felt because the lack of diversity of most picture databases, and in this new field, the time available for their growth to a size which makes good indexing essential, has not yet elapsed.

Before starting on database retrieval tests, some method for measuring and expressing the results must be devised in order that the performance of indexing languages may be compared – for example for comparing the effectiveness of word terms with query-picture "terms" applied to the same set of pictures. It is also desirable that the results should be indicative of the effectiveness of the chosen method when applied to a diversity of pictures so that precedents are set for testing picture collections of any kind in the future.

The performance of indexing languages used for identifying and retrieving documents from a collection, particularly scientific documents, was investigated some years ago by Cleverdon (1966, 1987), Salton (1971), and others.

Cleverdon has described his experiments, known as the Aslib-Cranfield tests, with a collection of 1400 aeronautical papers. He investigated retrieval effectiveness from sets of questions posed and documents retrieved by a team of subject experts (Cleverdon 1966).

The tests involved the preparation of an indexing sheet for each of the research papers showing the indexing terms used for three different languages with "importance weights", questioning the database with 221 questions, and then determining the relevance of each research paper to every question.

Cleverdon's work has withstood the passage of time quite well and his precision/recall ratio is still widely used. Efforts to find a single measure instead of a ratio have not been very successful although there have been a number of attempts.

The 2 x 2 contingency table and the Precision/Recall criteria described by Cleverdon may be applicable for expressing the results of picture collection tests, but new test methods must be devised for picture retrieval.

A paper containing a concept of interest cannot be retrieved unless all the concepts described in it have been indexed. Indexing Exhaustivity is therefore important. But unless the indexing language is sufficiently specific we may retrieve some items which are of little interest, so Indexing Specificity is also important.

These two indexing parameters are major factors controlling the Recall and Precision (see below) of an information system. Exhaustivity is the depth of indexing accorded to the topics in a document. For example, the terms "leukocyte", "interferon", "Hepatitis" and "Virus infection" plus terms describing diagnostic and analytical methods – say "Lowry's method of protein analysis" – might be used to index a life sciences document.

The potential for high Recall now exists because if a user wants high Recall, and is interested in articles indexed by any of the above four terms, the relevant documents may be found. However, high Exhaustivity reduces Precision because there is no means of knowing the treatment of the subject in the article. There may be 50 articles mentioning Lowry's method, but a complete description of the method is given in only one.

If low Exhaustivity indexing is used, "Lowry's method" will be used as a term only when the article is substantially about that topic. For instance its use could hardly be avoided for an article entitled "Lowry's method for protein determination". In this case a searcher using that term would be led only to such articles and not to articles in which Lowry is merely mentioned.

Specificity is the degree of precision of indexing terms. Thus the terms "hepatitis A" and "hepatitis B" are more precise then "hepatitis", just as "Telecoms", "Telecoms: satellites", and "Telecoms: satellite transponders" represent increasing degrees of precision. As might be expected, indexes containing many specific terms provide the potential for high Precision, while indexes with fewer, more general, terms do not.

The number of articles described by each specific term will be relatively small, so if the specific term "CRT resolution" is used, aspects of that subject contained in articles about "Image processing", had this less specific term been used instead, will be missed unless it occurs to the searcher to check all articles indexed by "Image Processing" in the hope that some may contain something about "CRT resolution".

Over-specificity – the use of a large number of different terms for indexing – will reduce Recall, although the average number of terms used to index each document does not much effect performance according to Cleverdon.

Cleverdon checked the Recall Ratio – that is the percentage of documents retrieved out of those known to be relevant, and the Precision Ratio – that is the percentage which were relevant out of those retrieved.

High recall means that almost all of the relevant items will be retrieved accompanied by unwanted documents – a user will have some sorting to do to remove the latter. High precision means that almost all the retrieved items will be relevant but some relevant documents will be missed.

The relationship between these factors takes the form shown in Figure 7.1 (After Cleverdon. The shift in the characteristic shape is caused by using different rules for searching the document collection).

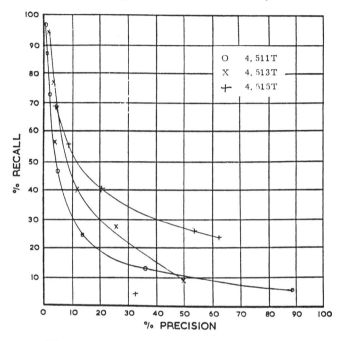

Figure 7.1 Recall and Precision relationship

The indexing method and the kind of question posed also affect performance. Broadly posed questions or unspecific indexing will retrieve many documents some of which will be relevant. Relatively few will be missed. Narrowly posed questions and a specific indexing language will retrieve fewer mostly relevant documents but more will be missed.

For collections of unambiguous data, as opposed to concepts, as just described, the recall/precision curve will be shifted towards the top right hand corner of the curve indicating high recall with high precision.

Since most collections of pictures are described by words inserted by indexers similar considerations are likely to apply to picture collections.

To produce meaningful results, a similar kind of exercise performed by Cleverdon for text needs to be performed for pictures. Cleverdon's documents have been assumed to be typical of the technological and scientific literature, so a "test collection" of supposedly typical pictures will need to be assembled. The scientific literature is heterogeneous enough, but the diversity of pictures is even greater – pictures may be so diverse that any results obtained using a single test collection would not be applicable across all collections.

Examples of systems where indexing is not discussed – is it needed?

The need to index collections of textual data is well appreciated and many books and papers have been published about it – for example Salton, with others, has described his life's work on the SMART system (Salton 1971). Similarly, major institutions have found it appropriate to devote years of effort in devising and executing ways of indexing large art collections, usually with the aid of large thesauri, as will be later described.

Since these large collections are indexed by words, the considerations worked out over many years for text retrieval apply. When picture retrieval by query-pictures is introduced, the basic principles will probably still apply.

However many system designers describing their collections of pictures in electronic form ignore indexing or regard it lightly. The image cultivated by designers is advanced technology – worlds apart from boring elderly indexers at work with their quill pens in some fusty old Victorian building. It has not yet become evident in many pixel-picture databases, mostly started relatively recently, that sheer size will make the resolving power of an efficient index essential before long.

Several papers delivered at the July 1992 Electronic Image and Visual Arts conference are discussed below, but indexing methods received no discussion. In the closing session I was able to ask a panel of speakers why this was so. The panel looked blank although afterwards one of the delegates said to me that "this was an interesting and important question", as if to say "I hadn't thought of that before".

In the short review which follows it will be noted that the idea of indexing is implied or mentioned but never receives detailed discussion.

Lunin (1990) refers to some comments made by Doszkocs (1984) and Nugent (1984). They seem to be the only people out of some 250 mentioned in this review which covers "electronic image information", who mention the need for new approaches to indexing. Lunin concludes:- "One of the main areas of concern is how to represent structural information in a database mode. This calls for thinking in terms of spatial continuous grey-scale information. The designs and techniques for image databases still have a long way to go before users can retrieve by the "language of the image" and browse among these databases easily and efficiently".

Lunin's "long way to go" seemed to imply that image indexing languages were at least starting to be used. So far as I am aware, even in 1993 the only systems which have passed the experimental stage and are actually being used are one or two using visual-thesaurus-controlled descriptive words. Some most interesting picture-query software, as discussed later, is likely to reach the market in 1994.

By 1989 interest in handling images was increasing as equipment improved and prices dropped. A number of articles were published about "image processing systems" often excluding any mention about finding an image. Reports about work on retrieval using automatic content-analysis systems was equally rare. In Lunin's review, she was only able to find two articles about the topic, 1983 vintage.

Issue 3 of the 1990 volume 29 of the *IBM Systems Journal* contains 13 articles about image technology and management. The cover depicts various art objects with the caption:- "One aspect (of ImagePlus) involves cataloguing... the other... locating pieces for loan. The combination of visual and textual information is beneficial for this application".

In this high-quality journal, which covers operational systems available today, indexing considerations are virtually invisible in its nearly 200 pages. The title "The image object content architecture" looks promising. An "object" is an area of a document containing "text, image, graphics, and fonts".

"To perform the indexing, the customer is identified through a standard data terminal. Then an "Index" transaction is executed to collect data about the document". The meaning of this phrase is obscure. And elsewhere:- "Each object directory is an indexed table in the database that is part of each object storage group. The relational characteristics and multiple index capability of the database allows objects to be selected and updated in different ways for different types of storage management with the expectation of reasonable performance. Efficient selection of objects that require processing is the key to automatic object storage management".

This is perfectly true, but who indexes an object and how do they do it in the first place? The omission of this information is partially explained because the general slant is towards Document Image Processing in business, and does not cover picture collections.

In an otherwise comprehensive article by Ryman (1990), among various functions such as "File", "Scan", "Print", "View" etc., indexing does not appear nor is "Find" or "Retrieve" discussed.

Menella and Muller (1990) state clearly that their major consideration in assessing tasks during the capture of compound documents for inclusion in an online database is the cost of "equipment used, and user expectations... Since our users indicated that figure captions were useful for queries and for locating the page containing the graphic mentioned in the text, our decision was to preserve graphic captions". In other words author's captions to signify the existence of a graphic were better than nothing.

Chaudhry and Roy (1990) describe the technology of a system running on an IBM mainframe for providing access to a collection of Indian visual art consisting of digitized representations of paintings, sketches, etchings, statues, sculptures, lithographs, etc. Users can access the data from terminals all over India via a packet switched network, and from London via an international gateway. A data field is provided for an "abstract giving details of the object". No further details are provided.

Pamela Danziger (1990), Director of information research services at Franklin Mint, writes:- "Designing an indexing scheme for a picture database is basically no different from any other indexing scheme... the special requirements for indexing images on optical disks are little different than designing any other database... To determine the descriptive criteria needed, identify only those elements that will be used to select pictures for the database". Later in this Chapter it will become evident that this is a naive viewpoint.

In Maurer's (1991) article about museum and "viewseum" systems for a collection of 100,000 images, it is concluded that "As the automatic integration of material depends on keywords, pictures alone are useless for the purposes of the viewseum... first discussions with organisations in other countries make it likely that integration problems are solvable". It seems that a great deal is being expected from these "first discussions".

Llewellyn (1991) from the Australian War Memorial Commission, describes a collection which includes around 800,000 photographs, 70,000 accession relics, nearly 30,000 works of art, 60,000 monographs and other items. A central bank of players outputs the stored images to a network for transmission to work stations. Records which satisfy the search criteria are displayed on the screen.

In referring to a handgun collection Llewellyn says:- "If our written records were sufficiently detailed to provide accurate descriptions... they would be very lengthy and to read one would take many seconds if not minutes. The mind can take in a picture at least with sufficient detail very quickly in order to decide if close inspection is needed. A user could scan our collection (of pictures) to make his identification in a little over 30 minutes".

Looms (1991) from the Danish Broadcasting System, discusses the creation of the National Picture database at the Royal Library, Copenhagen. The first phase is the production of 115,000 images on a budget approaching $3M. "We have commissioned the pilot version of an electronic catalogue based on approximately 5% of the pictures known to exist. The pictures themselves constitute one of the problems; (at present) a search is conducted... by thumbing through the originals themselves, each of which is kept in a brown envelope with handwritten details on the outside. The biggest uncertainty ...is finding people with the necessary background knowledge to be able to describe the content of historical photographs". No details about the proposed electronic catalogue are given.

Schmitt (1992), considers that for the foreseeable future image databanks of large numbers of works must have verbal information attached to them for retrieval. Whatever the advances of pattern recognition and other visual identification devices, words will remain indispensable in the retrieval of images. The information identifying the work (artist, date, country etc.) is seldom found in the image itself, and the meaning may often be expressed symbolically rather than literally. The absence of standards to guide consistent data entry is a much greater obstacle than such commonly claimed impediments as computer-phobia or a reticence to share information, Schmitt concludes.

Cappellini (1992), describing work in progress on a database at the Uffizi Gallery, Florence, reports that studies covering the definition of the file-structure and methods of information retrieval have been started.

Different solutions are being considered for file support (magnetic, optical disc) on the basis of the various uses – central filing system, multimedia peripheral systems, telematics, broadcasting.

A catalogue of 45,000 slides was put into a searchable database at the MIT Rotch library (Smith 1992). A collection of 30,000 images of Boston architecture is also mentioned. "Visual collections, archival collections and museums have been looking at new ways to provide access to their frequently very large collections of images .... employing emerging optical storage technologies", but indexing is not discussed.

Diana Hale (1992) describes the UK National Monuments record consisting of several million photographs. The City of York collection was chosen as the subject for the prototype. Site records and textual descriptions are incorporated in the system, complementing the images. This allows for the retrieval of text and image information, according to a wide variety of search criteria. Hale says that different users have different needs and aims for comprehensivity or selectivity which must be clearly thought out by the compiler. "A satisfactory way of presenting our whole archive of several million images in one undivided form has not been done".

Francis *et al* (1992), in two attractive-looking booklets published by the Arts Council curiously entitled *Very Spaghetti* refer to the use of interactive multimedia systems in museums. "Neither collection management nor interpretation is well funded and there have been in the past too often a resentment between the "dull" curators and the "populist" educators (both talk about the other with a sneering derision)".

In a section about "How to deliver a solution in museums" Francis et al say:- "Create means to catalogue collections and establish a consistent database method and technique that can be converted from computer to interactive access, in the first case, created on the simplest index cards". Out of several chapters about visits made and issues raised, and the state of the art in the United States, this is the only mention of indexing.

Moir (1992) writes that in a photographic collection covering the Port of Toronto "Negatives were listed in chronological order with a brief notation regarding their content, providing some measure of access for users who had specific data in mind, or were patient enough to wade through hundreds of pages of lists for a caption providing a glimmer of relevance"

In preparing an analogue computer-based system into which the photographs would be transferred, over 37,000 images were moved into an optical disc. Retrieval software "is predicated on the assumption that users will continue to follow the traditional route of starting with the textual description of an archival record and then proceed to request the original document or an image of it".

"However experience with historical photographs suggests otherwise. Users prefer to employ the database to prepare a general list of images that are selected using rather broad search criteria. They expect this list of photographs to be provided in a quick and responsive manner as they watch the monitor, turning to the textual record only when a suitable visual image has caught their eye... ironically, this treatment of archival finding aids is not too far removed from the time-honoured techniques that saw users browse through binders of photo-copies of reams of microfilm".

Indexing considerations

Some of the factors to be considered by researchers and research sponsors, assuming that their objective is the production of collections in electronic form which make economic and practical sense, are:-

- The performance expressed in an appropriate manner. It may be difficult to devise Cranfield-type tests (Cleverdon 1967), but on the other hand there is little point in developing alternative methods of image indexing unless there is some means of measuring their relative efficiency.

- The time taken to index a new image. The more elaborate the indexing method, the longer indexing will take. The longer it takes the less likely it is that the necessary time/effort will be devoted to doing it.

- The time taken for a user to learn how to use the system. Must the system require a skilled intermediary to operate it, like most online text retrieval systems, or is it feasible to make it easy enough for users with little training?

- Image collections may be very large, cover a wide area of interest, and may include complex images containing individual objects of interest to a large multi-disciplinary corps of users. At the other extreme there may be small collections of simple images of interest only to users with a common narrow interest. Different system designs appropriate for collections at and between these extremes need to be considered, not forgetting growth prospects.

Practical requirements

Nagy (1985) comments:- "Seldom can the developers devote sufficient resources to the user interface, to maintainability and reliability to data integrity, to device independence... etc".

The nature and support of academic research (most imaging research is academic) makes it inappropriate for researchers to become involved in mundane but necessary non-research activities of the kind mentioned by Nagy. Occasionally the researchers may become entrepreneurs and proceed through the stages necessary to produce a usable "end-product".

Otherwise, if the research looks as if a usable "end-product" could emerge, the potential has to be perceived by an "implementor", if not a commercial system provider, in order to proceed to "feasibility trials". The risks and cost of the effort needed to bring a product to the market require to be assessed. The researcher able to acquire the attributes needed for success in this very different activity is rather rare. An alternative is for an "ear-to-the ground" entrepreneurial company to take on the project. The EC may be able to help (Cawkell, 1992b).

Finally, "the first international imaging standard" (Blum, 1991), still under discussion, may contain something of relevance to image indexing.

Under the heading "elementary image data types" there are requirements for standards covering "image lists (ordered image sets)" because "individual images can be accessed only via successor/predecessor relations.... image records are collections of individually named data types or image data types. The attributes may be of different types and can be accessed via their names". The article includes a list of "image markets":-

- Computergraphics in medicine for the analysis of movement, flow etc.,

- Remote sensing in seismology, mapping, meteorology and military intelligence.

- Industrial vision for inspection, testing, process control, etc..

- Computer graphics art and animation incorporating draw-and-paint tools for graphic production, rendering animation etc.

- Document processing for converting printing pages or microfiche into electronic form.

Indexing Philosophies

There seem to be at least three possible methods by which images might be indexed – by words, by using a visual thesaurus, and by picture content. So far as I know only the "words" method is in use in real world situations.

Other "words" methods and the "visual thesaurus" and "content" (allowing picture-queries to be used) methods are still at the research stage although there are a few experimental systems running with small test collections. The alternatives for indexing methods are summarised in Figure 7.2

Besser (1990) says "images are rich and often contain information that can be useful to researchers coming from a broad set of disciplines. For instance a set of photographs of a busy street scene a century ago might be useful to historians wanting a snapshot of the times, to architects looking at buildings, to urban planners looking at traffic patterns or

BY WORDS

IN A HIERARCHIC CLASSIFICATION SYSTEM.

USING A SPECIAL LANGUAGE FOR DESCRIBING GRAMMATICAL RELATIONSHIPS OF WORDS.

USING A SPECIAL LANGUAGE FOR DESCRIBING SPATIAL RELATIONSHIPS OF OBJECTS:

BY CONTENT

PATTERN-MATCHING OF IMAGES IN A COLLECTION AGAINST A QUERY PATTERN

MATCHING STRUCTURES IN A COLLECTION AGAINST A STRUCTURES QUERY

Figure 7.2. Indexing pictures

building shadows, to cultural historians looking at changes in fashion, to medical researchers looking at female smoking habits, to sociologists looking at class distinctions, or to students looking at the use of certain photographic processes or techniques.... Even an enormous amount of descriptive text cannot adequately substitute for the viewing of the image itself".

Ragusa (1992) echoes Seloff's remarks:- "When anyone other than the cataloger reviewed the collection, it was discovered that similar photographs were given different descriptors at different times. It was concluded that an individual cataloguer's perspective changed from week to week. In addition, the viewpoint of the cataloguer varied from that of the NASA engineers and scientists who would later need to retrieve the images. As a result, as the collection expanded consistent classification and retrieval became nearly impossible".

A paper by Hogan *et al.*, (1991), draws on the experience of Besser, Rorvig, and Seloff, taking visual thesauri a stage further. It is based on the notion that "preliminary research has shown that images play an important part in the search process in both print and online formats. Therefore for an information retrieval system which includes graphical materials as well as text, the adoption of standard indexing and retrieval methods will result in far less retrieval precision for images, and, indeed, can hamper the information retrieval process of both images and text".

A number of thought-provoking points are made in the Hogan article.

"If an image carries a great deal of information for the user which is dependent on contextual and situational factors, the assumption that meaning rests in a pre-defined set of subject terms is of limited ability to control access to the contents of an image base".

"Like in the indexing of textual documents, the verbal descriptors available to describe the visual content of the image are often inade-quate to express meaning from the user's point of view..... In the case of images, the use of thesauri to control inconsistency is not effective due to responses prevalent in human reactions to visual materials..... inconsistency is the reflection of creativity and the diversity of human interests, situations, and contexts.

If inconsistency is to be overcome, system designers will need to relinquish the idea of the utility of using words to index non-verbal understanding.... We are looking for alternative ways of image retrieval, ways that are less dependent on familiarity with existing taxonomies and their assigned authorities".

In a criticism of Besser's IMAGEQUERY system, Hogan suggests that "there is no clear distinction between the image as a work in itself, a visual representation, or a copy of a copy (slide of a photograph etc.).

It seems to us that Besser is talking mostly about the media through which the user encounters the item and not some inherent quality of the item itself. According to him, with the written text, knowledge representation can be obvious even explicitly; the author's intention can be known. With images, representation is interpretive and textual".

Enser (1991) has in mind a variation of the visual thesaurus idea not dissimilar to Rorvig, Seloff, (cited by Enser), and Hogan. User's query words would retrieve reference images for various concepts, and hit reference images would be matched against images of objects segmented from a database of photographs.

Enser says:- "The delight and frustration of pictorial resources is that pictures can mean different things to different people".

"The content of a picture, whether from the realm of fine art or commercial photography, presents some potential difficulties. Since there may be a multiplicity of entities within a single image, and a multiplicity of attributes associated with any one of the entities, it is contended that the subject requests for which a given image may be deemed relevant, appropriate, or interesting, are much less predictable than is the case for textual material. A small scale survey has been undertaken with a view to providing some experimental evidence in support of this contention".

Enser then describes an experiment in which pictures of a street market, the Eiffel Tower viewed from the Seine, and a crucifixion scene were presented to library staff accustomed to indexing, and also to people of different genders and occupations (e.g. accountant, estate agent, hotelier, medical practitioner, etc). They were asked to write down any words or phrases describing contents or features of interest to them.

The interpretations of the pictures are listed in tables in the article indicating the effects of observer variables in producing a very wide range of alternative terms for indexing the same pictures. Enser concludes that "it would seem unlikely that indexing could produce an appropriate key by means of which more than a small proportion of the multi-faceted information stored within a given image could be unlocked".

Later, Enser and McGregor (1992) analysed over 2,700 requests made by users of the Hulton Picture Collection – a very large collection of photographs, resembling a newspaper morgue, originally used in the publication *Picture Post* during the nineteen forties and fifties.

They are critical of the indexing arrangements "offering a shallow indexing of concepts, which, with the exception of portrait photographs, lies at some considerable remove from the linguistic forms in which requests are expressed for the retrieval of pictorial material from the library's holdings".

Bearing in mind "the viability of automatic image retrieval in a large, general purpose image bank, akin to that of a host library", but with reference to the use of the Hulton collection, Enser finds that simple indexing is adequate for simple concepts. Thus when uniquely identifiable items, such as "Althorpe House" are requested, they are retrieved, as are items which include "refiners" such as "George V Coronation, BUT NOT procession OR any Royals".

Enser comments "the retrieval of appropriate pictures in such cases is equivalent to an exact match operation which is deterministic in nature and unlike the probabilistic operations conducted by textual information retrieval systems". "Precision" has no utility as a measure of effectiveness in such cases".

There are difficulties when trying to evaluate performance in collections such as the Hulton (or for that matter when evaluating the retrieval performance of any indexing system) associated with the problem of "misses"; the number of relevant pictures which are not retrieved is usually unknown so system performance is hard to measure.

But as pointed out by Eakins (1992) the work of Salton (1971), and, of course, Cleverdon's work (1966, 1987) is available for evaluation purposes (Eakins is unique among the imaging fraternity in making this point).

However both Cleverdon and Salton used special collections prepared for test purposes in which details about every document in the collection were known. Evaluating performance in real-world situations introduces human factors which Cleverdon excluded. In this situation, Eakins point (unless applied to image collections specially prepared for test purposes) about the usefulness of Cleverdon-type tests is less valuable.

As described by Enser and MacGregor in regard to the Hulton collection, the results, particularly in the case of "non-unique" item requests, were affected more by the presence of an expert intermediary than by the indexing arrangements. For example no "misses" (as far as was known) were recorded perhaps because the picture librarians, extremely familiar with the system, were sometimes able to find, after some "negotiations" with the client, a picture of some interest, even if substantially different to the original request.

In this connection Enser, reflecting his interest both in automatic indexing and in TELCLASS classification described elsewhere in this Chapter, says:- "requests for non-unique items, e.g. "girl with fair hair, 1940s/1950s, aged 7 or 8, with monkey" would be extremely difficult to satisfy by automatic means. The Hulton indexing scheme offers no help although an exhaustive scheme such as TELCLASS probably would. The caption - intrinsically iconic – is unlikely to be of assistance; indexing by keywords at such a depth is implausible, other than in a specialist, TELCLASS, environment".

"In an environment such as that of a host library, an extremely heavy dependency on the expertise and search time availability of the picture researcher in his or her role as intermediary, must continue to be the norm in the short to medium term".

Research in which indexing (by words) is considered important

Large indexing systems co-operatively established such as AAT and ICONCLASS, and TELCLASS established by one organisation but recently used by others, will be discussed on pages 122-125. Apart from comprehensive systems of this kind, driven by the need for developing methods for specialised fields, very little work has been done on indexing until the new systems described in the next Chapter came along.

Petterson (1984) describes a very simple system using words in a dictionary stored on an Apple II to retrieve associated graphics from a Laservision player controlled by the Apple. One Swedish indexing word appears to have been allocated to the content of each page (Figure 7.3).

Sustik and Brooks (1983) discuss problems of indexing graphics stored on interactive videodiscs. "Merely storing data on a videodisc does nothing to facilitate recall and precision; effective indexing does... Many people think that text is easier to index... the difficulty of indexing stems from the problem of identification and naming. Objects consist of an infinite number of embedded qualities. Very few are at any one time considered useful, interesting, or worth noting... Idiosyncratic nomenclature and cross-classifications will proliferate unless working agreements are made about categories... people categorize objects because they belong together and follow a rule". Sustik and Brooks provide examples of their proposed categories (Figure 7.4).

```
FLOD ...............................1635
FLODA..............................1636
FLODHÄSTAR.....................1637
FLODOMRADE.....................1638
FLODSPRUTA .....................1639
FLOEM.............................1641
FLOR .............................1642
FLORA.............................1643
FLORARIKE.........................1645
FLORENS...........................1646
FLORETT ..........................1647
FLORIDA...........................1648
FLORIN ...........................1649
FLORISTIK ........................1650
FLORSLÄNDA.......................1651
FLOSKLER  ........................1652
FLOSSA ...........................1653
```
Figure 7.3
Simple retrieval by words

Sustik and Brooks's comment:- "many people believe that text is easier to index" conveys the impression that there are some who think that images are easier.

Those who start indexing pictures for the first time are in for a shock. Text is not just easier, but far easier, unless the pictures to be indexed consist of a small,

CATEGORY	EXAMPLE
Descriptive: Possess same physical attribute	All six-legged crawling animals
Inclusive: One includes the other	All people who were U.S. presidents
Exclusive: One excludes the other	All wallpapers not pre-pasted
Identity: They are really the same thing	All pictures of John Kennedy
Ordinal: In a particular order	Stages of embryo development
Causal: Some things make others happen	Hiroshima after the bomb dropped
Probabilistic: Connected under certain conditions	Results of vitamin deficiency
Temporal: Connected in time	Impressionistic painting 1879-1880
Spatial: Connected in space	Buildings in the Federal Triangle

Figure 7.4 Graphic category rules

narrowly defined collection of simple objects.

Various phrases are used to describe the concept "picture indexing". One publication chooses the words "scene interpretation" to describe an article about "visual-scene understanding" (Sowizral 1985). Another phrase used when discussing graphics is "visual materials".

Special languages may be developed for the purposes of reducing the indexing effort, or making it more amenable to computer operations. They include various kinds of machine-processable shorthand with which to describe the structure of an image.

Leung (1990) has described experiments using a Picture Description

Language for the coordination of terms, object descriptions, object attributes, relationships and events. Boolean searching and thesaurus assistance will be incorporated. Picture data are stored in an SQL relational database. Leung claims that "In the context of still pictures... the main semantic concepts of entity, attribute, and relationship... closely correspond to the noun, adjective, and verb which are the essential components of a simple description of a picture". The allocation of these components to SQL relationship tables will enable more efficient searching to be carried out.

An addition to the system called "adaptive tuning" is due to be tested. When a picture is retrieved, its description could be augmented or adjusted by that user to provide improved access for the next user.

Wanning (1991) uses hypertext software to retrieve images from a database of "4000 photographs, 6000 artifacts, and 1000 archivals. How else could we have exhibited 4000 photographs in a meaningful way with several different forms of access and possibilities for combinations?" asks Wanning. In this case "database management", as is often the case in museums, means the organisation of keyword access and browsing.

One of the largest schemes in progress is the computerisation of the Archivo de General Indias – a collection of documents, maps, and drawings about Spanish America originating from the time of Columbus.

The collection is kept in its own building in Seville (Anon,1990); about 8 million pages were scanned by the end of 1992, representing about one third of the total archive. The storage requirements are terabytes. Little is said about indexing in the beautifully presented book about the project, with numerous illustrations in colour, but some information was obtained over the telephone from Juan Secilla who is managing the operation.

Secilla says that a huge fund of "indexing" already exists added over a period of time as the documents were collected, but it is not clear how this is organised. In a long press release dated 1992, IBM says that among the various benefits to historians and others wishing to use the system will be "rapid location of documents", without details of how this will be done.

The work is being conducted and financed by the Spanish Ministry of Culture, IBM Spain, and the Areces Foundation. IBM Spain is no doubt drawing upon experience gained from its work on digitizing and storing the Wyeth collection of pictures (Mintzer, 1991).

Turtur's (1991) system includes facilities for capturing, indexing and retrieving images. The textual data associated with each image is managed in a relational data-base. Free text searching carried out using logical operators generates a cluster of hits consisting of image titles which may be replaced by a cluster of the actual pictures of reduced size. Any one of these may be selected for enlargement to full screen size.

Hine (1992) describes a DVI system for storing over 100,000 images in optical storage. The incentive for taking the scheme beyond the research stage – it is now in regular use – was to improve the recovery rate of stolen paintings. A number of techniques have been developed. These are said to include image matching, fuzzy searching (i.e. to non-exact specifications) and several thesauri.

```
         ᴊ1ᴇ
    NOTE  Acʟ...ᴘa....ᴏu ᴅy ᴀ ᴘnotograpn and 4 pageᵥ ᵥ      ...entary ᵤaterial.
    NOTE  Contents:
          Cover sheet. With sketch map by Jay T. Liddle (b. 1906), Daniel A. Finlayson, Harry
          E. Weir (b. 1907) and Charles Dabbs Krouse (1A–39522)
          Sheet 1. Floor plan by Weir, Harry W. Phillips, A. Hays Town (b. 1903) and Liddle
          (1A–39523)
          Sheet 2. East and west elevations by Weir, Finlayson and Town (1A–39524)
          Sheet 3. North elevation by Krouse, Weir, Town and Liddle (1A–39525)
          Sheet 4. South elevation by Weir, Liddle and Town (1A–39526)
          Sheet 5. Detail sheet of cornice, corbel and baptismal font by Weir and Town
          (1A–39527)
          Sheet 6. Iron work details by Liddle and Town (1A–39528); LC–USZA1–784 (b&w
          neg.)
    NOTE  HABS/HAER Database Control No. MS0058.
    NOTE  B&w reference copies available in Prints & Photographs Reading Room; full size repro-
          ducible drawings also available.
    NOTE  Transfer, Historic American Buildings Survey, Department of the Interior.
    COLL  HABS–18
    DESC  CHAPEL OF THE CROSS (MANNSDALE, MISS.)
    DEꜱᵀ  ANGLICAN Cᴘ    ˙'ᴇ̣ꜱ
     ᵣ      ˙'ᶜᶜ˙ ˙ᵖ̣ᵎ
```

Figure 7.5 Example of Marc-type record used in the LC project

Large established systems for picture indexing and retrieval by words

The Library of Congress videodisc project

In 1982 the Library of Congress embarked on a programme to provide access to a portion of its collection of 12 million graphic items -original photographs, historical prints, posters, architectural drawings, and so on (Parker 1985). In a pilot project about 49,000 graphics were photographed and recorded on videodisc, with the videodisc player controlled by a microcomputer for searching.

Parker comments "The dilemma for custodians and researchers of graphic collections is that words cannot entirely represent an image, but the image cannot be comprehended entirely without some words of identity. Researchers must verbalize what they are looking for, however vague".

An example of a record is shown in Figure 7.5. The time taken to index an item varies greatly, but the average is believed to be about 5 minutes. No information is available about retrieval performance or about the effect of changes in indexing policy on performance.

The LC decided to index the collection using a modified shortened MARC format. At the time, a MARC format for visual materials was under discussion but had not been finalised.

A "Thesaurus for Graphic Materials" was due to be published in 1986. "The videodisc captions consist of fields from the MARC format with a concentration on the controlled vocabulary access point fields most useful for picture searching".

The Art and Architecture Thesaurus

The AAT originated at Rensselaer Polytechnic in 1979 (Peterson 1990). It was published in 1990 by Oxford University Press in three volumes and a floppy disc edition and contains over 40,000 terms "Hierarchically arranged according to a rigorously constructed, internally consistent structure", using standard thesaurus conventions, modelled on the National Library of Medicine MESH (Medical Subject Headings). During its development terms were drawn from the Library of Congress Subject Headings (LCSH).

As time went on it became clear that there was a need for an arrangement more in line with MESH. The Thesaurus is compiled and managed by art historians, architects, and information scientists.

The AAT is used at Rensselaer for indexing a collection of 65,000 slides (Keefe, un-dated). This report, kindly sent to me by Jeanne Keefe the Graphics Curator, appears to be for internal use. It should be made generally available; it clearly shows the magnitude of the undertaking. Keefe's estimate for the time taken to deal with 50,000 slides is 17 man years.

Keefe (1990) describes how the AAT is used in the Marc-like records of the publicly searchable INFOTRAX database covering a Rensselaer slide collection. Keefe says indexers needed "An initial training period of at least three months". After that training it took 47 minutes to complete a slide worksheet and enter the details into the database.

At the time the Keefe article was written 1300 slides had been indexed. One full time indexer would take 3.5 years to complete 10,000 slides. Unfortunately Keefe does not provide any information about retrieval performance. In Figure 7.6 the indexing for a number of slides has been consolidated in one record – a policy generally adopted during compilation which results in a substantial reduction in the number of records needed. Lunin (1990) describes the AAT applied to fiber art graphic databases. She considers that "There appears to be almost universal agreement that the image is desired in the database record together with textual information... Even with a mass of information available to apply to a work, it is difficult to describe the concept and other important aspects with just a few index terms or a classification".

```
  TITLE :  Sydney Opera House; post-1945, aerial view
     BY :  Utzon, Jørn
SUBJECT :  Opera houses, auditoria, auditoriums, ceremic tiles, performing arts
           buildings, concrete halls, music halls, music auditoria, symphony
           halls, movie theaters, theatres, cinemas, restaurant, ribbed vaults,
           ribbed arches
           concrete beams, concrete paint, podium, roof trusses, roofing, roofing
           tile, ribs, vaulted roofs, shell roofs, reinforced concrete, lattice
           roofs, shell structures, shell vaults, towers, steel trusses,
           ceremonial ways
           workspaces, workshops, wood walls, wood ceiling, wooden ceilings,
           concrete vaults, concrete structures, concrete pilings, concrete
           joints, glass, glass walls, laminated materials, cables, cable roofs,
           cable-stayed structures, ridge boards, precast concrete, granite,
           granite powder cement, bronze window mullions, ridge beams
    SITE :  Australia, Sydney, New South Wales, Benelong Point
   DATES :  1957 - 1973
    SIZE :  2x2 in. color
HOLDINGS :  3 plans, 11 sections/drawings, 2 aerial views, 29 exterior views,
            3 interior views, 3 details
```

Figure 7.6 AAT terms used to index a slide

A "Browser" for the Art & Architecture Thesaurus (AAT) has been developed at the University of California at Berkeley (Snow, 1991). The Browser runs under the X Window system on Sun 3/50 workstations. The preparational and development costs were paid for by a grant from the university; presumably a user's time to learn the system and the use of it will be considerably reduced compared to the printed version. For example the Styles and Periods hierarchy may be chosen followed by "The Americas" - a term which indicates the "children" at the next specific level below it, and so on, eventually arriving at one or more specific images.

The ICONCLASS system

Henri van den Waal (University of Leiden), the originator of ICONCLASS, said "the material offered for consultation should always be visual. Any other reference – either verbal or by means of codes – can never be more than the first stepping stone". ICONCLASS was published in the period 1973 to 1985. It consists of 17 volumes of hierarchically arranged codes associated with a textual description in English, designed for classifying the content and subject matter of fine art material.

Dr. Catherine Gordon, project director at the Courtauld Institute of Art, London, is using the system to index a collection of about 1.5 million paintings, drawings, and engravings, by some 75,000 artists. The project was started with the support of the J.Paul Getty Trust to compile the Witt computer index of the American section in the Witt library.

At first sight it might appear that ICONCLASS is simply a duplication of the effort put into the AAT. But a comment by Gordon (Gordon 1990) emphasises the order of difficulty of classifying pictures; even within the same general area, account must be taken of the need to accommodate nuances of human perception.

Gordon says (Gordon 1990):- "... ICONCLASS allows classification where we lack knowledge... where a specific narrative or topic is not recognised, it is still possible to classify what is seen.

In more traditional systems what cannot be identified may not be able to be filed". More information is available in Anon (1987) which summarises work going on at a number of other centres using ICONCLASS.

```
The Codes used to describe the Van Gogh painting

48C513                  Portrait, self-portrait of an artist
3283312( +3+52)         Japanese, costume, female
61B2(GOGH, Vincent van) Portrait of male sitter (identified)
48C5142( +76112)        Picture within a picture, (in Japanese style)
48C5151                 Artist's tools - easel
31A2213                 Parts of the body - ear
31A419                  Mutilation
31A464                  Emotional illness, derangement
49G3211                 Bandage


Example of a code used for the Tiepolo painting

94S32                   Hercules Galicas - he captivates his audience
                        with a golden chain going from his mouth to
                        their ears
```
Figure 7.7 Codes for the Van Gogh painting

These include the University of Leiden (for illustrated books, a collection of 10,000 Italian prints, and another collection of 65,000 engravings), at Marburg for a huge microfiched collection, for the Provenance Index to several collections at Santa Monica, at Utrecht for describing valuable objects in churches in the Netherlands, and for the Courtauld collection of paintings of the American school in the Witt Computer Index. (Anon. 1988).

In view of its quite wide use, a more detailed listing from ICON-

124

CLASS is shown in Figure 7.7 – the set of codes used for indexing Van Gogh's *Self portrait with bandaged ear.* The thesaurus is organised in a number of levels commencing with nine primary codes:- "1. Religion and Magic", "2 Nature", "3. Human Being Man", "4. Society, Civilisation, Culture" etc.

The first two characters of the code are digits and the third is always a capital letter permitting 25 sub-divisions (J is excluded) at the third level.

When a new word or phrase is added to the thesaurus in its correct alphabetical position, its notation is composed as a primary symbol and a succession of symbols representing successive levels of sub-divisions of the primary code. Notations at the same level may be combined, as indicated by a "+" sign.

Newly compiled codes are also entered into the associated "Key Number Index" which lists all codes allocated from the third level downwards, together with their associated lower-level codes thus:-

Key to 25F and sub-divisions
25F1   Animals used symbolically
25F11   Bestiaries "physiologus"
25F332   Antlers; horns

The arrangement of part of the thesaurus itself, showing the heading and sub-headings of the major divisions from which the Van Gogh indexing terms "easel" and "ear" were derived, is shown in Figures 7.8 and 7.9.

The indexer would, of course, have found the notation for each wanted description (e.g."ear", "easel" etc.,) by looking it up in the alphabetical index

During thesaurus composition the words "easel" and "ear" were allocated codes determined from the level they occupy under the appropriate primary heading. Thus "easel 48C5151" is a sub-division of "Tools of the painter 48C515" and so on, descended from "4 Civilization and Culture".

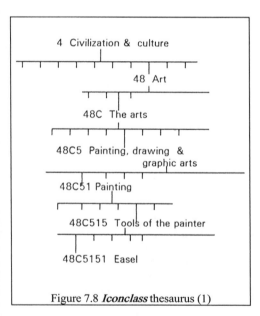

Figure 7.8 *Iconclass* thesaurus (1)

To the uninitiated it seems curious that lower level codes are so specific – see the code allocated to a picture by Teipolo (bottom of Figure 7.7). However to the cognoscenti the code representing "a picture showing Hercules Galicas captivating his audience with a golden chain going from his mouth to their ears" may be a non-unique concept. ICONCLASS indexing has been described by Gordon (1990).

125

Telclass

Another variation of the same principle called TELCLASS has been developed by Evans at the BBC's Film and Videotape Library (Evans 1992).

Evans says that the scheme "differentiates Words from Concepts... paying due regard to the relationships between categories and objects". Some clues to this principle as shown by the kind of subject terms used to label media material are indicated in Figure 7.10.

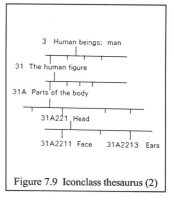

Figure 7.9 Iconclass thesaurus (2)

Evans (1991) takes an unusual philosophical view about classification systems:- "the totality of structural features for representing the three semantic relationships of any specific atomic concept (fact) together with strict application of Russell's principles of logical construction based on technique which distinguishes between the virtual and the actual, differentiates words from concepts and represents those "concepts" at both the molecular and atomic levels, paying due regard to the relationships between categories of objects. This is a viable methodology for organising the whole field of objective human knowledge, irrespective of subject area".

The TELCLASS system is an attempt to put these ideas into practice which is "radically different from other types of text-based or language-based systems such as free text or pure keyword". Evans uses six main groups of terms (which may be compared with the main groups in ICONCLASS) – verbal, schematic, actuality, simulation, technical, and formal.

The *Multimedia Encyclopedia of Mammalian Biology* published by Mc Graw Hill, Maidenhead, U.K., on CD-ROM uses three TELCLASS-type thesauri under the primary terms "Taxonomic", "Biogeographic", and "Thematic". It also embodies DVI – motion video and sound are available if you possess Windows 3.0 with multimedia extensions software and a DVI board. 300 clips of motion video with a total duration of 20 minutes are included.

R33	Scenes (Media)
R33:102.32	Unpleasant or shocking scenes
R33:101.32.1	Gruesome scenes (Media)
R33:521.003.1.002.923.1	Pithead scenes (Media)
R330	Aftermath scenes
R330:101.111:526.522.31	Aftermaths of lorry crashes (Media)
R331	Scenic shots
R331:461.232.232	Snow scenes
R331:461.232.232 (211.1)(117.2)	South of England snow scenes
R53	Primary camera movements
R531	Panning shots
R531:R556.2	Wide angle panning shots
R63	Editorial format (Media)
R639.3	Compilations (Media)
R639.31	Highlights (Media)
R639.311	Edited highlights (Media)

Figure 7.10 Some TELCLASS terms

Research on indexing and retrieval by content

Much research is in progress on image recognition. Unfortunately recognition techniques are still in their infancy. The eye-brain can recognize objects with such ease that machine vision systems seem to be, and indeed are, in a very early stage of development. However the advances and techniques described in Chapter 4 are now being applied to picture databases.

Many of the attempts being made to recognise images are still at the stage of segmentation – the division of an image into its constituent parts for further processing. The major processing activities involved in segmentation are "edge detection" using the continuous boundaries formed by adjacent black and white pixels (See Chapter 4) or abrupt changes in grey levels, and "pattern recognition".

Issue 12, volume 22 (1989) of *Computer* – a journal with high standards – carries on its cover a picture of an open photograph album showing period photos, with the legend "Image database management". There are five lengthy articles about the topic inside the issue.

In an introduction it is said that "In the computer vision community, interest has focused specifically on the design of image data-bases and efficient retrieval of iconic information".

The paper by Brolio *et al* (1989) is representative of state of the art research at that time and goes some way towards the realisation of methods which will enable the content of a graphic to be analyzed and matched with a user's query preceded by little or no indexing effort.

Brolio et al explain:- "ISR's fundamental object is the token... which can represent an image event such as a line or a homogeneous region in an image, or an aggregate of events such as a group of parallel lines, a geometric structure or the regions hypothesised to belong to some object... we have written functions for storing tokens in the appropriate cells and for retrieval based on eight types of spatial regions – point-to-point, line-to-line, region-to-region, etc."

Brolio *et al* show a halftone photograph in the paper of a forest glade, and a second photo showing a passable machine automatic representation of it using ISR processing software. Ross Beveridge, a co-author, told me that the analysis took about 30 minutes using a Sun workstation. The system is being up-graded to work up to 10,000 times faster.

The converse operation is to submit a rough outline drawing to the system for matching against a collection of photographs and the system will select the most similar photo. Fuzzy matching is used – an exact match is not required for a "hit". For example a halftone "edge" is defined by a fuzzier boundary than a line connecting the transitions from black to white pixels.

Weems (1991), in an excellent review, having mentioned that twenty three million instructions per second are needed for a typical video imaging requirement, says "many researchers believe that one hundred thousand times that amount is required. He considers that "pattern recognition techniques, by themselves are inadequate... it is clear that vision involves both sensory and knowledge-based processing".

To retrieve an image automatically by its content some method of formulating a query must be devised – but how? It is hard to visualise a system which automatically generates words or structural descriptions for search purposes when a search question is posed. Alternatively an actual structure resembling that of the required image must be input for matching purposes.

S.K.Chang describes a method of picture indexing in Chang (1984) and moves on to provide a description of a more fully worked out scheme in Chang (1988). The idea is that spatial relationships between objects may be represented by strings of characters enabling questions like "What objects are situated between a lake and a forest in the picture". Objects appear to be named ikons *representing* objects, not objects which have been automatically recognised and named – a far more difficult operation.

The idea is expanded in Chang (1990) where the segmentation of objects is indicated by data representing transitions when the system generates vertical and horizontal cutting lines which intersect edges in the image. Chang also suggests (In Anon 1988) that a combination of image keywords, pattern recognition, image processing, and image understanding might be used for retrieval. The user must inform the system in advance what methods are required and it will prepare indexes for the particular case. The more it is used for that application, the more it acquires knowledge to optimise its retrieval strategy.

C.C.Chang (1991) has taken the work further in order to use the data in S.K.Chang's "2-D strings" as a similarity measure for retrieving those images containing features similar to a known image.

Bordogna (1990) describes a method of identifying images by parts having a specific shape. For example the silhouette of a structure would be described in terms of the co-ordinates of its width, body length, arms, endpoints etc.

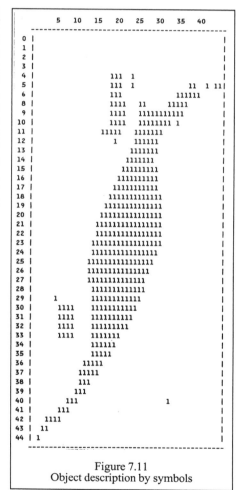

Figure 7.11
Object description by symbols

The images chosen to demons--trate the technique are Galaxies exhibiting various features such as "arms" etc. (Figure 7.11) This scheme could equally well be called a "descriptive word" scheme because each item is retrieved by "picture data

128

words" used to describe objects.

There must be some doubt about whether the various schemes of this kind, only a few of which have been described here, will function for more complex objects. At present only the simplest kinds of objects are chosen for description/recognition. Their ultimate effectiveness will depend on the extent to which more power (which is undoubtedly on the way) will bring about improvements, and whether the time taken for human descriptive indexing, which is likely to become prohibitively large, can be automated in some way.

A measure of similarity has been proposed by Lee (1991) for classifying irregular areas of similar shape and size by pattern matching involving strings of pixels. This kind of operation is computer intensive; a 256 x 256 pixel image took more than two hours on a Mac II. Another type of application is to find the best match between an input image and an image in the database stored in the machine. One such case is the recognition of human faces. Obvious applications have prompted research in this area, as described by Govindaraju (1990) and Hines (1989).

A system based on Aleksander's (1982) work on human face recognition done in the early eighties is now being further developed by Rickman and Stonham (1991) at Brunel University, UK (Figures 7.12 and 7.13). It is one of the few content recognition systems which is demonstrable. Since it works by pattern matching a collection of images in a database against an input image, a suitable image for inputting must be available in the first place.

The Brunel system can be tested on a facial image database consisting of 500 black and white images, each of 32 x 59 pixels. Each node in a neural network locks on to a particular feature of an image by a consolidation or rejection learning process during successive presentations of the test image.

Interconnected nodes learn by being encouraged to collect more data about a group of elements which they have already amassed. This identification of the "Principal Components" of an image is achieved by the adjustment of a weighting function associated with each node, each having "locked on" to a feature (Figures 7.12 and 7.13, with the permission of Brunel University).

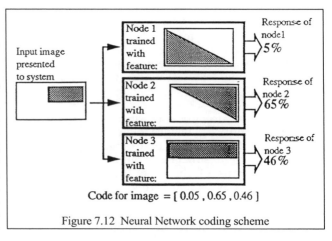

Code for image = [0.05 , 0.65 , 0.46]

Figure 7.12 Neural Network coding scheme

After learning, each node will generate output data whenever presented with that feature. Several such nodes will output signals when several features representing the complete image are presented to the system. The objective is to maximise discrimination of the Principal Components across the data set so that features of the image are identified with minimal overlap. Any other image in the collection sufficiently similar to the learnt image will produce similar output signals enabling image selection by matching to be performed.

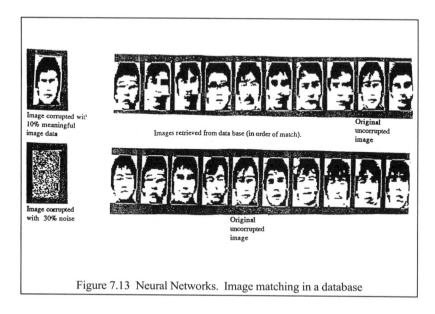

Figure 7.13 Neural Networks. Image matching in a database

The work at Brunel and by Dr. Eakins who is working on shape recognition at Newcastle University, is fairly typical of the state of the art in the UK. Eakins is working with a small image database consisting of a collection of two dimensional objects containing a limited amount of detail. Items may be retrieved from it by "example-based questions".

The more complex the images the more difficult it is for the user to produce a usable visual example and the more difficult it is to effect pattern matching. Three-dimensional patterns may need to be matched; the difficulties are then increased. The order of difficulty is further increased if the user is interested in retrieving pictures containing a particular object within a picture.

For instance if a user wants to retrieve "all pictures containing a motor car", it should not be too difficult to depict a car aided by currently available software embodying "clip-art" files (containing a large selection of already-drawn objects) and "drawing tool" software. When the "image-query" is submitted to the database for matching, it must be possible to retrieve a car from within any other picture no matter how it is represented, and whatever its attitude – a not impossible, but currently a slow computer-intensive task using expensive equipment.

Items within an image could be pre-processed to some degree in order to facilitate pattern matching. Someone would have to decide which items required to be pre-processed in order to make them retrievable. "Segmentation" –

that is the isolating of particular image components from others – is a research area where some success has been achieved. See below for a review of some 1993 work in this area.

In Eakins's (1992) Safari Project drawing tools are provided for building up a query shape by using coordinates, direction, length, arc angle etc., commands. The resulting object is compared with database objects for the best match. While at present it caters only for a restricted domain of 2D shapes, plans for a full 3D version are well developed.

"Are such systems needed at all?" asks Eakins. In reply, he discusses issues in the engineering field. With regard to wider issues of image description and indexing Eakins says "a more fundamental issue .... is that of defining the wider aspects of picture meaning in a way that makes sense to database users. The experimental systems described above have concentrated on deliberately simplified situations.... they are unlikely to be able to cope with general collections of images such as newspaper photographs most of which are incapable of any but the most trivial interpretation without the aid of external cues".

On feature extraction Eakins says:- "the overhead of this option would be considerable and its advantages largely illusory since no body of expertise yet exists to judge which types of feature are likely to be most successful in answering any given type of query".

"Existing spatial and image paradigm systems use pattern recognition techniques developed for computervision applications such as identifying "unknown" objects in noisy images. In the majority of cases these techniques have been developed using ten or fewer reference shapes for matching. There is little evidence that such techniques work effectively in discriminating between the much larger number of image types likely to be encountered in the general environment".

These comments have been overtaken by events to a considerable degree, largely due to the rapid development of inexpensive complex technology, as will be noted later in this chapter.

"One surprising feature of the image database field", continues Eakins "is the reluctance of many systems designers to submit their prototypes to any systematic evaluation. All too often, prototype systems are designed and tested by a member of the team, and the new system's features reported with no more than an indication of the type of output expected. Objective evidence on system effectiveness is sadly lacking -despite the fact that evaluation techniques adapted from the bibliographic retrieval field (e.g. Salton 1971) are readily available".

In computer vision there is a major problem in recognising three dimensional objects. So far as is known little work has been done on the question of using query-pictures to recognise three dimensional objects in a database.

Eakins is not alone in his interest in this topic. Dickinson *et al* (1992) cite a number of earlier works in their article about the subject. They suggest that collections of 3D "volume" objects should be defined in terms of their component parts such as cylinders, pyramids, truncated cones, etc. A database is queried to find out which objects contain component parts which match one or more of the indexing primitives.

Truesdell (1992) describes a system called Excalibur in which "the computer automatically extracts patterns from the data and learns the storage location with the resulting pattern identifications.... to retrieve data the user obtains a sample image .... and the computer repeats the same process used for learning".

A version, called Pixtel/EFS, was available, while a more advanced product, Pixtel/VRS, was said to be at an experimental stage. Excalibur Technologies (McLean Va) has been working on pattern recognition for ten years, but filed for Chapter 11 protection in 1985. The Japanese then put money into it in return for certain exclusive rights.

EFS works on the recognition of binary patterns generated from ASCII text – for instance OCR generated ASCII – and then fuzzy-matches queries against stored text. It runs on a VAX/VMS with a starting price of around £30,000. The software includes "automatic Indexing" facilities (text strings which match query strings). It will retrieve images from the descriptive text associated with them.

Pixtel/VRS was not available as a ready to use product in 1992. It will recognize patterns in images and match them using neural network techniques against input images. Software suites and programming expertise are available but cost and effectiveness are hard to assess from Excalibur literature and telephone conversations. The Truesdell article needs careful reading to distinguish between its "review" content and its "what Excalibur will actually do" content.

However, work on the system has continued and the latest version was seen in the UK in 1993. Some comments about it follow in the section "Indexing by query pictures" later in this chapter.

Davcev (1992) describes a system where images are broken up into elementary two-dimensional areas and curves. The areas are classified as either geometrical or fractal objects. For each fractal object an iterated function system is calculated by Barnsley's method (Barnsley, 1985). For geometrical objects, characteristic points are determined. Any open curve would be presented as a collection of pixels. The image is a collection of fractal and geometrical objects.

A description of "query vector creation" required for retrieval purposes is given. A technique called "cognition correction" automatically "determines the optimal cognitive network centre for spreading activity initiation according to the user query information".

The system performs quite differently from the well known relevance feedback techniques, requiring user intervention, as described by Salton. In conclusion it is stated that the system can provide an efficient "query-based mechanism for diverse information retrieval" and "our research is continuing in a number of directions".

Vaxiviviere (1992) describes a system for converting drawings on paper into a format suitable for Computer Aided Design (CAD). Having explained methods of converting bit maps into vectors, he then discusses the "complete decomposition of a drawing as a set of structures at a level higher than vectors – that is at the level of minimal closed polygons, or blocks, drawn with thick lines and their thin line attributes".

O'Connor (1991) is considering motion video images. "Among many forms of recorded documents in the bibliographical universe are those such as film, videotape, and videodisc, which rely primarily on moving pictures. In considering how we might describe these documents for access and analysis several issues arise".

O'Connor discusses a system for representing patterns of change within picture frames. It tracks attributes from the time at which an object first appears, and its size, location, and position relative to other objects. The objective of this idea is the selection of a single image containing information from a long sequence of motion video images. A way of handling such "abstracts" in alpha-numerical and graphical terms is described so that frames containing similar information may be discarded.

Work in progress at the MIT Media Laboratory on a language called Mnenosyne is described by Chakravarthy (1992). Most visual descriptive languages consist of lines, shapes, arcs etc., but the authors write:- "Our hypothesis is that while it might be possible to define visual primitives over limited domains, it is hard to define satisfactory primitives for the real-world images encountered by an archival system".

In Mnenosyne an Image is described by a number of descriptive entities each called an "index" of the form "Root/Image 1/Element 1/ shape" etc. Every index can therefore be referred to by listing its path from the root.

"Mnemosyne clusters functionally equivalent but structurally dissimilar descriptions leading to a more expressive visual description language than is possible through the use of visual primitives". Development of the idea continues.

Cumani (1991) discusses a method of describing images of dynamic scenes in terms of contour segments. A contour is a string of pixels with clearly defined end-points. A clustering of contours denotes an object and the distribution of the clusters provides information about their relative positions. "Tests on real images have shown very good results allowing almost all segments to be classified as belonging to some object".

An automatic content retrieval system has been described by O'Docherty (1991). It analyses the shape and dimensions of image objects and produces a description in terms of "webs" of codes representing arcs, nodes etc. The system is in the process of development at Manchester University.

A system with facilities for dealing with pictures and objects within a picture has been described by Strack (1992) and Schneider (1992).

According to Strack "A digital image can be classified within a database as one image object, which is composed of the following components; the original image in maximum quality and resolution, image derivatives for the graphical-interactive presentation and/or retrieval, and image related attributes (e.g. resolution, channels, colour map).

A new image type inherits all image attributes of its direct and indirect predecessors within the graph and can be extended with additional user-defined attributes. Thus, the image database can be structured according to application-specific requirements".

Each image object is an instance of a user-defined image type, which describes, besides the above-mentioned components, specific semantic attributes of the attached image objects. The image types of one image database form a directed acyclic classification graph which can be extended by using inheritance mechanisms.

Image data may be classified within the database in three categories:-

- Raw data – a digital image as an unformatted byte sequence.

- Registration data – data such as details of resolution, colour, coding, etc., for interpreting the raw data.

- Description data – describing the content of the image and/or administrative data.

Figure 7.14 (by courtesy of Magnifye, Ltd., on behalf of Proficomp Gmbh, Munich) shows a screen display during operations with a software package called "Screen Machine II". It shows (on the left) the user's instructions for reproducing the picture on the right. It was decided that an enlarged version of the picture was required following the display of the "thumbnail hit strip" shown along the bottom. The wanted picture is on the extreme left.

Some more information about Hine's system (Hine 1992) has been received in a personal communication from Dackow (1992) who developed the software. Semantic matching is performed between words describing pictures in the database and words associated with a query picture. Of greater interest is the method used to match the content of a query file containing a representation of a picture, and representations of pictures in the database.

The data used for matching is a tonal representation derived from a picture scanned into the system. Hit pictures are output according to the degree of tonal data matching between the input picture and database pictures. The need to already possess a picture (e.g. a photograph or a copy of the wanted picture) limits applications, but, given appropriate drawing tools, it might be possible for a user to produce a sketch good enough to pull hits out of a database for consideration.

Lee (1991) is also working on a method for the classification of areas

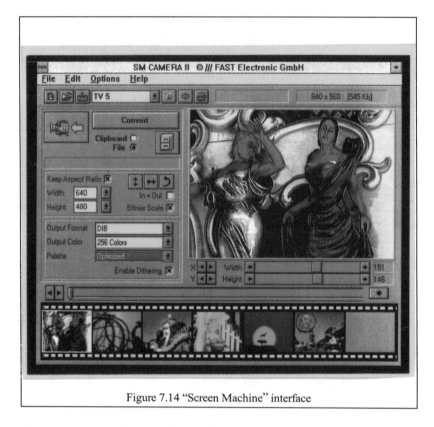

Figure 7.14 "Screen Machine" interface

from Landsat images by tonal matching. "Every sequence of pixels within a test image region is matched against areas to be classified. If the test sequence matches a texture primitive in all spectral bands, there is said to be a match". In plain language this means seeking matches between strings of pixels containing similar grey-scale data.

At Carnegie Mellon University, Michael Horowitz (Information Technology Centre) put forward some proposals for "The Alexandria Project" in July 1992. The proposals draw on work in progress at the Universities of California at Berkeley, Wisconsin-Madison, Brown, and Edinburgh, and at Altair (France), MCC, Servio Logic, Hewlett-Packard, Ontologic, and Bell Labs. (Horowitz, 1991a).

In an introduction to the proposals, Howowitz writes that "At the ITC we envision a future where scholars, artists, and other professionals use computers to create, manage, and communicate information as naturally as they use telephones... our mission is to gain international recognition as a center for excellence for distributed multimedia systems and to transfer our technology to our sponsor, IBM.

The system will incorporate an object-oriented database as described in Horowitz's report (Horowitz 1991b). Many of the features of this ambitious proposal bear a strong resemblance to the features outlined by Bush for his

Memex machine. Different types of data such as raster, audio, and video are included; it is planned to "generalize information management from textual to multimedia domains, specifically those involving multimedia indexing technologies". Presumably this means indexing by content.

In view of the resources available to Carnegie Mellon and others, their intention to launch a large scale project in this area is likely to be of considerable interest.

Research on indexing and retrieval using a visual thesaurus

Some new ideas, with some experimental work to back them up, have been put forward in support of the notion that the use of words for image retrieval is unsatisfactory. This confirms what is already known and encourages the pursuit of alternatives to schemes like ICONCLASS, TELCLASS, or AAT.

Technology which would enable visual thesauri, particularly "wordless" systems, to be implemented, is advancing slowly. Recent work in the United States indicates a move towards systems described as "Visual Thesauri" or "image query-by-example" systems. The major protagonists in this new field include Besser, University of California at Berkeley (1990), Rorvig (1993) and Seloff (1990), both at NASA, Houston, and Hogan et al (1991) at Syracuse University.

Besser, Rorvig, and Seloff are moving towards Visual Thesauri but without abandoning the use of words.

Besser describes the "IMAGEQUERY" software in which text-based information will be used to narrow down a search and the user will then browse through surrogate images of a retrieved set associated with the query words.

A range of "popular images" is linked to the thesaurus terms and "selection of a descriptive term from the thesaurus retrieves its associated image, as well as broader, narrower and related terms along with their associated images".

Seloff (1990) describes a system devised to manage a collection of more than one million transparencies and films and about 10,000 motion video and audio reels in the Johnson Space Centre (JSC) collection in Houston, growing at the rate of up to 65,000 new images per year. Seloff mentions the indexing Syndrome which indexers know so well:- "The viewpoint of the cataloger invariably changes from one week to the next and is always different from the perspective of the engineer or the scientist... the wider the disparity in the points of view, the less likely the appropriate item will be retrieved".

The JSC thesaurus was compiled by automatically processing a number of existing catalogues but it was felt that a visual thesaurus was also necessary. Seloff discusses thesaurus compilation (based on Salton's automatic thesaurus term selection work), to deal with film catalogue cards in the JSC augmented by further terms derived from the NASA thesaurus of scientific and technical terms.

A Hypercard system was developed enabling "a descriptive term from the thesaurus to retrieve its associated image as well as broader, narrower, and related terms along with their associated images". The "data retrieval engine", Personal Librarian, used in this work, ranks hits in order of relevance. This is obviously a very large project and future plans for its further development are described.

Word-labels may be inadequate for images but they are the conventional labels. Hypertext software is often the software used for image databases. It is word-oriented but may also be used for image management – for example for retrieving images from peripheral equipment such as tape, CD-ROMs, etc.

Seloff's prototype system was eventually set aside because "subsequent analysis of this visual thesaurus approach indicates that it is of more interest than utility to casual, or less experienced users, while the textual thesaurus approach is of more use to experienced users.

However Besser concluded that "descriptive text alone was often inadequate to provide intellectual access when attempting to locate a precise visual image". He proposes a browsing approach using standard, text-descriptive information to narrow the search to general categories; next, surrogate or miniature images are viewed, and finally "the user selects an appropriate image to view in full detail".

Ragusa et al (1992) are taking on NASA's information system problems in research at the Intelligent Multimedia Applications Laboratory (IMAL) at the University of Central Florida. The objective is to arrange for classification and retrieval of photographs taken during a space shuttle operational cycle. 35,000 photographs are taken during each cycle.

In the NASA Photographic System to Aid Classification (NAPSAC) a cataloguer views existing space shuttle photographs arranged in a 4-level hierarchy from complete system down to component level.

When a photograph of the appropriate subsystem is retrieved, new images accompanied by routine new textual data about that subsystem generated during the new operational cycle are entered automatically on an associated new dBase III record under operator supervision. The operator may add additional data.

Retrieval is either by textual query or by selection from the image hierarchy. Hits are shown in miniature sets on the screen, any of which may be enlarged to a full screen image. "Working tests of the prototype modules have been promising".

In multimedia presentation systems or publications, explicit indexing may not be needed. Images appear as an enhancement of the text, and it is the text which is ordered. For example in the previously mentioned CD-ROM/DVI publication "*Multimedia Encyclopedia of Mammalian Biology*" (McGraw Hill), about 3500 colour pictures and some motion video clips accompany text entries. Forms of indexing have of course been incorporated into the design so a user is not directly involved with it.

Indexing by query pictures

Almost all collections of images have hitherto been indexed and retrieved by words although various other approaches have been attempted as described above. But it has become evident during 1993 that the arrival of cheap processing power and the development of special software will soon result in the availability of a new generation of picture indexing methods.

This subject is discussed at length by Cawkell (1992b, 1993b). The following quotations are taken from the 1993 paper.

"In the case of images, the use of thesauri to control inconsistency is not effective due to the individual responses prevalent in human reactions to visual materials. That inconsistency is a reflection of creativity and diversity of human interests, situations, and context. If inconsistency is to be overcome, system designers will need to relinquish the idea of the utility of using words to index non-verbal understanding".

"The delight and frustration of pictorial resources is that pictures can mean different things to different people".

"it would seem unlikely that indexing could produce an appropriate key by means of which more than a small proportion of the multi-faceted information stored within a given image could be unlocked".

In the case of the next generation of picture database it is assumed that query-images will often be used for retrieval so that the enormous effort involved in creating, controlling, up-dating, and learning to use the thesauri and indexes will be reduced. The justification for this assumption is based on the remarkable advances made since the Cawkell (1993b) paper was compiled.

The system developed at Brunel University is one of the first to use alternative methods. It will match an input picture of a male face against a database of 500 faces, each of 32 x 59 pixels (Rickman and Stonham, 1991) as previously described.

Rorvig (1993) describes a method for "Automatically abstracting visual documents". The work represents a change of method compared with Seloff's "Visual Thesaurus" just described. Frames from film sequences of space shuttle launch operations are digitized and a range of features such as grey levels, edge slopes, line lengths, angles, etc., are extracted.

Data from these features are summed into a single value representing the structure of each frame and the values for a sequence of frames are compared.

A proportion of the numbers from the tails of the curves showing the distribution of these values are selected in order to provide a smaller set of significantly different images. A reduction, typically in the ratio of 700:1, from a mass of images, many of which are similar, to a set showing significant changes, is obtained.

Niblack and Flickner's method

Niblack *et al's* (1993) Query By Image Content (QBIC) prototype system runs on an IBM RS/6000 Risc machine. Queries may be asked in terms of full-scenes or within-scene objects by using questions about colour, texture, shape, or by drawing an edge-sketch of the object of interest. A test database of 1000 images and 1000 objects from a clip-art file is used.

The RS/6000 workstation called "Powerstation 530" delivers 10.9 Mflops and 34.5 Mips. It incorporates 128 Mbytes of memory and a 2.4 Gbyte internal disc; it uses Aix version 3 Unix-standard software. Its price is £42,747 with mouse, keyboard, and 3D graphics board. This board on its own costs £6731. A 19" colour monitor with 1280 x 1024 resolution and 24-bit colour is extra at £2350. However a commercial version of the software will run on much less costly PS/2 equipment.

In the edge-sketch query method, the user draws a shape, however crude, on the screen, and the machine obliges by presenting those thumbnails which most nearly resemble the sketch, as hits. The user may then narrow the choice if he or she chooses by improving the sketch in an attempt to reduce the noise retrieved by reason of the sketch's inadequacy. In Figure 7.15 a simple sketched query-picture is shown on the left with some of the hits produced by matching it against the content of the database

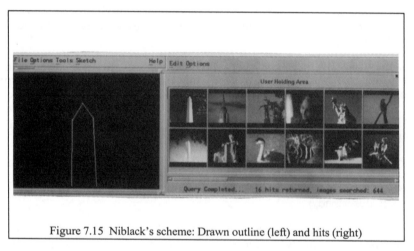

Figure 7.15 Niblack's scheme: Drawn outline (left) and hits (right)

The system is used for approximate matching between an input query-picture and a database picture. It works as an information filter to eliminate pictures which do not match the input picture sufficiently well. The thumbnails are 100 x 100 pixel reductions of the main pictures.

When the database is loaded, objects within pictures which might be supplied as hits must be outlined. The indexer approximately outlines an object or a number of objects within a picture and the system uses *Snakes* (see Chapter 4) to refine the outline so that it closely follows the outline of the required object. A choice of 256 colours is available to be used as a query as is the texture of an object as described in an associated paper by

Equitz (1993).

The shapes of objects to be searched are assumed to be non-occluded planar shapes. Algebraic moment invariants are computed. For retrieving sketches, edge maps are created for all pictures and objects within them. "Full scene" queries may be input based on colour and texture features, thereby avoiding the need to provide a sketch. Alternatively a set of colours and textures in selected proportions may be input as queries.

A "colour picker" screen with selection sliders is provided for colour selection. The method of retrieving "hit" pictures from an input drawing is based on edge matching. A drawing is reduced to 64 x 64 pixels, partitioned into a set of 8 x 8 blocks, and each block is correlated with a search area of 16 x 16 pixels in the image. The result is scored for similarity.

These "fuzzy matching" arrangements are designed to reduce what may be hundreds of thousands of images in the database to a small number which are retrieved as thumbnail hits for browsing.

A query may consist of at least 20 separate questions. To identify and match objects in this type of question a method related to Quad-trees called R-trees is used. Computed values for objects and images are processed in a relational database called Starburst.

The user interface is shown in Figure 7.15 above. A range of drawing tools are provided. Perhaps the most useful is the polygon tool with *Snake* outlining. The desired object is roughly outlined and the *Snake* software provides a "shrink-wrap" effect upon the outline. The effect is shown in Figure 4.4, page 55. Any weighted combination of colour, texture and shape may be used as a query and the results are displayed in order of matching commencing with the best match.

Hirata and Kato's method.

Hirata and Kato (1993) claim that the user has only to draw a rough sketch to retrieve similar images from a picture database. Similarities between the sketch and images in the database are automatically evaluated and the most similar candidates are shown to the user.

A painting is reduced to a standard size of 64 x 64 pixels. Gradients for the RGB intensity values in four directions are then calculated. The database index is formed by inputting the RGB colour values of each painting. The gradients are used to generate edges in two stages – firstly to produce an edge-image for further processing and secondly to process the edges derived from the first process in order to produce an edge-image more suitable for representing the original picture. The hinned edges from this last image are used as an "abstract" image in the "pictorial index" against which input pictures are matched.

To search the database using an input sketch, both the sketch and all the database pictures are divided into 8 x 8 pixel blocks. Every picture so sub-divided in the database is then matched against the input sketch, but the blocks from the input sketch are shifted around the area of a candidate image to attempt "fuzzy matching". In other words the sketch

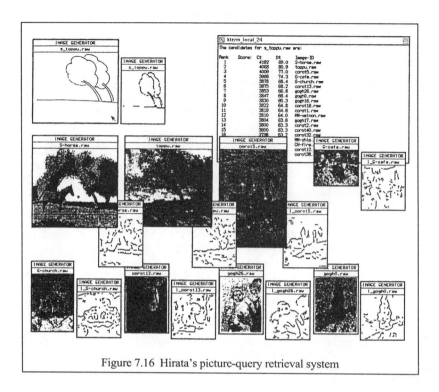

Figure 7.16 Hirata's picture-query retrieval system

could be appreciably different from an image in the database, but the latter could still be generated as a "hit". The most similar are rank ordered and presented for "hit" consideration.

The error between an input block and the database block of pixels may be up to about 12.5%. Figure 7.16 (by permission of NEC) shows the pictures and their corresponding edge representations retrieved by the sketch shown top left, with its edge representation immediately on the right of it.

The system was tested using a database of 205 paintings of full colour landscapes and portraits. A table is provided showing how well the sketches recall the best candidates from the collection. When 18 different sketches were used as test pictures, the intended image was received as one of the 5 best candidates in 94.4% of the tests.

The authors say that when the algorithms are applied to a large database, the time taken to retrieve images would become lengthy. The algorithms used are general enough to be applied to figures, diagrams, photographs, textile patterns and artistic paintings.

Swain's method

Swain (1993) has described a tool called "FINDIT" being tested at the University of Chicago. At the time of publication work in progress was based in the matching of a query image against a database image by the intersection of colour histograms. A histogram may be visualised as a bin whose size depends on the number of times a particular colour occurs in the image array. It has been shown that colour histogram intersection is fairly insensitive to changes in image resolution, histogram size, depth and viewpoint.

Each picture in the database is indexed by its characteristic set of histograms. These are matched against the histograms for a query-image input to the system. Some pictures of the results obtained with the system are given.

Pictures of objects taken from a 45 degree angle, showing a degree of perspective distortion, are matched against objects photographed from the front. However the degree of perspective distortion does not appreciably affect the shape of images in the photographs. Experiments are continuing on larger databases.

Dowe's method

Dowe's paper (1993) describes further developments of the commercially developed system called Excalibur, already mentioned in this chapter. Originally, patterns of text in text images stored in the database were matched against patterns in the in query text. Matching is described as "multiple layer neural net operation". The neural net learning feature, normally managed by inter-connected nodes, is implemented in software, but the principle of operation is not described.

Although this paper contains very little substantive data, it had been claimed during the preceding year that the system would work equally well on images, but that the image recognising system was only available to special order.

However at an exhibition at the Wembley Conference Centre during June 1993, a prototype of the image-recognising version of Excalibur was shown. Images were input to the system as photographs placed in front of a video camera. The database was searched, and if a matching photograph was found, it was displayed. Insofar as one can judge the effectiveness of the system on an exhibition stand, it appeared to work satisfactorily, and should be recognised as an impressive achievement. More information is awaited.

The papers by Samadani, Han and Katragadda (1993) and Shann (1993) describe methods of selecting images within one domain. Samadani selects pictures of fossils in rock and Shann pictures of the Aurora.

Since the curved structure of fossils in samples is fairly similar the detection and characterisation of such fossils is amenable to image filtering of a relatively simple kind because the system is only required to identify objects within a narrow domain. The same remarks apply to the system used for recognising Aurora images.

Graphical methods of information retrieval

There is some activity in work designed to match the similarity of images where objects in images have similar spatial relationships. Graphical nodes can be used to represent the position of objects and the direc-tion and length of their interconnections may be described.

In one case (Wakimoto, 1993) the recognition of similarity between the whole, or sections of diagrams of engineering plants, is described. The same principle is mentioned in Ozsoyoglu (1993). Kitamato (1993) describes a graph-matching system where each graph describes the relationship between cloud patterns in photographs taken by a satellite. Oakley *et al* (1993) describe a language of geometric construction to enable a user to specify groups of features of interest in an image.

QUERY PICTURES WILL NOT ALWAYS BEAT WORDS

Not a great deal is known about the kind of questions that users are likely to put to a picture collection. What kind of users and what kind of collection are we talking about? Examples have already been given of a number of collections of various kinds, but there is virtually no analysis of the kind of questions asked or the success of the system in responding to those questions in any of the published papers.

There is one exception, and that is Enser's work on the Hulton picture collection. The reasons for Enser's work on this collection have been described (Enser, 1991) and were discussed earlier in this Chapter. Retrieval problems are well illustrated by his comment:- "one of the many entities recorded was a perambulator; the photograph provides useful visual evidence of this seemingly bygone form of transport in ordinary use. All such information is lost, of course, when the picture is indexed by the caption such as "market day in Kirby Lonsdale".

In this case a "hit" would have been recorded by inputting a query-picture.

The Hulton picture collection is enormous, and in Enser's words "such is the scale of the Hulton Company's operation, so varied is their customer base and so catholic their collection, that it would seem reasonable to expect the findings of this project to be generally applicable to non-domain-specific picture collections".

Enser's findings were, in fact, that in such an environment "an extremely heavy dependency on the expertise and search time availability of the picture researcher in his/her role as an intermediary must continue to be the norm in the short-to-medium term" (personal communication).

Unfortunately we do not have any results on "failure analysis". Users may not have always found what they wanted, or following a user-librarian dialogue and more searching, a user may have departed with a picture which was not a genuine response to his or her question.

Since then a relatively very small part of the Hulton collection has become available on CD-ROM and "hit thumbnails" are available on the disc. (see Figure 8.1 in next Chapter). The method of indexing and the thumb-nails may call for some revision of this last statement, and comments on the system are expected.

Although the idea of inputting a query picture has much to recommend it, had such a system been available for Enser's tests, it would not necessarily always have been more successful than existing indexing arrangements. It would have been difficult to devise query-pictures for some of the questions asked during the test – for example "great personalities of the 20th Century", "Street Scenes in 1850", or "Smog/Pollution in London".

Query-pictures do not always replace the descriptive power of words which may be better for some abstract concepts. For instance it is hard to see how a query-picture could be devised for "great personalities of the 20th century, nor would it be likely that a question using those actual words could be used.

The need for effective indexing systems

Indexing an image may be a time-consuming process to be carried out by subject experts. In the AAT work described by Peterson and Keefe, for example, refinements took several years. In addition to the investment made in compiling a thesaurus, there will be an on-going investment to up-date it.

One might expect that this kind of effort would be needed to deal only with a large, diverse, collection. The AAT system is designed only to handle Western art and architecture out of the totality of art and architecture. ICONCLASS covers a similar area with a difference in emphasis.

Objects in collections indexable by these systems, a part of the totality of art and architecture, in turn represent only a minute fraction of all possible objects – for instance the range of objects that might be encountered in a newspaper's library of photographs. In many image col-lection projects, recognition of the "indexing problem" is noticeable for its absence.

How many collections are awaiting digitization or are already in digitized format waiting to be indexed and placed in a database for the greater benefit of users? What proportion would form a small database of simple images amenable to indexing, and what proportion would form a large database of hard-to-index complex images?

Are numerous collections awaiting to be represented in electronic form in such places as libraries, museums, art galleries, private houses etc., together with various kinds of "non-art" collections? Would a latent demand be revealed if relatively inexpensive technology and effective methods of indexing were brought together?

In response to questions about the demand, evidently there are a number of quite large image databases covering *objets d'art* in existence. Many contain complex images. At least twenty are described in the Proceedings of the Pittsburgh conference and in the "EVA" Royal Academy 1992 meeting proceedings, both cited a number of times in this Chapter.

References to many other collections are also included in this chapter, but why is it that indexing is so often not taken seriously?   Some possible reasons are:-

- Some organisations seeking to assemble picture collections seem to prefer to extol the virtues of the technology with which they are experimenting at the expense of involvement with indexing.

- The systematic indexing of images is not considered to be of great importance. Equipment suppliers support this view by default.   Drawing attention to indexing problems negates sales prospects for the positive technical people who sell image handling hardware, so they simply do not mention it.

- At present the number of collections which have grown large enough and diverse enough to throw up indexing shortcomings is small.

- Perhaps those organising new collections, particularly when they are at the feasibility or prototype stage, are content with indexing their experimental collections in a simple way, adequate for their size.   The inclusion of provision for effective indexing – a costly, hard to argue component – in proposals to proceed with the main collection may not improve the chances of proposal acceptance.

- The people who are developing the means of managing a collection do not know about the problems of providing, and about the need to provide effective indexing for growing collections. This notion may seem extraordinary in view of the general competence of such people.   However there is a good deal of evidence to support it.

CHAPTER 8

MULTIMEDIA SYSTEMS AND PICTURES; DATABASES; COPYRIGHT,

Multimedia in museums and art

Multimedia systems are used in many museums and art galleries and pictures are the most important component in many of them.

Although "multimedia/hypermedia (M/H)" used to mean systems for providing on-screen presentations with text and line drawings, it now often means presentation systems with text, graphics, still or motion pictures, and sound.

There is still a considerable gulf between the usefulness of M/H as claimed by the hardware/software hyper-authors responsible for pushing it into the market, and its actual useful practical applications. This gulf is gradually narrowing.

Visser (1993) defines four different types of art/museum multimedia systems:-

- Documentary, providing library/encyclopaedic information primarily for professional users.
- General information covering a wide range of topics intended for the general public.
- Supporting information system, for instance for use at exhibitions, etc., for providing limited information.
- "Point of information" stand-alone system associated with a collection.

Apple's hypertext system called *Hypercard* was an important contribution to M/H-image symbiosis; it is described in Chapter 6. The facilities for controlling peripheral equipment on which pictures are stored makes *Hypercard*, or one of the competitive products which are also available, a convenient and frequently used control method.

Cards contain "buttons" which, among other things, may be mouse-selected and "clicked/pushed" to execute an external command or XCMD, routed through the appropriate "driver" (software compatible with particular external peripherals such as a videodisc player, CD-ROM etc.).

Hypercard was developed primarily for the manipulation of cards containing text, with image-control as a bonus. The principle has been developed further for systems designed specifically to manage images and component parts of images.

For example with the Macromind *Director* multimedia software, the system is frame-based rather than card-based, with the means for controlling both external equipment and objects within a frame on the screen. The role of *Director's* "XObjects" is to a frame similar to the role played by *Hypercard's* XCMDs to a card.

Lunin (1990) says:- "Increasingly museums and art departments are investigating the tremendous potential of videodisc and optical disc technology for projects such as collections management, research, fund raising, visitor interpretation and education, and exhibition design"

According to Besser (1991):- "Many museums, archives, and libraries have fine arts collections of either original objects or of surrogate images (such as slides) of original objects. The items in these collections (be they original objects or surrogate images) are often either too large (wall sized), too small (slides), or too fragile both to attract textual explanatory material to them and to retrieve them easily when someone needs to examine them".

In an introductory piece to the proceedings of a recent conference Bearman (1991b) says:- "Since the early 20th century museums have tried to be more than "cabinets of curiosity" to be viewed passively. In this volume we witness the latest efforts to interact more assertively with visitors, but despite the introduction of new technology, they represent a continuity more than a radical departure".

Woolsey and Semper (1991) of Apple (San Francisco) point out that there are over 10,000 museums and visitor centres in the US and Science Centres are visited by more than fifty million people every year. "Multimedia offers to people working in public space a set of new and exciting tools to augment their 3D displays and a way to extend the experience of visitors to greater depth and other environments. Through access to rich interactive kiosks in museums, for example, it is possible for visitors to move from a glancing experience to a deeper involvement with an underlying idea.

Electronic imaging is probably used in museums and for *objets d'art* at least as much as in medicine, both being exceeded only by military applications. There are a number of journals and newsletters covering this field, for example:-

Archives and Museum Informatics
5501 Walnut St.,
Suite 203
Pittsburgh PA 15232-2311
USA

Art Documentation
Art Libraries Society of America
c/o Rutgers University Art Lib.,
New Brunswick NJ 08903
USA

Chart Newsletter
Computers and the History of Art
43 Gordon Square
London WC1
England

MuseMedia
Sharon Kayne Chaplock
557 North 68th St.,
Milwaukee WI 53213-3954
USA

Museum Management & Curatorship
Butterworth Heineman
Linacre House
Jordan Hill
Oxford OS2 8DP
England

Visual Resources
Fine Arts Library
Fogg Art Museum
Harvard University
Cambridge MA 02138
USA

This list is a selection from a larger list published in *Archives & Museum Informatics.*

A publication from the Museum Documentation Association (Anon 1993) lists a large number of software and database software packages with the names and addresses of suppliers and a list of the two or three hundred museums, colleges, universities, trusts, and other organisations using them. *MODES* for cataloguing is the most widely used package by far, followed by *MIS* for inventory and *Recorder* for biological locality recording. *DBase* is easily the most widely used database.

From this data, we may extrapolate to perhaps 20,000 museums and like organisations world-wide, of which perhaps 3000-5000 are running computerised systems. Some hundreds of these are probably using or contemplating using images with many more thinking about their introduction.

Examples of proposed or existing systems

The proposed Globe Theatre system

To quote a recent feature article "The potential now exists to extend at least part of the public experience with all its drama and senses into the private world of the home... A visitor produced multimedia presentation which can be recorded at a public space site on to videotape can be taken home for viewing... the development of the Globe theatre project will serve as a good set of concrete examples of what we are discussing here".

This system is to be used in the International Shakespeare Globe Centre which includes the re-built Globe theatre. The original Globe, built in 1598, was closed by the Puritans in 1642 and demolished to make way for tenements in 1644. Sam Wanamaker decided to rebuild it. A plaque on a brewery wall on the south bank of the Thames commemorates it. Rebuilding started in 1988 and Phase II is in progress.

A museum and research centre is being built on the site as well as the theatre. In October 1993 the building was being held up by a shortage of suitable oak beams. Sam's most untimely death means that he will not see it opened in 1994.

Some preliminary work on a multimedia system for use by visitors was done by IBM. Several modules were considered including one to provide general information for visitors, a second to assist students, and a third to provide for several research options.

An ambitious scheme described by Friedlander (1991) received Apple encouragement and is gradually being developed. Historical advice has been supplied by Andrew Gurr, Professor of English at Reading University. Part of the design provides for the production of animations using *Macromind Director.*

Another part will enable Shakespearian plays to be made available as multimedia presentations. The plays could, for example, be "edited" into various stage settings.

The Berkeley prototype

Besser (1990) describes the *imagequery* software implemented at the University of California at Berkeley. It will run on workstations including SUNs, PS/2s with AIX, or MACs with AU\X.

Besser talks about the often inadequate availability of rich information sources such as collections of photographs. His remarks about the problems of indexing objects in, or aspects of photographs were quoted in Chapter 7.

UC Berkeley already run campus-wide online library services so it is proposed that *imagequery* be made available as a kind of enhanced Online Public Catalogue (OPAC) over the existing network and workstations. This would allow users "to browse visually through the group of small surrogate images associated with an initial hit list". Images would be taken from the Architectural Slide Library, the Department of Geography's Map Library, and the Lowie Museum's Anthropology collection of photographs of their objects.

A form (spreadsheet) is first displayed, forcing the user to make the appropriate entries by selecting options from pull-down menus.

Thus the "fields" menu for the architectural database offers the option "place". If "Venice" is chosen, that word appears in the upper part of the spreadsheet. If the "Authority List" is then chosen, classes of existing images are displayed for selection by the user e.g. "piazzas".

At this point a more complex Boolean logic query may be added or the "do query" button pressed and a hit list displayed in the bottom part of the screen. For example "Venice...San Marco" might be selected from the list.

Upon selection of "browse", thumbnail-size images are displayed on the right hand side of the screen. The display area may be expanded to include the whole screen if necessary, allowing up to 30 thumbnails to be displayed together. Finally, any of these images may be replaced on command by a high resolution colour enlargement.

The proposed Visual Thesaurus at Syracuse University.

The Globe project is one of a number of museum systems described in the Proceedings of the 1991 Pittsburgh conference. However, arguably the most interesting idea discussed in the Proceedings is the visual thesaurus.

Hogan *et al* (1991) say "Many current information systems used to access images simply transfer the text-based methods of information storage and retrieval to computerized systems. Because the multiple aspects of visual access to images has long been neglected its development is still woefully inadequate... The inter-relationship between text and graphics needs to be thoroughly explored as does the creative possibilities in visual-based retrieval systems... Visual thesauri and their applications to the museum community incorporate a complex mix of political, economic, and design issues".

Hogan reminds us that picture thesauri have been around since Joh Amos's *Visible World*, published in London in 1672. I remember being given a book called *The English Duden* many years ago. I believe it was originally published in German. Every other page represented a scene showing many numbered objects. These pages were entitled "The Car", "The Farm", "The Bank", "The Railway Station", etc. The opposite pages contained the names of the numbered objects.

This was the basic arrangement but there was also some kind of logical ordering of pages and the number of objects in each picture was very large. I don't remember whether there was any cross referencing or duplication of objects in different scenes.

Hogan says "It is relatively quick and easy to browse the page of a visual dictionary even though the book may have a large number of pages... This type of browsing is difficult in a visual environment... rapid traversal of displays is difficult... what is lost to the user is the ease of determining the underlying structure which becomes quickly apparent with the use of a print dictionary", and so on.

However there are some on-going attempts to extend this principle into computer-based system and Hogan briefly discuss Besser's *imagequery*, the NASA visual thesaurus, and the event display system used by physicists at CERN.

Advances in this area would, of course, be of great interest not just for museum collections but for all kinds of collections. Hogan et al review research and then describe a prototype visual thesaurus being developed at Syracuse University.

They make the point "...visual images make it possible simultaneously to compare all the features of two patterns. Therefore information is matched in parallel... in contrast to features described verbally which are not all accessible at the same time and must be compared serially". They also suggest that a computer can rotate images for pattern matching much faster then the brain can.

This is not a good comparison to bring into the part of the paper headed "Human Information Processing" which contains some otherwise interesting reflections. Brain-computer object-rotation comparison are not very helpful. Computer pattern matching as a method of retrieval by similarity, which is implied here, is infinitely less effective than the human brain

A computer is unable to recognise the similarity between two quite simple objects when one of them is viewed from a different angle or when they are presented with a different perspective unless a complex computing-intensive operation is put in hand – an operation currently receiving considerable attention. The ease and speed with which a human accomplishes this task and can deduce the appearance of a complete object from a single viewing are unlikely to be matched by a computer in the foreseeable future.

The other point is that it has only just become feasible (1993) to pose a question in the form required by a pattern matching system, namely "here is the kind of image I am seeking – which image in the collection most nearly matches it?".

The authors propose one way out of this difficulty, eliminating text entirely by, in effect, providing a user with the tools of the kind which are already used now – e.g. rotation, scaling, mouse dragging, curve construction, etc., for modifying a simple image drawn from, say, a "clip art" collection. The question is now "is there an object in the database resembling this one?"

The user's simulation has now become the formulated query which he or she asks when it is felt that artistic attempts have produced a reasonable simulation for presenting to the database for matching. The machine signals the number of hits which may then be visually browsed by the user. Prompted by the resemblance, or lack of it, between his or her sketch and hit images, the sketch is adjusted and the query repeated.

Hogan *et al* follow these ideas with the comments "When considering information retrieval in general we are reminded of an old Russian proverb (quoted at the beginning of Chapter 7). We are looking for alternative ways of image retrieval, ways that are less dependent on familiarity with existing taxonomies and their assigned authorities. Accomplishing this end is less clear-cut."

A working system at the Smithsonian Institution

In April 1992 I saw part of the Smithsonian's "Information Age" multimedia exhibition at the National Museum of American History on Constitution Avenue, Washington. It is appropriately housed because this part of the Smithsonian contains such relics as Morse's original telegraph, examples of Bell's first telephones, and the ENIAC computer.

The system has been running since May 1990. The visitor's inter-active PCs are linked by an IBM token-ring LAN. A number of the PCs embody touch-screen windows with choice provided by touching the image of a frame from a video clip.

Allison and Gwaltney (Allison, 1991) say that "the most popular program in the exhibition relates to code breaking. It runs on two stations. Visitors played it 314,564 times in the first year so it had approximately 471,846 viewings. With this program, visitors can encipher their name using a simulation of the German ENIGMA cyphering machine. They then decode it by remembering the machine rotor settings they used to encode it.

Finally they can see actual German messages that were intercepted and decrypted during World War II... We believe that the subject attracts visitors and so does the fact that they can encode their own names. Making programs personally relevant to visitors clearly increases their popularity".

The monitoring equipment, linked by an Ethernet LAN, handles the bar-coded guide used by visitors for logging-in to terminals, and is also used for checking operational status and collecting statistics about visitors' behaviour.

Treasures of the Smithsonian on CDI

Woolsey's idea that a videotape derived from the Globe system "might be taken home for viewing" has been implemented in a different way by Hoekema (1990) and others.

"Treasures" was designed in 1987/1988 from the data then available about CDIs. CDI players became available in the US at the end of 1991. Motion video will become possible some time this year.

From the description of CDIs given in Chapter 6 it will be noted that interactivity and motion are achieved by shifting relatively small amounts of new data on to the screen against a background of larger amounts of "old" data which changes infrequently.

This mechanism is not particularly useful for the "Treasures" presentation. The CD-I facilities for combining commentary, music, and text as used here, will enable users to change a limited number of full-screen images but this is still a considerable advance on CD-ROM.

Hoekema says "we would try to give every treasure (about 150 are included) its due in the form of audio-visual presentations with the best images we could find, a lively narration marked by wit and personality, and a full soundtrack with music and sound effects which would reinforce the interpretation of the object being presented. "Another feature of the system is user selection of a treasure by date, by museum, by category, or by associated person.

A "tour" of several different sets of treasures connected by some common theme may also be selected. The CD-I was published in October 1991, having earlier won an award from the American Association of Museums. The price is $49.95.

The historic textile database at the University of Maryland

The imaging system described by Anderson (1991) shows that image collections do not necessarily introduce difficult indexing problems as discussed in Chapter 7.

In this case the database consists of images of coverlets (decorative loom woven bed-coverings) and carpets. "Design motifs found in coverlet centerfields, borders, corner blocks, cartouches, and logos are coded on the back of the information sheet and then entered into the motif database. This makes it possible to search for specific design motifs".

Nothing more is said about the coding scheme except that "untrained students would be hired to enter the data... so it must be easy to update records and learn the basic tasks of entering, appending, and editing the data". Presumably an efficient coding scheme for all possible patterns has been devised and is easy to use.

The problems which arose in this case were not in the indexing area but in the imaging equipment. They sound predictable because "the lack of funds forced many difficult compromises". *PicturePower* software enables images to be imported from a video camera into a database running on a PS/2 via an image capture board, and integrated with text. Formats are compatible with *DBASE III*, chosen for the database. However modifications were required because of the inconvenience of searching with this database.

Inadequate picture quality was improved by two methods. A standard camera was replaced by a professional camera and lens. System resolution was improved and colour was replaced by a 4-bit greyscale. It seems that 16 levels of grey were preferred to poor colour. The impression conveyed by Anderson is that the system does the job in spite of the cost constraints.

History information stations at the Oakland museum

A number of "History Information Stations" for the use of visitors have been installed at this museum. Each consists of a microcomputer, 19" monitor with touch screen, disc drive, videodisc player, and stereo amplifier and loudspeakers. The primary goal of the scheme is to "provide, identify, and interpret, information about each of the 6000 artefacts on exhibition" (Cooper and Oker, 1991).

However "A clear favourite" say the authors, is the interactive map. The map includes "landmark icons to help visitors select the area in which they found the item in question". A montage of display cases is shown, and the visitor selects the case and then the artefact. "The map allows the visitor to filter out most of the gallery from the decision making process with one touch of the finger".

The information is contained on videodisc (i.e. motion video to the NTSC standard) with large-size text stored on the hard disc. The authors say that "we chose to use a 286 class of computer because it has just enough speed to load full pages of text at an acceptable rate".

The CMC (Delhi) Art Records prototype

Chaudhry and Roy (1990) describe a government of India scheme called the *Arts Record Treasury System* operated by CMC. A prototype art object imaging system is now in use at the Indian Centre for Cultural Relations.

The objective of the scheme is to enhance an existing online Art Object Catalogue with images. The online catalogue is organised as an SQL/DS relational database running on an IBM 4361 in Bombay. It is accessed over the INDONET SNA network which has nodes at a number of centres in India with a connection to CMC's London office via a gateway to an international packet switch network. The catalogue covers a collection of Indian paintings, sketches, etchings, statues, sculptures, lithographs etc., exhibited at various locations in India and abroad.

Significantly, and in common with image collections elsewhere, a problem "prevalent in the Indian scenario is the lack of uniformity in categorising various schools of thought, styles, etc., leading to an ad hoc classification scheme.

Unlike books in the libraries the objects in a museum's collection are physically diverse and they have to be named before they can be added to the catalogue. A nomenclature for naming these objects has yet to evolve in India".

The image capture system consists of an Eikonix CCD type 850 camera for producing 4000 x 4000 pixel images in colour from standard size 22.5 x 15 cm photographs, a PC/AT microcomputer, and Philips optical disc storage. Compression is not used for fear of degrading the images. Each image is accompanied by a textual description of image attributes managed using Oracle RDBMS SQL software with interactive menu-control for user searching.

Hits are picture identification numbers each associated with an image displayable on a 500 x 500 pixel Mitsubishi colour monitor. Details of how the contents of pictures are described or indexed are unfortunately not provided.

Multimedia systems running in 1992

The following brief extracts covering the twenty five different systems running mainly in the UK but including five different countries as described by Hoffos (1992), provide a good overview of recent multimedia activities:-

Bank of England
> A Public Relations exercise because "there is a steady demand for our products without advertising". However the presentation is seen by about 100,000 visitors a year.

Birmingham Museum
> A guide to the South Pacific collection.

Bradford Cartright Hall (Bradford, England, attractions).

British Golf Museum, St.Andrews
> An elaborate system comprising eight laserdisc and three CD-I systems in an audiovisual theatre. Includes many early video-clips.

British Museum
> Several presentations covering Saxon England.

Cambridge (Nagas Tribes).

Design Museum, London
> Includes an interactive computer-assisted design package (CAD) inviting visitors to design a toothbrush.

Imperial War Museum, London
> Features a number of interactive databases with touchscreen access covering two world wars.

Jersey Museum
> A comprehensive CD-ROM based system covering museum objects and places of interest on the island.

Manchester Museum
> Covers scientific and technical subjects.

Musee Carnavalet, Paris
> Several guides to major musical compositions.

Museum of Civilization, Ottawa
> Includes several Arctic themes, in particular "The Living Arctic" designed for children.

Museum d'Histoire Naturelle, Paris
> Three separate systems covering mammals, reptiles and birds.

Museum of Natural Science, Taiwan

Multimedia packages produced by MPI, London, to be followed by a large diorama of flora and fauna to be introduced during 1993.

National Gallery, London
Described in a separate section later in this Chapter.

National Museum of Racing, USA
An installation at Saratoga Springs featuring a "Hall of Fame", designed by Tempus (London) and based on a scheme already working at Newmarket.

National Waterways Museum, Gloucester, England
Interactive presentations covering canal building and features.

National Museum of Photography
Film and Television, Bradford, England.

Natural History Museum, London.

Norwich, England (Tourist Information).

Royal Britain, London.

Royal Museum of Scotland, Edinburgh
Includes a hypertext presentation "The Wealth of a Nation" and a prehistoric touch-screen presentation.

Glascow Exhibitions Guide.

Tate Gallery, Liverpool
A "Sculpture Interactive" package covering the work of Henry Moore.

Victoria & Albert Museum, London
Aspects of Chinese art.

Wellcome Institute, London.
A large scheme which includes over 50,000 photographs of prints, paintings, and sculptures.

Multimedia systems running in 1993

A number of papers were delivered at a conference "Electronic Imaging and the Visual Arts" (EVA) held at the National Gallery, London, in July 1993 (Hemsley, 1993). They covered descriptions of systems in use, existing and proposed telecommunications, and the acquisition, storage, display, and publication of images.

The images often form parts of a multimedia system. Such systems are now becoming quite widely used in art galleries and museums. They may be interactive in order to encourage the participation of visitors who are otherwise passive observers. Multimedia is often labelled "a technique looking for an application" – a label which is no longer applicable in the arts field. Four of the projects described in the papers are supported by CEC, ESPRIT, RACE, or IMPACT funding.

The variety of projects described illustrates the current range of electronic imaging activities. Three papers are about multimedia projects in museums. There are also three papers covering the subject of the inter-communication of imaging data. Other papers cover conservation, high quality colour reproduction of pictures, historical applications, copyright and indexing. The Apple Macintosh microcomputer is often used - it comes across as the dominant platform. Kodak Photo-CD receives a mention as a very promising newcomer.

The articles about telecommunications are to do with the Remote Access to Museum Archives (RAMA) telecom system to be used for inter-museum access to databases. The telecommunication links remain a problem, an FDDI network being mentioned for communication between French museums, with ISDN/X25 for inter-country telecom links.

One of the most informative papers is by Friso Visser (1993) a member of the team formed from 8 museums – 3 in Germany, 1 in France, 1 in Spain, 1 in the Netherlands, 1 in Portugal, and 1 in Denmark, and 4 research or industrial organisations – 2 in Germany, 1 in Spain, and 1 in Portugal.

The objective is to provide a multimedia visitor's programme in English entitled "Discoveries – traces of Europe's cultural integration". It is to be a test for inter-communicating interactive multimedia to be made available to the public at each of the participating museums. The project, called the European Museums Network (EMN) project, ran from 1989 to 1992 with the support of the CEC through the RACE programme of application pilot projects.

The inter-communication aspect could not proceed as planned since suitable telecoms were unavailable. It is interesting that in this and other related projects conceived in the late eighties, unrealistic assumptions appear to have been made about the availability of European broadband telecommunications. Perhaps by sponsoring projects requiring that the telecoms would be in place, the CEC felt that its optimistic forecasts would seem more plausible. Alas they were not in place, but this did not stop other aspects of Museum and Arts systems from being tried out.

The EMN's objectives were to provide the museum's administrators with the opportunity to get to grips with multimedia authoring and to try out the results on the public. To this end, data covering about 800 museum objects was input and the multimedia machine chosen was an Apple Mac IIfx with System 7.0 and Quicktime, and a Unix operating system. The machine includes a 24-bit video card, and viewing is done on 13" Trinitron monitors.

The information about the 800 objects is up-dated periodically by the museums, the main feature being digitised TIFF 1280 x 960 pixel 24-bit pictures. This is backed up by text, sound, and other images, with 30 second video clips and animation to be added later. Appropriate compression will be included when the video is added. The text includes basics, facts, explanations, titles and labels, copyright data, etc.

The system includes "A short tour on.... " facilities and button selection of functions. Navigation is assisted by the ongoing display of a "personal keyword list" with thumbnail pictures and step-back operation as needed.

Visser states that "the average manpower to describe one object to its full extent and store it digitally involved one full week of work. The average data referred to consists of the main image, some 15 pages of text, 15 additional images, and one or two fragments of sound".

Assuming the cost of labour and overheads to be a conservative £30,000 per annum the weekly cost (48 week year) is £625. Describing the 800 objects therefore cost about £500,000. This does not include video or animation. The total cost of the EMN project was 10 million Ecu (1M ECU = £770,000). This multi-national multimedia project would cost substantially more then a project undertaken by a single organisation but it provides an idea of the authoring effort and finance needed to mount a multimedia "visitor's system" for a museum.

Delouis (1993) describes problems encountered when communicating images between museums. The idea is to enable people studying the history of arts, fine arts generally and museum objects to obtain the necessary information without having to consult archives in different museums. In many museums only part of the collection can be presented at the same time because of lack of space.

A few museum archives are already accessible – for example the Beazley Archive in the Ashmolean Museum and in France The National Museum's collections of paintings which are partly accessible through Minitel. Presumably only data about images, not the images themselves, are available.

A large number of plates, drawings, and prints are available for viewing on "a high definition screen" at The Musee d'Orsay running on a Vax computer for local viewing. Remote access to a collection at the Louvre from the Musee d'Orsay is being considered.

"The concept of an electronic museum will be achieved through a work station which can access various bases or databanks inter-linked by gateways". The inter-linking will be by a broadband network. "Eventually in Europe, ATM networks might bring a single solution ... compliance with property rights on images and other related rights such as copyright are the most important aspect; these rights differ from one country to the other. Compliance with museum pricing policies is another essential point".

The article ends with the question "is a virtual museum conceivable"? The answer provided is that the "future shall decide whether the virtual museum can be achieved". Evidently RAMA is at a very early stage of its development.

According to van der Starre (1993) the early stage of the European Museum Network described by Delouis is confirmed since "it does not work as a network because of the lack of telecommunication facilities". The Van Eyck Project, involving a number of partners in the U.K., Ireland and the Netherlands is intending to use RAMA for "access to major scientific art documentation collections in an easy and cost effective way for users such as academic researchers, art museum staff, lecturers and students, collectors, art dealers, auction houses, journalists, public libraries and the general public". The meaning of "a scientific art documentation collection" is not given.

"It is hoped that the EC will fund the second phase for building the system and the expansion into other countries". An Irish partner (Trinity College, Dublin) is still in the process of defining an indexing system. "It has been proven that it is possible to relate the Witt (ICONCLASS) and AKD (Netherlands Institute for Art History) systems... and to build a concordance which will be suitable as the basis for the development core record structure ... the system will form yet another step towards a global network of data files which may be consulted by anyone at any time and any place".

A further description of current Multimedia systems in the Arts in reference book form has been published by the International Visual Arts Information Network (1993).

Jeremy Rees (IVAIN, Ipswich) points out that although CEC funding is very welcome, the tackling of projects jointly by several institutions, encouraged by the CEC, adds to costs and complexity. Rees also says that funding under IMPACT is "very modest". He continues:-"one of the biggest problems facing any serious interactive multimedia project is one of distribution. As yet there is not a well developed means of point of sale access to such resources". He asks whether people will be prepared to spend at least £100, sight unseen, on a CD-ROM or CD-I purchased at a bookshop or electrical shop.

As at a similar conference which took place in the previous year – EVA'92 – little was said in any of the papers about indexing problems. I attempted to rectify this omission with a short paper about some of the requirements. I could only find mention of it in one other paper at the '93 meeting – by Lewis and Draycott (1993) describing the preparation of 56,000 pictures to be included in the Wellcome Institute's history of medicine project. A "cataloging" operation is included in the flowpath diagram provided, but that is the sum total of the comments about indexing.

In some organisations very large collections require to be managed. Sulger (1993) reports that at the New York Office of Mental Health there may be one hundred million documents. For files averaging up to 32 Kbytes in length, 16 2 Gbyte drives would be needed to store one million images. Removable optical storage will be needed. Sulger describes a search algorithm and provides listings written in C++ to handle very large numbers of files.

1993 PCs are capable of a remarkable performance for special tasks with appropriate software. Miller (1993) describes the arrangements made to handle oceanographic images from the Advanced Very High Resolution Radiometers (AVHRR) aboard weather satellites. The PC's ability to display rapidly special types of high resolution image indicate the potential for displaying high quality pictures.

Using a software package called *Figment* the time taken to calculate scale and offset for a display of 2048 x 1616 pixels was (in seconds) 159 for a 3240 concurrent multiuser multitasking mainframe, 21 for a Sun SPARC 1 workstation, 22 for a PC with 486 33 MHz processor, 59 for a PC with a 386 33 MHz processor, and 330 for a PC with a 286 10 Mhz processor.

The most suitable method of storing image data was found to be transportable Bernoulli cartridges, each with a capacity of up to 90 Mbytes.

Picture databases

The idea of forming, indexing, retrieving, and communicating data over a wide area from a large picture database is new because technology at the right price is new.

One of the first large databases of this type being developed is being tackled in two stages — the first stage is a computer-based index to separately available pictures, and the second includes pictures with the index.

Sir John Beazley's archive of Greek figure-decorated vases -Beazley spent much of his life collecting and researching — is held at the Ashmolean Museum, Oxford (Moffett, 1992). It comprises 250,000 photographs and thousand of drawings indexed using relational DBMS Ingres on the University's VAX cluster of computers. This data occupies (1992) 80 Mbytes of storage.

```
BEAZLEY ARCHIVE DATABASE
REPORT ON VASE    7043
-----------------------------------------------------------------
Technique : R                        Shape  : CUP B


   Signature : EUPHRONIOS EGRAPH[SEN] (EG)
   Provenance :

   Attributed to EUPHRONIOS Painter  by SIGNATURE
   Attributed to 525-475 by x
Decorated Area : A  HYPNOS AND THANATOS WITH SARPEDON, AKAMAS
Decorated Area : B  PYRRHIC, YOUTH PLAYING PIPES, YOUTH AND
WOMAN
Decorated Area : I  FLORAL COMPLEX, PALMETTES


Cataloguing history
-------------------
  1      TEXH5            Texas, Hunt Collection
  1      MALGLOAN7043     Malibu (Ca.), The J. Paul Getty Museum
  2      NEWSXXXX7043     New York (N.Y.), Market - Sotheby's

Publication record
-------------------
  J. Paul Getty Museum Journal, 9 (1981) 24-26, FIGS.1-6
  (I, A, B)
  Wealth of the Ancient World, the Hunt Collections (Fort
Worth, 1983), 54-57, NO.5, FRONTISPIECE (I, A, B, PARTS)
  Sotheby's, The Nelson Bunker Hunt Collection, New York,
  19.6.1990 (New York, 1990), NO.6 (A, B, I, PARTS)
```

Figure 8.1 Beazley archive vase indexing report

Each vase is indexed in several ways — by Vase Identity data, by Attribution, by Cataloguing History, by Iconography, by References (published illustrations), by Published References, and by Terms based on the iconography. By entering SQL commands a report programme generates output in the form shown in Figure 8.1 (by permission of the Ashmolean Museum).

The archive has been available for use via the JANET UK University network, IPSS, and NSF-NETRELAY. The intention is now to supply 40 Kbyte thumbnail pictures of vases together with the retrieved data, estimated to consume 4 Gbytes of storage. The RAMA inter-museum network, mentioned earlier in this Chapter, will be used. Experimental transmissions between the Ashmolean and the Musee d'Orsay have already taken place using the ISDN.

There is another European programme sponsored as part of the CEC DG XIII programme called the Electronic Library Image Service for Europe (ELISE) operated by the IBM UK Scientific Centre, De Montfort University, Leicester, The Victoria & Albert Museum, and Bibliotheque Publique D'Information, Paris (Black, 1993).

The database will be accessed via the ISDN. The image archive will be composed of TIFF high resolution images. These are normally unavailable on-line – compressed images up to 1024 x 768 pixels and 120 x 90 pixels be available to users. It is intended to index the pictures using the AAT when appropriate.

"Images will be retrieved by their textual descriptions and so work is under way to investigate the difficulty of articulating in textual terms the search for a visual item".

Relational database management systems were rejected, and three other packages "are being evaluated further against a system specification and a choice will be made in the near future". Unfortunately this description tells us little about the way in which the system will be indexed. The ISDN will be used for communications.

Software for image collections

Document Image Processing (DIP) for business documents is making rapid progress and systems for that field might be pressed into service for some kinds of picture collections. However DIP systems are usually designed to manage a very large number of relatively small, not a relatively small number of large records.

The Canonfile 250 desktop electronic filing system, from Canon (Crawley) is a typical example. It includes a scanner, magneto-optical disc drive, paper output delivery guide, display screen and attached keyboard in one box. It will scan documents up to about 9" x 14" at 200 x 200 dots per inch (monochrome) at a claimed speed of 40 pages per minute.

Images are stored on a removable disc of 256 megabytes per side. The system costs about £9,500, and an associated laser printer costs £1,600. It will display retrieved pages on its LCD screen which is about 5" x 10". Provision is made for simple indexing by words which are matched against query words for retrieval purposes.

A number of general-purpose microcomputer software packages for dealing with relatively small numbers of documents and/or pictures, usually including provision for rather basic indexing methods using words, are also available.

One of the earliest picture database system was Picture Power (Figure 8.2, next page) from Pictureware – a software package for the IBM PC. It enabled a user to design an indexing form and to capture and edit a picture from a television camera.

Picture Cardbox is a package including provision for indexing by words using a "Term Manager" which enables a thesaurus to be constructed and operated; existing thesauri may be imported. Images may be displayed together with descriptive text and an image may be enlarged to fill a VGA display. It is claimed that a 300 megabyte hard disc will hold up to 15,000 images; an optical disc may be used if needed (Gray, 1992). Picture Cardbox costs from £900.

Aldus *Fetch* 1.0 is a multi-user database for cataloguing images, animations, QuickTime Movies and sound files on Macintosh machines running QuickTime. It is suitable for various image packages including PICT, TIFF, Illustrator, Photoshop, Kodak Photo-CD, Sound Edit etc. Images may be imported from various sources. In a recent review of *Fetch* its author says:- "you can search for files by description or keywords rather than just file names, but generating this information can

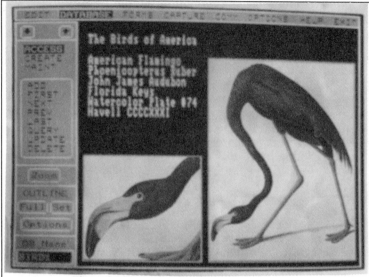

Figure 8.2 Picture Power picture database screen

be quite a chore ... with some procedural discipline all your files could have keywords and descriptions built into them, allowing *Fetch* to use all of its Apple searching capabilities". *Fetch* costs $295.

The main feature on Kudo, an Image Browser from Imspace Systems (San Diego) is to scan forward or backwards through a thumbnail collection by pressing the "riffle" button. Each thumbnail of 16K bytes per colour, represents "mixed-media" image files of unspecified quality. The browser "is aware of the human eye's ability to perceive un-related images at approximately 10 frames per second" says the blurb. The system will hold 32,000 or more images. Indexing is not mentioned.

The Kodak Company has been particularly active and all or parts of its various "photo-CD" systems might be pressed into use for the requirements being here discussed.

A Kodak Photo-CD transfer station, which costs £85,000, includes a high-resolution film scanner, Sun workstation, disk-writer and Ektatherm thermal colour printer. It became available in the UK in September 1992. It is used by Photo-CD bureaux for the graphics industry, and the intention is to extend the service to the general public.

A client will bring in a reel of exposed colour film containing pictures taken on an ordinary 35mm camera, for conversion at the bureau into a CD-ROM containing up to about 100 images for running on a CD-XA drive and display on a TV receiver. A print of thumbnail size images, supplied with the CD, will act as an index to it. Alternatively the image files from the CD may be input to a computer directly.

A 35mm frame film is scanned at very high resolution, generating 2000 x 3000 pixels with 24 bit colour – a total of 144 Mbits (18 Mbytes) of data. By compressing this to 4.4 Mbytes, over 100 images may be stored on one CD-ROM disc. The pixels in each image are reduced according to application requirements. For example the reduction may be set to provide an image of, say, 150 x 100 pixels. A large number of such images take up a file of easily managed size.

This system could be used to provide an indexed thumbnail browser for displaying pictures by "hit-screenfuls". 16 pictures of 150 x 100 pixel size could be displayed on a 800 x 600 Super VGA screen leaving enough room for short keys. This size should be adequate for a user to identify any picture – to be subsequently supplied as a high quality image – out of a large collection.

Each thumbnail would total 150 x 100 x 8 = 120K bits or 15 Kbytes if displayed in 8-bit colour. Compressed by 10:1 each would occupy 1.5 Kbytes of storage. Thus 600/.015 = 40,000 could be stored on a single 600 Mbyte CD-ROM. Compression/decompression of 10:1 using current methods should still provide adequate quality for human recognition purposes.

Figure 8.3 shows a full resolution Kodak Photo-CD photograph. The photo in Figure 8.4 (next page) has been reduced by pixel sampling to provide a thumbnail of about 100 x 75 pixels which is superimposed on an enlargement.

Figure 8.3 Kodak Photo-CD print

The enlargement of Figure 8.4 is of the very small part of the original picture outlined within the thumbnail. It is remarkably sharp even when printed at this size – motion by the riders in the original photograph is responsible for some of the slightly blurred reproduction. It is hard to believe that it was produced on a thermal printer.

Kodak can also supply an image software package called PhotoEdge which costs $135. It works on Photo-CD, TIFF, and Macintosh PICT files. It will present a Photo-CD thumbnail display, and enables any full resolution image to be displayed in any one of five resolutions laid out in a chosen number of columns. It includes various tools such as a tool for outlining an object within an image. The object may then be lifted out and managed as a separate image.

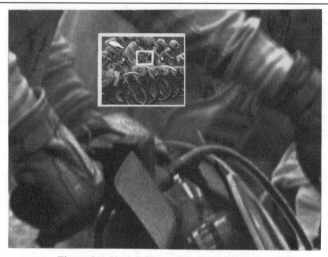

Figure 8.4 Kodak Photo-CD: Enlargement quality

Existing picture database systems

A good example of a picture collection, although using equipment which is already out of date, is Mintzer and McFall's (1991) IBM-devised art catalogue system which will accommodate up to 10,000 pictures -it has been used to manage a collection of artworks by John Wyeth. It also demonstrates the scale of such operations.

The database contains 1024 x 1024 x 16 bit colour (16.8 Mbit) pictures. Thus when 10,000 pictures are in place, 16.8 x 10,000 = 168 Gbits (21 Gbytes) of storage is used. When 32 bit colour comes into wider use, 10,000 pictures would occupy 336 Gbits (42 Gbytes). In an associated relational database, each picture is represented by 200 x 200 pixel by 8 bit (320 Kbit) colour thumbnail pictures, together with the artist's and the curator's notes for information or for retrieval by word matching. A number of thumbnails may be displayed on a screen together.

Browsing through a succession of rapidly presented blocks of thumbnails immediately brings to bear the most efficient selective system by far – the human eye/brain. Unlike a computer, a human can almost instantly ignore unwanted pictures. The number of thumbnails per screen depends on the amount of detail needed to identify a wanted picture, and on the screen size and resolution. 25 to 30 could be accommodated in many cases.

If a person can discriminate between pictures in this manner, the need to provide an elaborate indexing scheme for discrimination purposes is reduced.

Since the indexing review was prepared (Cawkell 1993b) quite a number of picture collections have been described. The collections, and the hardware and software are diverse. A few are mentioned here since they illustrate trends and methods currently chosen to manage different kinds of collection.

The slide collection in the Hong Kong Polytechnic Library (Yeung, 1992) is housed in 108 filing cabinet drawers. There are 70,000 slides with sufficient storage space for 100,000. The slides cover paintings, sculptures, fashion, architecture, product design, aspects of Hong Kong and other topics. The slides are catalogued according to the Anglo-American cataloguing rules (second edition) supplemented by U.S. MARC formats for bibliographic and authoritative data. Slide titles may be searched on a computer keyword file.

The photographic library at British Petroleum, Britannic House, London, has been described by Patel et al. (1992). It contains 300,000 photographs covering BP sites and activities. The library is currently entering the photographs on to optical discs capable of storing about 25,000 photographs. The equipment consists of Macintosh II workstations, archive server and document server together with Panasonic WORM drives and Archis software.

Archis (commercial software) screen presentations consist of a picture and a photograph accompanied by various data in words including a caption describing the photograph. It is intended that workstations will be installed at major sites world wide, so the system may be searched online before branches request particular photographs from the library.

As at September 1992 an Apple Macintosh system with scanner, optical disc and Archis software could be purchased for less than £10,000. Archis "enables users to input, store, retrieve, and output any type of document such as text, computer files, images (colour or black or white) slides, X-rays and digitized video, directly onto the desktop. .....users can search for information through a hierarchical structure or through the use of keywords".

The system running in the new Sainsbury wing at the National Gallery has been described by Rubinstein (1992). It took 2.5 years to prepare. It is a visual image catalogue to the National Gallery's collection in 5 sections – a painting catalogue, artists' biographies, an historical atlas of Western art, a types index, and a general reference index. It covers each of the 2,200 paintings in the permanent collection.

Paintings may require 8 pages of description covering the subject, technique, restoration, gallery position etc. Thumbnail images abstracted by special software from the main images are provided for all the paintings. There are twelve 19" touch screen displays in the micro gallery, any of which may be used by a visitor without prior arrangement. Each screen is driven by a Macintosh II with its own 1.3 gigabyte hard disc. The software was purpose designed, and the display tubes provide a resolution of 82 dots per inch.

164

The National Gallery already possessed 10" x 8" transparencies of almost the whole collection. They were scanned into the system by a Sharp JX-600 scanner in 24 bit colour. 8 bit colour is used on the displays. The system is said to include 21,000 articles with 7 hours of sound together with animations, music clips, and other items. Images may be displayed at 1024 x 768 pixels with 8 bit colour and the system contains 7,000 photographs, charts, and graphics. Consideration is being given to a CD-ROM version.

Hulton Deutsch (Anon (2) 1993) have recorded 2,500 out of its collection of pictures of the 1930s on a CD-ROM. Searching is by associated keywords (Figure 8.5). The kind of indexing words chosen reflect Action, Background, Location, Mood, People, Scene and Subject. Screenfuls of thumbnail hits are provided, any of which may be used to select a main image. Another disc called the People Disc is available containing 10,000 pictures of personalities and public figures. Further discs are planned.

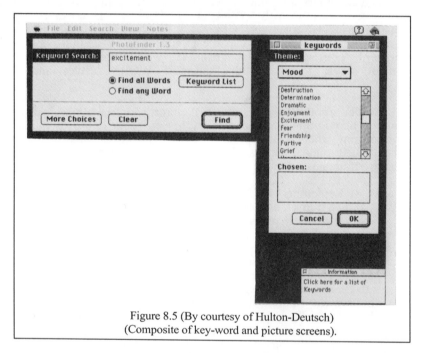

Figure 8.5 (By courtesy of Hulton-Deutsch)
(Composite of key-word and picture screens).

The University of Oslo Library (Aabo, 1992) houses the Nansen Collection of photographs, art work, drawings, and prints which are being scanned into an Apple computer. The resolution of the system is up to 150 dots per inch. As the operation continues, provision will be made for using a 1 Gbyte hard disc for storing the compressed pictures. The hardware includes a Macintosh II fx machine operating on an Ethernet network, and Apple's QuickTime software is being used. Searching is by words using Boolean logic.

The Aviador (Anon 1993) is an interactive system linking a videodisc of over 40,000 architectural drawings from the Avery Library to their online catalogue descriptions in the Research Libraries Group (RLG) on the RILN network. Searching is carried out using special software developed for use with Windows on a PC which includes an analogue video disc-player. Telecoms software connects the PC to the RILN database.

The database covers building projects each of which requires a large number of drawings. A user who possesses the appropriate PC, videodisc drive, and the Aviador videodisc together with the Telecom software, may search RILN catalogue records for descriptions of drawings held on the disc, and immediately view them.

The National Railway Museum in York (Heap, 1993) is aiming to incorporate its collection of 75,000 photographs eventually growing to over 1.25 million on to WORM optical discs each capable of storing 1 Gbyte of data. Each WORM will store 950 Mbytes equivalent to about 1000 2048 x 3072 compressed monochrome images. The complete system was supplied by a company called Primagraphics. The major purpose is to make the collection more accessible since it is currently stored in air conditioned archives which are not available to the public.

Pictures are managed at 2048 x 3072 pixels with an 8-bit grey scale, and are JPEG compressed, normally at 13:1. They are indexed on a searchable "image description sheet".

The University of Kent (Bovey, 1993) holds about 80,000 original British newspaper cartoon drawings. They are accessible with Prism, a purpose designed UNIX system implemented on Sun Sparc-stations using the X-windows interface. Little is said about the indexing effort but judging by the amount of data shown in examples of retrieved records it must be considerable. Retrieved cartoons are displayed together with associated data.

Several so-called "multimedia encyclopaedias" have been produced which are of interest as they show what can be done with existing inexpensive software, hardware and storage capability.

For example Encarta from Microsoft for 386 or higher machines, and which runs on Windows, is supplied on a CD-ROM. It is said to include 21,000 articles with 7 hours of sound together with animations, music clips, and other items. Images may be displayed at 1024 x 768 pixels with 8 bit colour and the system contains 7,000 photographs, charts, and graphics. It costs $395.

Conclusions about working systems

Much of the available software appears to cater for the storage and retrieval of selected pictures to be incorporated in other material – for example in multimedia presentations, Desktop Publishing, etc. The software examples provided here are a small fraction of available packages for microcomputers.

The examples of operational collections are also only a fraction of the total in use. Almost all are indexed in some way using descriptive words keyed to each image by an indexer. Retrieval methods are usually similar, if not identical, to the methods which have been used for many years for text retrieval – the text forms part of, or is associated with a picture which is retrieved by searching the text associated with it.

The fact that computer systems are used to manage such a variety of collections indicates a considerable general degree of interest in picture databases.

The absence of critical comment about the various systems is very noticeable. Most are described with the "I gotta picture system" enthusiasm by their originators or custodians – the enthusiasm which characterised the people enthusing "I gotta text system" twenty years ago. Test results are not provided and the idea of "failure analysis" is never discussed.

Organising a large database of diverse pictures

To generalise the database idea, suppose that there is a general requirement for users to transmit a question to a database for picture retrieval, and for the "hit" pictures to be sent back to them. A user may wish to change the question and repeat the operation if the first set of hits is unsatisfactory. Each complete operation needs to be quickly concluded – each picture should be received within a few seconds of posing a question.

Let it be assumed that the collection is large and consists of paintings, artworks, historic illustrated manuscripts, photographs, drawings, museum objects, images of items which are not normally accessible, and like items. These classes could reside in separate databases or could form a sectionalised single database.

It is also assumed that the collection is large enough to require an index with a considerable power of discrimination, using a language which does not require a time consuming indexing effort, or learning-to-use effort, and that the whole system may be amended or augmented and is capable of being scaled up to accommodate a larger collection and more users.

The effort and money expended in forming, indexing, operating and maintaining a picture database depends on its planned size and diversity. Indexing, as explained in Chapter 7, and which is often neglected. requires special attention.

Query-pictures will augment word queries as the techniques are refined for many kinds of questions; not all concepts can be better queried in this manner. Query-pictures will be introduced in due course to pose questions like "What pictures are there showing ladies wearing medals?", or "Are there any 17th century pictures which include animal pets?".

The system should be able to handle "information discovery" questions as well as "information recovery" questions – that is questions about data known to exist like "Show me a selection of cartoons by Leonardo da Vinci".

The attributes and functions of a large diverse picture database could appropriately include:-

- An up-datable collection possibly divided into mutually exclusive sections, containing high-resolution full colour images.
- Careful consideration about ways of moving collections which may be available in original, photographed, or other forms, into a computer system.
- The inclusion of "thumbnail" (miniature representations of each picture) pictures which contain sufficient legible detail to represent parent pictures unambiguously.
- Queries by word terms or query-pictures.
- An indexing system.
- A mechanism for matching queries against contents and selecting hits.
- An optical multi-platter or a multiple magnetic disc store.
- A compression/decompression system.
- If necessary a staging mechanism to move data automatically from remote to local storage locations.
- A telecommunication network for transmitting questions and hits.
- A community of users in different geographical locations with appropriate workstations.

Because imaging per se is "fashionable", systems of all kinds and capabilities have been developed usually disregarding the need for effective indexing and retrieval but employing methods of storing, transferring, communicating and displaying pictures with technology which increases in sophistication almost daily.

Storage arrangements

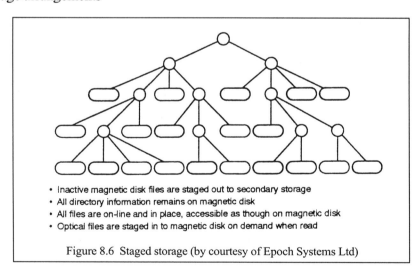

- Inactive magnetic disk files are staged out to secondary storage
- All directory information remains on magnetic disk
- All files are on-line and in place, accessible as though on magnetic disk
- Optical files are staged in to magnetic disk on demand when read

Figure 8.6 Staged storage (by courtesy of Epoch Systems Ltd)

For large volumes of data, one idea is to store it hierarchically in order to position the data most likely to be needed close to the user in order to minimise the time taken to retrieve and transmit it. A number of storage units are arranged so that archival least-used files are stored in the bottom row of stores which are accessible relatively slowly (Figure 8.6, previous page).

Files are moved upwards in stages to the local disc at the top, located in a user's workstation. All files are logically on line. Staging is managed so that storage units never fill up. A user's activities are monitored and his or her most active files moved into local storage.

Alternatively if the database contains data which may be stored in more or less mutually exclusive sections, one section per disc, then a user's question may be routed directly to the appropriate disc. The retrieval speed will obviously then be faster than if the wanted picture is somewhere within one large store.

The idea of supplying blocks of hits as small thumbnails held in a store of moderate size for preliminary assessment, representing full-screen displays showing pictures from the whole collection, has much to commend it. The selected picture may be subsequently retrieved in its high-resolution full colour format at a more leisurely pace.

The Kodak CD Jukebox system, for example, will provide rapid access to 30,000 thumbnail ("ikon") images, and slower access (5 seconds storage response time) to 60 GBytes of storage on 2 x 50 CD jukeboxes containing associated high resolution images. 60 Gbytes amounts to 3333 3000 x 2000 x 24 bit (18 Mbyte) uncompressed images, or 13,330 of the same images compressed by 4 times.

In fact, CD-ROM is likely to be a more convenient method of storage than large optical discs or jukeboxes. A considerable advantage of the CD-ROM is that a new disc may easily be produced for up-dating purposes. Moreover individual CD-ROMs may be despatched for use anywhere as needed. Parts or all of the Kodak Photo-CD system could be pressed into service as part of the system to be described in the next section.

However there is yet another option, for which Kodak provide, and that is to store the pictures on CD-ROM at full resolution, with provision for calling them off at some lower resolution as "thumbnails". This has the advantage, assuming that telecom problems and costs can be overcome, of concentrating all activities at the database end and dispensing with the off-line CD-ROM indexed-thumbnail arrangement operated at the user's premises.

A feasible database system

There are several major considerations when designing a database system to provide online access to a large collection of pictures.

Transmission costs and line bandwidth availability being what they are, it makes no sense to clog up the system when a number of users simultaneously want to pose questions, receive hits, modify the question and receive some more hits, finally requesting the online delivery of one or more high quality pictures.

Assuming that users have a CD-ROM player and a microcomputer or workstation, the initial selection procedures could be performed off-line on the user's premises. For example if the collection houses 20,000 images, 20,000 thumbnails must be indexed; they could be comfortably accommodated on one CD-ROM for in-house viewing. Provision could be made for word searching, just as it is in the inexpensive ready-made software previously described. Indeed, a software package might be selected from the widely available commercial packages for use in this system.

It is not known, at present, how good the indexing facilities must be, if the user is able to scan, say, 20 hits at a time before deciding on a wanted picture. Nor is it known whether software incorporating facilities for query-picture searching and matching could be easily integrated into the off-line system. It seems likely that they could be. There is a wide choice of ready-made software for drawing, painting, clip-art selection, etc., which would provide the user with the means of posing query-pictures. Scanned images could be input for this purpose as well if necessary.

In any event, local off-line thumbnail searches of this kind are feasible. The only traffic and operations left for the main on-line database are then to deliver requests for one or more individual pictures, perhaps when requested by a number corresponding to the number of the previously selected thumbnail. In this case no indexing or matching facilities are required on the database site. The system is simply concerned with retrieving a picture of the required number and despatching it down the line.

If each picture contains $1000 \times 1200 \times 24 = 28.8$ Mbits which is 3.6 Mbytes, and 2.9 Mbits or 360 Kbytes when compressed by 10:1, then a 2.9 Mbit picture transmitted at 500 Kilobits per second will take 5.8 seconds to reach a user.

The storage requirements for 20,000 compressed pictures will be $20,000 \times 0.36$ Mbytes $= 7,200$ Mbytes or 7.2 Gbytes. If a CD-ROM contains 540 Mbytes, then 14 such discs would be needed to house the entire collection.

The database system must include the means of retrieving and despatching pictures from these 14 CD-ROM drives with their discs. A server containing a 80486 processor and EISA bus, connected to the drives by a SCSI interface would be satisfactory. It would be accompanied by a 486 microcomputer or a machine of greater power, as a monitoring workstation, and as the device required to process image-query pictures if this method is used.

Such a combination would be capable of outputting data at a rate of up to 25 Mbits per second. The server must contain a card suitable for despatching data down the chosen line – say a SuperJanet line. A SuperJanet plug-in telecoms interface card for a microcomputer does not yet exist, but it seems safe to assume that it soon will.

A server such as the DEC Infoserver 150 or an Attica server would be suitable. A diagram showing an Infoserver 150 on an Ethernet LAN is shown in Figure 8.5 (Next page, by courtesy DEC Ltd).

The server would be capable of delivering data to a number of users simultaneously. It is assumed that those users would receive the data down SuperJanet, and that at each user site there would be a Hub with a LAN, or direct lines, to each user's terminal. The server's delivery rate of 25 Mbits per second may be sub-divided into the equivalent of separate channels (see page 172) each running at 500 Kbits per second. The system would be capable of handling requests to supply numbered pictures at that rate to each of 50 terminals.

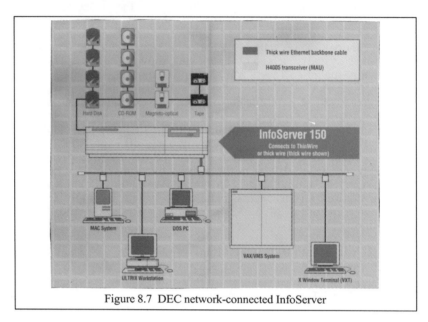

Figure 8.7 DEC network-connected InfoServer

50 terminals/users simultaneously accessing the system represents a large total population of users. For example if 50 users at a time each has a two hour session on the machine each week, and there are, say, 36 hours available per week, there could be 18 two hour sessions providing a service for 900 users.

All of the above numbers are theoretical, and would doubtless not be realised in practice, although they are probably of the right order.

A standard CD-ROM and drive delivers data at a rate of 170.2 Kbytes = 1.36 Mbits per second, comfortably exceeding the assumed rate of 500 Kbits per second. Faster "Quadraspin" drives are now available from Pioneer, rotating at 4 times the normal speed and capable of delivering data at 612 Kbytes = 4.9 Mbits per second. Such an arrangement would seem to be able to cope with a large user population with something in reserve if it was required to be scaled up at a later date.

To summarise, the system would consist of the following items:-

- CD-ROM drives
- 80486 microcomputer
- Attica CD-ROM server
- Software

An installation consisting of 14 CD-ROM drives, and a server with input interface cards, in two tower-type cases with 16 Mbytes of memory and a 125 Mbyte disc, 486 processor, EISA bus and cabling, together with a 486/EISA microcomputer for monitoring and auxiliary functions, but excluding an interface card to SuperJanet and also excluding installation and maintenance would cost about £10,000 (Attica Cybernetics Ltd., approximate quotation).

This company has had experience of supplying installations resembling the above, and the quoted figure should be correct to plus or minus 20%. The server is capable of handling a maximum of 32 drives. It is claimed that it will support up to 100 simultaneous users.

Users's access time to any CD would be about 14 milliseconds and only a simple inter-disc directory is assumed to be needed. Thus if a user specified picture no. 5282, the CD containing that picture would be selected.

No inter-disc directory at all would be needed if the collection was divided into as many sections as there are CDs, and user's know in advance on which section their picture is contained, posing questions in the form of the CD-ROM number plus the record number.

A number of companies would be capable of providing a suitable database system of the kind discussed here. They include Origin, Trimco, Epoch Systems, DEC, and IBM.

Telecommunications

The communications links between a picture database system and its users, assuming that they work in different parts of the country, could represent a severe bottleneck. Users must be able to participate in a question-answer fast-response session in order to home-in to, receive, and display wanted pictures using the remote system by trial and error.

The response time depends mainly on retrieval from storage, telecoms transmission time, and the time it takes to present a high-resolution full-colour picture on a workstation.

The advent of wideband nationwide networks running at speeds of up to one Gigabit per second or more will eventually reduce the telecoms bottleneck. In the UK, the ISDN provides relatively fast data delivery and the SuperJanet nation-wide inter-university network capable of running at speeds of over 600 Megabits/second started operating in 1993.

In order to consider the effect of the time taken in telecommunication transmission, the time to retrieve data from storage etc., it will be assumed that a large diverse collection is to be accessed by people in different parts of the country. It will consist, as has already been assumed, of about 20,000 pictures each occupying a picture file of 28.8 Mbits, or 3.6 Mbytes. The total compressed size of 20,000 such files would be 7200 Mbytes or 7.2 Gbytes.

Loeb (1992), from the Bellcore Laboratories, discusses the problems of sending large files over networks and concludes that "very little effort has been made ... to examine the network aspects of hypermedia applications". After providing some tables showing the order of magnitude of "P-objects" – that is a range of items from magazine articles to motion video frames – Loeb concludes that large amounts of information would be delivered unnecessarily, and fast unpredictable shifts in end-user requests for service would be very hard to fulfil.

It is worthwhile quoting another of Loeb's conclusions, although they are already well-known, namely that "studies show that for response time, toleration of delays depends on how the user perceives the communication. If the user expects the system to be of a type that has no internal complexity (one which responds to stimulation without going through computational states) then the response time expected is in the order of 0.2 seconds.

However if the user views the system as performing computations after a request is issued, then an average delay of 2 seconds is acceptable. Also it is of interest to note that users tend to give up waiting for a response after about 20 seconds".

A not unreasonable time to wait in the telecoms part of the system under discussion could be about 5 seconds. There will be other delays from the moment the user poses a question to the time he gets a picture retrieved from the system and displayed on his workstation, but if, say, the telecoms link can deliver the data at the rate of 500 Kbytes or 4 Mbps, then a 3.6 Mbyte image would take 7.2 seconds in transit.

SuperJanet will use Switched Multimegabit Data Service (SMDS) under its immediate future telecoms regime until the regime changes into Asynchronous Transfer Mode (ATM) protocol.

SMDS is a "bandwidth on demand" system enabling what amount to "closed user group" transactions to be processed. It will also incorporate a billing system so that if necessary, charges may be made for services. SMDS is a "cell based" not a "packet based" system (Cawkell 1993a), so picture data would be transmitted as a virtually continuous data stream to arrive in one piece.

Under SMDS in the database system under discussion, "user channels" would in effect be set up between a terminal on the SuperJanet network and the server at the data-base end. It will appear to the user as if he has a dedicated line to the database.

The ISDN would be an alternative way of connecting a user to the database although it would be substantially slower than SuperJanet. Picture delivery speeds of 500 Kbps have been assumed in this Chapter although of course SuperJanet permits substantial data speed increases if required. The ISDN, if used at its maximum "2 x B" channel = 128 Kbps data rate, would increase picture delivery times to about 28 seconds.

If a user is at an organisation connected to a "30 x B" = 2.048 Mbps total capacity ISDN – the arrangement used, for instance, for connecting PABX's to the ISDN – then data speeds could be 500 Kbps or more as with SuperJanet.

User population and system peak handling capabilities

The maximum number of users who would be querying a system of this kind at any instant is a matter for conjecture. It would depend on the general usefulness of the collection, the way in which users connect to it, and the total population of users able to get access.

As already suggested if 50 terminals/users, each with a two hour session, simultaneously access the system in a 36 hour week, there could be 18 two hour sessions providing a service for 900 users – a population and activity rate probably large enough for the moment.

In reality, the access pattern would probably resemble Bradford's law – i.e. 5 people (say) would account for 20% of the total use, 10 for the next 17%, 20 for the next 15%, 40 for the next 12%, etc.

The telecommunication delays would depend on the way the connecting links radiate outwards from the database centre to the users, and the ability of the retrieval mechanism to handle questions put by a number of users simultaneously.

It is well known that most local area networks, where the most popular data rate is nominally 10 Mbits per second, slow down appreciably when a number of users are exchanging data – the bandwidth must be shared by the network users.

LANs work perfectly well in most cases when short bursts of data, such as electronic mail messages, are being exchanged. However the maximum speeds of such networks are on the increase and existing LAN users do not have to change the cabling or the software to use them. These faster systems, which run nominally at 100 Mbytes per second, are more expensive than ordinary LANs but much less expensive than FDDI optical networks (Clarkson 1993).

There are currently two groups working on fast LANs both suggesting different standards. The situation is likely to be resolved in September 1993 when the IEEE Committee working on the problem proposes a solution.

With the advent of SuperJanet, to be capable of transmitting data at a rate exceeding 600 Mbits per second, presumably those establishments connected to it will use local area networks for distributing data received from the local SuperJanet node.

A set of local area networks, each with a few users, could be connected to a node via a Hub station. Users with heavy traffic could connect to the Hub with their own dedicated line.

Copyright problems

The advent of a technology enabling text and images to be electronically created, easily reproduced, and then copied with a quality quite closely approaching the original, introduces many new copyright problems.

Emerging problems became evident in the seventies. Warnings were officially promulgated when the list of exclusive rights was extended in a 1980 amendment to the US 1976 Copyright Act. Following a description of "derivative works" the following phrase was added "...or any other form in which a work may be recast, transformed, or adapted".

This is intended to extend protection from the print-on-paper medium to any form of media – notably current and future media enabled by new technology. There have been a number of image-related examples illustrating the point.

In June 1990 a judge found in favour of Lotus against the *VP Paperback Planner* because of similarity between a Paperback and the *Lotus 1-2-3* spreadsheet interface.

In 1-2-3 the choice, structure, and presentation on the screen were found to be original and non-obvious and therefore copyrightable. VP-Planner had been deliberately copied from 1-2-3.

In March 1991 there was some further support for the idea that "look and feel" could be copyrightable in the well publicised case of Apple versus Microsoft and Hewlett-Packard. These companies claimed that Apple's iconic interface infringed Xerox's copyright covering, for instance, features in the Star machine which caused a sensation in the late seventies.

A judge gave Apple permission to pursue its copyright suit, considering that there was no evidence of Apple's infringement of Xerox's "look and feel" copyright. In regard to Apple's claim that Microsoft and Hewlett Packard were infringing Apple's own look and feel copyright, the judge obviously thought that this was too wide a concept. His permission to allow Apple to proceed was based on the point that there could be specific features of the two companies' software which infringed.

In June 1991 there was a case of copyright infringement which was so evidently blatant that arrests in the United States followed an investigation. Those arrested were employed by a number of Taiwanese companies making or using copies of Nintendo's chips for computer games.

There is a quite a different aspect which affects the earnings of museums and art galleries. How can museums and art galleries earn revenue by selling reproduction rights for multimedia products containing thousands of images without hampering the market? They currently earn up to $500 per picture for allowing reproduction in commercial publications. These kinds of prices per image applied to multimedia would encourage infringement.

In 1991 (Bearman 1991a) an informal meeting between several major museums was held and a "Model Agreement" was proposed to cover conditions of use and royalty payments for multimedia usage.

Shandle (1991) says that *The Sporting News* wanted to purchase the rights to the cards showing football players owned by the Topps Company. They were trying to publish a CD-ROM about football. Because this would involve negotiations with up to 1000 player's lawyers, the idea was abandoned. Project viability required a royalty of 0.15%

At the Multimedia and CD-ROM conference in March, exhibitors claimed they were put on notice by the American Society of Composers, Authors, and Publishers (ASCAP) that "spotters" would be at the show listening for copyrighted music in multimedia presentations.

Keates and Cornish (British Library) raise the problems of access and protection in terms of copyright at the EVA '93 conference (Hemsley 1993). "The intellectual property industry cannot afford to allow its products to be copied, packaged, pirated or distributed without insuring adequate economic compensation", they say. They propose a system called CITED to list and standardise a number of aspects and to deal with the relationship established by the actions taken by people such as owners, distributors, and end-users.

REFERENCES

Aabo, S.
> IFLA Journal, 18(3), 243-251, 1992.
>> A picture database; conservation needs and electronic access to the Fridtjof Nansen picture archive.

Aleksander, Igor.
> Art Libraries Journal. 7(2), 61-66, Summer 1982.
>> Modern pattern recognition and the classification of works of art.

Allison, David, K., and Gwaltney, Tom.
> In Bearman D. (Ed.), 1991 (q.v.) pps 62-73.
>> How people use electronic interactiveness.

Alsberg, Peter A.
> Proc IEEE 63(8), 1114-1122, 1975.
>> Space and time saving through large database compression and dynamic restructuring.

Anderson, Clarita S.
> J. Amer. Soc. Info. Sci., 42(8), 597-599, 1991.
>> A user's applications of imaging techniques: the University of Maryland's Historic Textile database.

Anon.
> Visual Resources 5, 205-258, 1988 (Gordon & Breach).
>> Report of the ICONCLASS workshop, November 1987. Symbolic projections.

Anon.
> Report, Ministerio de Cultura, Fundacion Ramon Areces, and IBM Spain, 1990.
>> Computerization project for the Archivo General de Indias.

Anon.
> Report. The Museum Documentation Association, 347 Cherry Hinton Rd., Cambridge CB1 4DH, England. 1993.
>> Who's using what software for documentation where?

Anon.
> Leaflet (1993) from the RLIN Information Centre, 1200 Villa Street, Mountain View, CA 94041-1100, U.S.A.
>> The Avery video disc index of architectural drawings on RLIN.

Anon.
> Leaflets from Hulton Deutsch, 21-31 Woodfield Road, London W9 2BA. 1993.
>> Decades – the 1930s.

Apiki, Steve.
> Byte 16(3), 309-314, 386-387, March 1991.
>> Lossless data compression.

Badaoui, S., Chameroy, V., and Aubry, F.
   Medical Information 18(1), 23-33, 1993.
      A database manager of biomedical images.
Barnsley, M.F, and Demko, S.
   Proc. Royal Soc. A., London. 399, 243-275, 1985.
      Iterated function systems and the global construction of
      fractals.
Barnsley, Michael F., and Sloan, A.O.
   Byte, 13(1), January 1988.
      A better way to compress images.
Bearman, D.
   Archives and Museum Informatics 5(2), page 9-10, 1991.
      Model agreement for owners of images licensing to multimedia
      producers.
Bearman, D.
   In Bearman, D. (Ed.). Proc. Int. Conf. Sheraton Station Square,
   Pittsburgh, October 14-16 1991. Hypermedia and Interactivity in
   Museums. Archives & Museum Informatics, Pittsburgh.
   Pps 1-16, 1991.
      Interactivity and hypermedia in museums.
Beaumont, J.M.
   BT Technol.J., 9(4), 93-109, October 1991.
      Image data compression using fractal techniques.
Besser, Howard.
   Library Trends, 38(4), 787-798, Spring 1990.
      Visual access to visual images; the UC Berkeley
      image database project.
Besser, Howard.
   J. Amer. Soc. Info. Sci., 42(8) 589-596, 1991.
      Imaging: Fine arts.
Black, Kirsten.
   Aslib Information, 293-295, July/August 1993.
      ELISE – an online image retrieval system.
Blair, Nancy.
   Advanced Imaging 7(4), 36-38, April 1992.
      Device independent desktop colour: Kodak's new management
      tool.
Blum, Christofer, Hofmann, G.R., and Kromker, D.
   IEEE Computergraphics and Applications, 61-70, March 1991.
      Requirements for the first international imaging standard.
Bodson, Dennis, and Schaphorst R.A.
   IEEE Trans. Communications COM-31(1), 69-81, January 1983.
      Error sensitivity of CCITT standard facsimile coding.
Bolt, R.A.
   Report: Massachusetts Institute of Technology number 77 (Architec ture
   Machine Group). MIT. 1977.
      Spatial Data Management System (SDMS).
Bordogna, G., Carrara, P., Gagliardi, I., Merelli, D., Mussio, P., Naldi, F.,
   and Padula, M.
   J. Information Science, 16(3), 165-173, 1990.
      Pictorial indexing for an integrated pictorial and textual IR
      environment.

Bove, Tony. and Rhodes, Cheryl.
    Que Corporation, Carmel, Indiana. 1990.
        Que's Macintosh multimedia handbook.
Bovey, J.D.
    Journal of Information Science 19(3), 179-188, 1993.
        A graphical retrieval system.
Brolio, John, Draper, Bruce. A., et al.
    Computer 22(12), 22-30, December 1989.
        ISR: A database for symbolic processing in computer vision.
Bryan, M.
    Information Services & Use 13(2), 93-102, 1993.
        Standards for text and hypermedia processing.
Burger, Jeff.
    Addison-Wesley, 1993.
        The desktop multimedia bible.
Bush, Vannevar.
    The Atlantic Monthly, 101-103, July 1945.
        As we may think.
Cappellini, Vito.
    Proc. Conf. Electronic Imaging & the Visual Arts (EVA). The
    National Gallery Sainsbury Wing, London.   Brameur, Aldershot, July
    1992. (No pagination).
        The Uffizi project.
Carey, James W.
    Journal of Communication 31(3), 162-178, 1981.
        McLuhan and Mumford: the roots of modern media analysis.
Cavagioli, C.
    Advanced Imaging, 44-48, March 1991.
        JPEG compression: spelling out the options.
Cawkell, A.E.
    Electronic Engineering 36(433), 142-149, March 1964.
        Cathode ray storage devices: TV by telephone line.
Cawkell, A.E.
    Critique, 2(6), 1-12, Aslib (London) April 1990.
        Information theory is thriving.
Cawkell, A.E.
    Critique 3(3), 1-12, Aslib (London) 1990.
        Multimedia: hardware, software, costs, and applications.
Cawkell, A.E.
    J. Documentation 47(1), 41-73, March 1991.
        Progress in documentation: electronic document delivery
        systems.
Cawkell, A.E.
    Journal of Information Science 18, 179-192, 1992.
        Selected aspects of image processing and management: review
        and future prospects.
Cawkell, A.E.
    Report to the British Library R&D Department, reference
    RDD/GC/901, January 16th, 1992.
        Review of British Library R&D Department's Image Handling
        and Multimedia Programme.

Cawkell, A.E.
   Information Services & Use 12, 301-32, 1992.
      Imaging systems and picture collection management: review
Cawkell, A.E.
   British Library Research Review No. 15. August 1993.
      Indexing Collections of Electronic Images; A review.
Cawkell A.E.,
   IT Link, 3-4, (Aslib, London), April 1993.
      SuperJanet for information delivery
Cawkell, A.E.
   In Hemsley, J (Ed). Proceedings of the 1993 Electronic Imaging and
   and Visual Arts Conference (EVA 93). Published by Brameur and
   VasariEnterprises, Aldershot, England, 1993. Pages 171-180.
      Developments in indexing picture collections.
Chakravarthy, A. S., Haase, K.B., and Weitzman, L.M.
   Euro. Conf. on Artificial Intelligence, Vienna, Austria, August 1992.
      A uniform memory-based representation for visual languages.
Chang, S.K., and Liu, S-H.
   IEEE Trans. Pat. Anal. & Mach. Intell. PAMI-6(4), 478-483, July 1984.
      Picture indexing and abstraction techniques for pictorial
      databases.
Chang, S.K., Yan, C.W., et al.
   IEEE Trans. Software Eng., 14(5), 681-688, 1988.
      An intelligent image database system.
Chang, Shi-Kuo, Jungert E., and Li. Y.
   In Lecture Notes on Computer Science. Pps 303-323. Springer
   Verlag, New York, 1990.
      The design of pictorial databases based upon the theory of
      symbolic projections.
Chang, C.C., and Lee, S.Y.
   Pattern Recognition 24(7), 675-680, 1991.
      Retrieval of similar pictures on pictorial databases.
Chaudhry, Anjali and Roy, Arup.
   In Proceedings of the 14th International Online Meeting. London.
   369-378, December, 1990. Learned Information, Oxford and New
   Jersey.
      Art records treasury system: picture retrieval through image
      databases.
Cherry E.C., and Gouriet G.G.
   Proc.IEE 100, part 3, 1953.
      Some possibilities for the compression of TV signals.
Clark R.S. (Ed)
   Frost & Sullivan. New York. 1992.
      Image Market '92. A strategic assessment of the international
      image and graphics management marketplace.
Clarkson, M.A.
   Hitting warp speed for LANs.
      Byte, 18(3), 123-128, March 1993.
Cleverdon, C.W. and Lesk, M.E.
   Aslib-Cranfield research project reports (2 vols). Aslib
   (London). 1966.
      Factors determining the performance of indexing systems.

Cleverdon, Cyril
Aslib Proceedings 19(6), 173-194, June 1987.
The Cranfield tests on index language devices.
Cookson, Clive.
Financial Times, October 11th 1990.
First auditions for the multimedia show.
Cooper, Deborah, and Oker, Jim.
In Bearman, D. (Ed.). Proc. Int. Conf. Sheraton Station Square, Pittsburgh, October 14-16 1991. Hypermedia and Interactivity in Museums. Archives & Museum Informatics, Pittsburgh. Pages 90-113.
History information stations at the Oakland Museum.
Cote, Raymond; Diehl, Stanford.
Byte 17(5), 208-234, May 1992.
Monitors; beyond VGA.
Cowen, A., Hartley P., and Workman, A.
Image Processing, 44-46, Autumn 1989.
Medical archiving: a picture of health.
Cumani, A., Guidicci, A., and Grattoni, P.
Pattern Recognition, 24(7), 661-673, 1991.
Image description of dynamic scenes.
Dackow, Tom
Personal Communication from Q Systems Research Corporation, 75, 6th Avenue, New York, NY 10012.
Daneels, D., Van Campenhout, D., Niblack, W., Equitz, W., Barber, R., Bellon, E., and Fierens, F.
In Niblack, W. (Ed), Storage and retrieval for image and video databases, Proceedings of the SPIE, Volume 1908, pages 226-233. San Jose, California, February 1993.
Interactive outlining: an improved approach using active contours.
Danziger, Pamela N.
Database, 13-17, August 1990.
Picture databases; a practical approach to picture retrieval.
Dash, R.K.
Dr. Dobb's Journal, 44-49, July 1993.
Image processing using quadtrees.
Davcev, D., Cakmakov, D., and Kabukovski, V.
Computer Communications, 15(3), 177-184, April 1992.
Distributed multimedia information retrieval systems.
Delouis, Dominique.
In Hemsley, J (Ed). Proceedings of the 1993 Electronic Imaging and Visual Arts Conference (EVA 93). Published by Brameur and VasariEnterprises, Aldershot, England, 1993. Pages 70-82.
Telecommunications in Museums.
Dickinson, Sven J., Pentland, A.P., and Rosenfeld, A.
CVGIP Image Understanding, 55(2), 130-154, March 1992.
From volumes to views; an approach to 3-D object recognition.

Doszkocs, T.
>In Cochrane, P.A. (Ed.), American Libraries 15(6), 438-441, 443, 1984.
>>Modern subject access in the online age (untitled comments with W.R. Nugent).

Dowe, J.
>In Niblack,W. (Ed), Storage and retrieval for image and video databases, Proceedings of the SPIE, Volume 1908, pages 164-167. San Jose, California, February 1993.
>>Content-based retrieval in multimedia images.

Eakins, J.P.
>Paper presented at the British Computer Society (BCS) Information Retrieval Specialist Group Research Colloquium, Lancaster, April 1992.
>>Pictorial information systems – prospects and problems.

Enser, P.G.B.
>In McEnery, T. (Ed). Proceedings British Computer Society (BCS) 13th Information Retrieval Colloquium, London April 1991. BCS, London 1991.
>>An indexing-free approach to the retrieval of still images.

Enser, P.G.B., and McGregor C.G.
>Personal Communications, August 1992.
>>Analysis of visual information retrieval queries.

Enser, P.G.B.
>Journal of Document and Text Management 1(1), 25-52, 1993.
>>Query analysis in a visual information retrieval context.

Equitz, W.
>Research report, IBM Almaden Research Centre, San Jose, CA, 1993.
>>Using texture for query by image content in QBIC.

Evans, Adrian.
>Report. BBC Film & Videotape Library, Brentford, England, 1991.
>>BBC TELCLASS; basics of concept classification.

Feldman, T.
>BNB Research Fund Report 54. British Library, 1991.
>>Multimedia in the 1990's.

Fink, E.
>Pages 229-232 in Raben, J., et al (eds), Proc Int. Fed. for Information Processing conference on databases in the humanities and social sciences, August 1979, Dartmouth College. North Holland. 1980.
>>Subject access to photographic reproductions of American paintings at the national collection of fine arts.

Francis, R., Nairne, S., and Pring, I.
>Booklets from The Arts Council, London, July 1992.
>>Very Spaghetti; the potential of interactive multimedia in art galleries.
>>Very Spaghetti; background notes for a report on interactive multimedia in art galleries.

Friedlander, L.
In Bearman, D. (Ed.). Proc. Int. Conf. Sheraton Station Square, Pittsburgh, October 14-16 1991. Hypermedia and Interactivity in Museums. Archives & Museum Informatics, Pittsburgh.
Electrifying Shakespeare: modern day technology in a renaissance museum.

Fromont, J.
Information Services & Use 13(2), 155-158, 1993.
State of the art regarding the various standards for contents related to text, still images, sound and video.

Fromont, J., Creff H., and Marie, X.
Information Services & Use 13(2), 159-170, 1993.
The AVI initiative; functional requirements analysis and proposed framework for standardisation.

Gale, John C.
In Proceedings of the 14th Online Information Meeting. London. December 1990. Learned Information. Oxford & New Jersey.
Multimedia – how we get from here to there.

Gonzalez, R.C. and V. Wintz.
Digital image processing (second edition).
Addison-Wesley Publishing Company, Reading Mass. 1987.

Gordon, Catherine.
In Roberts, D.A. (Ed.) Proc. 2nd Conf. Museum Doc. Assoc., 233-244, 1990.
An introduction to ICONCLASS.

Govindaraju, Venu., and Srihari, R.
Advanced Imaging, 5(11), 22-26, November 1990.
Automatic face identification from news photo databases.

Gray, L.
Aslib Information 20 (4), 164-165, 1992.
Information retrieval software; recent developments in the Cardbox family.

Haddon, J.F. and Boyce, J.E.
Electronics and Communication Engineering Journal, April 1993.
Co-occurrence matrices for image analysis

Hale, Diana, and Grant, S.
Proc. Conf. Electronic Imaging & the Visual Arts (EVA). The National Gallery Sainsbury Wing, London. Brameur, Aldershot, July 1992. (No pagination).
A multimedia database for heritage information systems.

Hales, Keith and Jeffcoate, Judy.
Report, Ovum Ltd., 7 Rathbone St., London. 1990.
Document Image Processing: the commercial impact.

Haskell, Barry G., and Steele, R.
Proc. IEEE 69(2), 252-262, February 1981.
Audio and video bit rate reduction.

Heap, C.
Advanced Imaging 8(2), 36-39, 1993.
Photo negative database at the UK's National Railway Museum

Helms, R.M.
IBM Systems Journal 29(3), 313-332, 1990.
Introduction to image technology.

Hemsley, James (Ed.).
    Proceedings of a Conference "Electronic Imaging and the Visual
    Arts". ("EVA 93") The National Gallery, London, July, 1993.
    Published by Brameur & Vasari Enterprises, Aldershot. 1993.
Hine, Graham.
    In Proc. Conf. Electronic Imaging & the Visual Arts (EVA).   The
    National Gallery Sainsbury Wing, London.   Brameur, Aldershot, July
    1992. (No pagination).
        The international art & antique loss register.
Hines, E.L., and Hutchinson, R.A.
    IEE Conference Publication No. 307. 3rd International Conference
    On Image Processing. London. 39-43, July, 1989.
        Application of multi-layer perceptrons to facial feature
        location.
Hirata, K. and T. Kato.
    NEC Research & Development, 34(2). 263-273, 1993.
        Rough sketch-based image information retrieval.
Hoekema, James.
    Interactive Multimedia 1(1), 7-22, October 1990.
        Multimedia design for consumers: the case of Treasures of
        the Smithsonian.
Hoffos, Signe.
    Library & Research Report 87, The British Library Publications
    Unit, Boston Spa., West Yorks., England.
        Multimedia and the interactive display.
Hogan, Matthew, Jorgensen, C, and Jorgensen, P.
    In Proceedings of a Conference on Hypermedia and Interactivity in
    Museums, October 1991, Pittsburgh, published by Archives and
    Museum Informatics, Pittsburgh, 1991, pages 202-221.
        The visual thesaurus in a hypermedia environment; a preliminary
        explanation of conceptual issues and applications.
Hollis, Richard.
    The Electronic Library 11 4/5, 307-309, 1993.
        CDROM versus online: the UK perspective.
Horowitz, Michael L.
    Project Proposal, Information Technology Center, Carnegie Mellon
    University, July 1991a.
        The Alexandria Project.
Horowitz, Michael L.
    Report No. CMU-ITC-91-103, Information Technology Center, Carnegie
    Mellon University, August 1991b.
        An introduction to object-oriented databases and database
        systems.
Huffman, David A.
    Proc I.R.E. 40, 1098-1101, 1952.
        A method for the construction of minimum redundancy
        codes.
Jagadeesh, J.M. and Ali, M.
    Computer 26(8), 86-88, August 1993.
        Framegrabber velociraptor.

Jain, Anil K.
> Proc. IEEE 69(30), 349-389, March 1981.
>> Image data compression: a review.

Karmouch, A., Goldberg M., and Georganas, N.D.
> L'Onde Electrique, 71(4), 7-12, July/August 1991.
>> Design considerations for a multimedia medical communications system.

Kass, M., Witkin, A., and Terzopoulos, D.
> Int. J. Computer Vision, pages 321-331, 1988.
>> Snakes: active contours.

Keefe, Jeanne
> Library Trends 38(4), 659-681, Spring 1990.
>> The image as a document; descriptive programs at Rensslaer.

Kitamoto, A., Zhou C., and Takagi, M.
> In Niblack,W. (Ed), Storage and retrieval for image and video database Proceedings of the SPIE, Volume 1908,
>> pages 60-73. San Jose, California, February 1993.
>> Similarity retrieval of NOAA satellite imagery by graph matching.

Lee, J.H., and Liu, H.T.
> In Anon. IEE Conference Publication No.307. 3rd International Conference on Image Processing, University of Warwick. IEE, London. 1989. Pps 595-598.
>> Digital image coding with high compression ratio.

Lee, J.H, and Philpot, W.D.
> IEEE Trans. Geosci. and Remote Sensing, 29(4), 545-554, July 1991.
>> Spectral texture pattern matching: a classifier for digital imagery.

Le Gall, D.
> Communications of the ACM 34(4), 46-58, April 1991.
>> MPEG: a video compression standard for multimedia applications.

Lelewer, Debra A., and Hirschberg, D.S.
> ACM Computing Surveys 19(3), 262-296, September 1987.
>> Data Compression.

Leonard, Milt.
> Electronic Design, 49-53, May 23rd 1991.
>> IC executes still-picture compression algorithms.

Leung, C.H.C.
> Information Services and Use 10, 391-397, 1990.
>> Architecture of an image database system.

Lewis, M., and Draycott, C.
> In Hemsley, J (Ed). Proceedings of the 1993 Electronic Imaging and and Visual Arts Conference (EVA 93). Published by Brameur and Vasari Enterprises, Aldershot, England, 1993. Pps 160-169.
>> The retrieval, display, and publishing opportunites for a visual database.

LLewellyn, Richard.
> In Bearman, D. (Ed.). Proc. Int. Conf. Sheraton Station Square, Pittsburgh, October 14-16 1991. Hypermedia and Interactivity in Museums. Archives & Museum Informatics, Pittsburgh.
>> Image storage and retrieval: a tool for museum collection management.

Loeb, S.
> IEEE Communications Magazine 30(5), 52-59, May 1992.
>> Delivering interactive multimedia documents over networks.

185

Looms, Peter O.
  In Bearman, D. (Ed.). Proc. Int. Conf. Sheraton Station Square,
  Pittsburgh, October 14-16 1991. Hypermedia and Interactivity
  in Museums. Archives & Museum Informatics, Pittsburgh.
      Economic and design issues of large scale multimedia databases.
Loveria, Greg.
  Byte 18(6), 176-192, May 1993.
      Making the MPC upgrade.
Low, Adrian
  McGraw Hill (Europe), Maidenhead U.K. 1991.
      Introductory computer vision and image processing.
Lunin, Lois.
  Optical Information Systems, 114-130, May-June 1990.
      An overview of electronic image information.
Makins, M. (Managing Editor).
  Harper Collins. 3rd Edition, Glascow U.K. 1991.
      Collins English Dictionary.
Marcus, Aaron., and Van Dam, A.
  Computer, 24(9), 49-66, September 1991.
      User-interface developments in the 90s.
Maurer, H. and Williams, M.R.
  J. Microcomputer Applications, 14, 117-137, 1991.
      Hypermedia systems and other computer support as infra-
      structure for museums.
McLuhan, Marshall.
  University of Toronto Press. Toronto, 1962.
      The Gutenberg Galaxy: the making of typographical man.
Menella D., and Muller A.
  In Proceedings of the 14th International Online Meeting. London.
  55-60, December, 1990. Learned Information, Oxford and New
  Jersey.
      Data capture of compound documents: solutions to the problems.
Miller, R.L.
  Int. J. Remote Sensing 14(4), 655-667, 1993.
      High resolution image processing on low-cost microcomputers.
Mintzer, Fred, and McFall, John D.
  In Proc. SPIE Image Handling and reproduction systems integration,
      San Jose, 1991. Vol.1460, 38-49. SPIE Washington.
      Organization of a system for managing the text and images
      which describe a collection.
Moffett, Jonathan.
  Bulletin of the John Rylands University Library of Manchester
  74(3), 39-52, Autumn 1992.
      The Beazley Archive; making a humanities database accessible
      to the world
Moir, Michael B.
  Archives & Museum Informatics, 6(1), 5-15, Spring 1992.
      The use of optical disc technology to improve access to
      historical photographs.

Mooers, Calvin N.
> American Documentation 5(2), (Editorial), July 1960.
>> Mooers law – or why some retrieval systems are used and others are not.

Mussman, Hans G., and Preuss, D.
> IEEE Trans. Communications COM-25(11), 1425-1423, Nov.1977.
>> Comparison of redundancy reducing codes for facsimile transmission of documents.

Mumford, Lewis.
> Harcourt Brace & World. New York, 1963.
>> Technics and civilization.

Nagy, George, and Shirali, Nagesh.
> Advanced Imaging 6(3), 49-53, March 1991.
>> Automated segmentation of printed pages for browsing.

Nagy, G.
> Image & Vision Computing 3(3), 111-117, August 1985.
>> Image databases.

Neville, Peter.
> MacNews, October 2nd, 1989, 12-15.
>> The Mac shows its true colours.

Niblack, W., Barber, R., Equitz, W., Flickner, M., Glasman, E., Petkovic, D., Yanker, P., Faloutsos, C., and Taubin, G.
> In Niblack, W., (Ed.) Proc. SPIE, Volume 1908, 173-187, 1993.
>> The QBIC project: querying images by content using color, texture and shape.

Nightingale, Charles.
> Chapter 14 in Pearson, Don (Ed.). Image Processing. McGraw-Hill, Maidenhead, U.K. 1991.
>> Image processing in visual telecommunications – a light-hearted critique.

Nugent, W.R.
> In Cochrane, P.A. (Ed.), American Libraries 15(6), 438-441, 443, 1984.
>> Modern subject access in the online age (untitled comments with T.Doszkocs).

Nyquist, H.
> Bell System Technical Journal 3, Page 324, 1924.
>> Certain factors affecting telegraph speed.

Oakley, J., Davis, D.N., and Shann, R.T.
> In Niblack, W. (Ed), Storage and retrieval for image and video databases, Proceedings of the SPIE, Volume 1908, pages 104-114. San Jose, California, February 1993.
>> Manchester visual query language.

O'Connor, Brian C.
> Microcomputers for Information Management 8(2), 119-133, June 1991.
>> Selecting key frames of moving image documents; a digital environment for analysis and navigation.

O'Docherty, M.H., Daskalakis, C.N., Crowther, P.J., Goble, C.A., Ireton, M.A., Oakley, J., and Xydeas, C.S.
> Information Services & Use 11, 345-385, 1991.
>> The design and implementation of a multimedia information system with automatic content retrieval.

Ohlgren, T.H.
    Pages 245-250 in Raben, J., et al (eds), Proc Int. Fed. for Information
    Processing conference on databases in the humanities and
    social sciences, August 1979, Dartmouth College. North Holland.
    1980.
        Subject access to iconographic databases. Theory and
        practice.
O'Mara, William.
    Physics World, 36-41, June 1992.
        LCD dividends.
Ozsoyoglu, G. and H. Wang.
    Example-based graphical based query languages.
        Computer 26(5), 25-37, May 1993.
Parker, Elisabeth Betz.
    Information Technology and Libraries, 289-299, December 1985.
        The Library of Congress non-print optical disk pilot progam.
Patel, P. and C. Underhill.
    Aslib Information, 333-335, September 1992.
        Preview at B.P.; finding the right image.
Pearson, Don (Ed.)
    McGraw-Hill, Maidenhead, U.K. 1991.
        Image processing.
Petersen, Toni.
    Library Trends 38(4), 644-658, Spring 1990.
        Developing a thesaurus for art and architecture.
Peterson, Gwen.
    Advanced Imaging, 6(4), 76-79, April 1991.
        When image meets text; partners at last.
Petterson, Rune.
    Videodisc/Videotex 4(1), 33-36, 1984.
        Laservision videodisc player and personal computer interaction.
Pratt, W.K.
    John Wiley, New York. 1991.
        Digital Image Processing (second edition).
Preston, J.M. (Ed).
    Deventer Kluwer, (2nd Ed.), Antwerp. 1988.
        Compact Disc Interactive – a designers overview.
Price, Mike.
    PC User, 66-72, 25th April, 1990.
        The big squeeze.
Pring, Isobel (Ed.)
    Image Technology in European Museums and Art Galleries Database
    ("ITEM"). Issue 5, April 1993. Published by IVAIN, Suffolk College,
    Ipswich. 1993.
Pring, I.
    Information Services & Use 13(2), 93-102, 1993.
        Video standards and the end user.
Ragusa, J.M., Dologite, D.G., Orwig, G.W., and Mockler, R.J.
    Private   Communication,   June,   1992.   /   (University   of   Central
    Florida).
        Adding   knowledge-assistance   to   PC-based   photographic   image
        database management system.
Rash, W.
    Byte 17(2), 85-87, February 1992.

Multimedia moves beyond the hype: products finally arrive that   solve real business problems.

Reeves, A.H.
IEEE Spectrum 2(5) 58-62, 1965.
Past, present, and future of PCM.

Rickman, R. and T.J. Stonham.
Coding images for database retrieval using neural networks.
3rd NERVES Neural Network Workshop (Grenoble, January 1991).

Rorvig, M.E.
J. Amer Soc. for Information Sci., 44(1), 40-56, 1993.
A method for automatically abstracting visual documents.

Rubinstein, Ben
Private Communication from Cognitive Applications Ltd.,
4 Sillwood Terrace, Brighton BN1 2LR. October 1992.
The micro gallery and the National Gallery.

Ryman, A.
IBM Systems Journal 29(3), 408-420, 1990.
Personal systems image application architecture: lessons
learned from the ImagEdit program.

Salton, Gerard (Ed.).
Prentice-Hall, Englewood Cliffs, New Jersey. 1971.
The SMART retrieval system.

Samadani, R., Han, C., and Katragadda, K.
In Niblack,W. (Ed), Storage and retrieval for image and
video databases. Proceedings of the SPIE, Volume 1908,
pages 50-59. San Jose, California, February 1993.
Content-based events selection from satellite images of the
Aurora.

Samadani, R. and Han, C.
In Niblack,W. (Ed), Storage and retrieval for image and
video databases. Proceedings of the SPIE, Volume 1908,
pages 219-226. San Jose, California, February 1993.
Computer assisted extraction of boundaries and images.

Sandbank, C.P. (Ed).
John Wiley, Chichester and New York. 1990.
Digital Television.

Schmitt, Marilyn.
Proc. Conf. Electronic Imaging & the Visual Arts (EVA). The
National Gallery Sainsbury Wing, London. Brameur, Aldershot, July
1992. (No pagination).
Art historians and the computer; the context for electronic
imaging.

Schneider, Uwe, and Strack, R.
In SPIE Image Processing Interchange, Vol. 1659, 288-298, 1992. Int.
Soc. Optical Eng., Bellingham, WA.
APART; system for the acquisition, processing, archiving,
and retrieval of digital images in an open, distributed
imaging environment.

Seloff, Gary.
    Library Trends 38(4), 682-696, Spring 1990.
        Automated access to the NASA-JSC image archives.
        Retrieving information with interactive videodiscs.
Sezan, M. Ibrahim, and Tekalp, A.M.
    Optical Engineering 29(5), 393-404, May 1990.
        Survey of recent developments in digital image restoration.
Shandle, Jack.
    Electronics, 48-53, June 1991
        Multimedia computing hits a sour note.
Shann, R., Davis, D., Oakley, J., and White, F.
    In Niblack,W. (Ed), Storage and retrieval for image and
    video databases. Proceedings of the SPIE, Volume 1908,
    pages 188-197. San Jose, California, February 1993.
        Detection and characterisation of Carboniferous Foraminifera
        for content-based retrieval from an image database.
Shannon, C.E.
    Bell System Technical Journal 30(1), 50-64, 1951.
        Prediction and entropy of printed English.
Shetler, Tim.
    Byte, 221-226, February 1990.
        Birth of the Blob.
Smarte, Gene.
    Byte 17(5), page 42, May 1992.
        Active-colour notebooks arrive.
Smith, Merril W. and Purcell, P.A.
    Proc. Conf. Electronic Imaging & the Visual Arts (EVA). The
    National Gallery Sainsbury Wing, London. Brameur, Aldershot, July
    1992. (No pagination).
        Developments in image technology for arts information.
Smura, Edwin J.
    Computer 16(3), 41-50, March 1983.
        Record structures for advanced information systems.
Snow, Maryly.
    In Petersen, Toni (Ed.). AAT Bulletin Number 19, 1991. AAT,
    Williamstown, Mass.
        The AAT browser at the University of California, Berkeley.
Soares, L.F.G., Casanova, M.A., and Colcher, S.
    Information Services & Use 13(2), 131-139, 1993.
        An architecture for hypermedia systems using MHEG standard
        objects interchange.
Sowizral, Henry A.
    In Williams M.E.(ed). Annual Review of Information Science and
    Technology. Knowledge Industry Publications, White Plains. Volume
    20, Chapter 7, 179-199, 1985.
        Expert Systems.
Sperling, George.
    Science 210(4771), November 1980, 797-799.
        Bandwidth requirements for video transmission of
        American Sign Language and finger spelling.

Stern, Barrie T., and Campbell, Robert.
Chapter 8 in Oppenheim, Charles (Ed), CD-ROM: fundamentals to
applications. Butterworths. London. 1988.
ADONIS; the story so far.

Stewart, B.K., Honeyman, J.C., Dwyer, S.J.
Computerized Medical Imaging and Graphics 15(3), 161-169, 1991.
Picture archiving and communication system (PACS) network-
ing: three implementation strategies.

Stoneman, Geoffrey.
The Electronic Library 11, 4/5, 299-302, August/October 1993.
Worldwide trends in CD-ROM publishing.

Strack, Rudiger and Neumann, L.
Proc. Conf. Electronic Imaging & the Visual Arts (EVA). The
National Gallery Sainsbury Wing, London. Brameur, Aldershot, July
1992. (No pagination).
Object orientated image database for an open imaging
environment.

Sulger, Art.
Dr. Dobbs Journal, 60-106, August 1993.
Indexing Image Databases.

Sustik, Joan M. and Brooks T.A.
J. Amer. Soc. for Information Science 34(6), 424-432,
November 1983.
Retrieving information with interactive videodiscs.

Swain, M.J.
In Niblack,W. (Ed), Storage and retrieval for image and video
databases. Proceedings of the SPIE, Volume 1908, pages 95-103.
San Jose, California, February 1993.
Interactive indexing into image databases.

Taira, R,K., Stewart, B.K., and Sinha, U.
Computerized Medical Imaging and Graphics 15(3), 171-176, 1991.
PACS database architecture and design.

Thompson, Tom, and Smith, B.
Byte 18(10), 81-90, September 1993.
Apple, SGI, blaze video trail.

Tonge, G.J.
In Anon. IEE Conference Publication 307 (as above). 257-263.
Current trends in image processing for broadcast
television.

Toth, A., Bellisio, J.A., Bogels, P.W., and Yasuda H.
IEEE J on Selected Areas in Communications, 11 (1), 1-5, January
1993.
Guest editorial; high definition television and digital video
communications.

Truesdell, Dan.
Advanced Imaging, 7(5), 26, 28, 80, May 1992.
Content based retrieval; imaging in multimedia.

Turtur, A., Prampolini, F., Fantini, M., Guarda, R., and Imperato, M.A.
IBM J. Res. Dev., 35(1/2), 88-96, January/March 1991.
IDB; an image database system.

Van der Starre, J.H.V.
>   In Hemsley, J. (Ed). Proceedings of the 1993 Electronic Imaging
>   and Visual Arts Conference (EVA 93). Published by Brameur and
>   Vasari Enterprises, Aldershot, England, 1993. Pages 84-92.
>>   Visual Arts Network for the exchange of cultural knowledge
>>   (Van Eyck project).

Vaxiviviere, Pascal and Thombre, K.
>   Computer 25(7), 46-54, July 1992.
>>   Celestin; CAD conversion of mechanical drawings.

Virgo, Philip.
>   The Daily Telegraph, November 12th, 1990.
>>   Putting true costs into the frame.

Visser, Friso E.H.
>   In Hemsley, J (Ed). Proceedings of the 1993 Electronic Imaging and
>   Visual Arts Conference (EVA 93). Published by Brameur and Vasari
>   Enterprises, Aldershot, England, 1993. Pages 204-217.
>>   The European museums network; an interactive multimedia
>>   application for the museum visitor.

Wakimoto, K., Shima, M., Tanaka, S., and Maeda, A.
>   In Niblack,W. (Ed), Storage and retrieval for image and
>   video databases. Proceedings of the SPIE, Volume 1908,
>   pages 74-84. San Jose, California, February 1993.
>>   Content-based retrieval applied to drawing image databases.

Waltrich, Joseph B.
>   J. Lightwave Technol., 11(1), 70-75, January 1993.
>>   Digital video compression – an overview.

Wanning, Tyne.
>   In Proceedings of a Conference on Hypermedia and Interactivity in
>   Museums, October 1991, Pittsburgh, published by Archives and
>   Museum Informatics, Pittsburgh, 1991, pages 57-61.
>>   Image databases for museum staff, visitors, and the outside
>>   world.

Weems, Charles C.
>   Proceedings of the IEEE, 79(4), 537-547, April 1991.
>>   Architectural requirements of image understanding
>>   with respect to parallel processing.

Wilson, Roger.
>   Report from Dragonflair Ltd., PO Box 5, Church Stretton, Shrop-
>   shire SY6 6ZZ, England. 1991.
>>   The market for multimedia.

Yeh, C.L
>   In Anon. IEE Conference Publication 307 (as above). 599-603
>>   A lossless progressive transmission technique for image
>>   browsing.

Yeung, T. and B. Burton B., and Wong, N.
>   Aslib Proceedings, 44(11/12), 386-392, Nov-Dec 1992.
>>   Management and visual resources in Hong Kong Polytechnic
>>   Library; the case of the slide collection.

Woolsey, K., and Semper R.
In Bearman D. (Ed.), 1991 (q.v.) pps 46-52.
Multimedia in public space.

GLOSSARY AND LIST OF ACRONYMS

Note about use

An acronym may appear alphabetically ordered by its letters, and also alphabetically by its words followed by a more complete explanation.

....

Example 1
ISO
          International Standards Organisation

....

This entry only appears once, ordered by ISO.   No further explanation is included.

....

Example 2.
CLUT
          Colour Lookup Table

Colour Lookup Table
          A table containing a limited number of locations, say 256 or 8 bit locations, each controlling a set of RGB values which produce...

....

In this case it is considered that an explanation is needed.   Having found the meaning under **CLUT**,   a user will find the explanation under **Colour Lookup Table (CLUT)**

AAT
          Art & Architecture Thesaurus.

Adaptive Delta Pulse Code Modulation
          A method of encoding audio signals from changes between amplitude levels. It is used in CD-I systems.

ADPCM
          Adaptive Delta Pulse Code Modulation

Aliasing

A jagged appearance noticeable on curves or diagonals displayed on a CRT screen, indicating inadequate resolution. The cause may be the use of data originally inadequately sampled. "Anti-aliasing" can be provided by passing signals through a low pass filter to smooth fast transitions, or by automatically adjusting the brightness level of pixels near an edge.

AMLCD

Active Matrix Supertwisted Nematic Liquid Crystal Diode.

Analogue Digital (A/D) Convertor

An electronic circuit used to convert a smoothly varying waveform (as, for example, a television picture waveform) into digital values.

ANSI

American National Standards Institute.

Art & Architecture Thesaurus

A thesaurus to assist in the indexing of images originated at Rensselaer Polytechnic in 1979.

Ascender

The upper part of the characters "bdfh".

ASCII

American Standard Code for Information Interchange.

Barrel shifter

Graphic software capable of manipulating pixel arrays *en bloc*, performing extremely fast shift operations in a single cycle; it can shift as many bits to new locations as it has bits. For example, a 32-bit barrel shifter can shift a 32-bit word by up to 32-bit locations in a single cycle. It also enables a field of pixels to be rotated.

Bezier Curve

A means of creating a smooth curve on a displayed image often with a facility comprising turning or levering "handles". A handle is a tangential line connecting to the curve. By moving handle the radius of the curve may be "levered" to assume a new radius.

Bi-level

A term used to describe a display in which pixels are either on or off – that is the system is able to reproduce only either "black" or "white" pixels.

Bit Map

A method of organizing a CRT display where (in a black-and-white display) each pixel in a particular position on the screen is controlled by a 0 or 1 bit in an associated memory. In grey-scale or colour displays there are as many memories ("Bit Planes") as there are bits to define the value of a screen pixel. Thus there would be one bit in each of 8 memories in order to represent the value of an 8 bit pixel.

Bit Planes

Memories which store the component digits of a pixel in order to speed up changes in a CRT display. For instance, a four-bit code could control a pixel to display any one out of 16 grey levels on a CRT. Four digits delivered simultaneously from four bit planes in parallel can be delivered four times faster than serial delivery from a single store.

BLOB

Binary Large Object. A description of an object which may be of any type, including an image, occupying a field in a database particularly in relational database management systems. BLOBs are indexed with words. For retrieval and storage purposes they are managed like any other record although they may be very large.

Bradford's Law

Bradford's Law states that the number of scientific periodicals in a collection for the nucleus and succeeding zones will be as 1, n, n^2 ....etc. This effect is described by similar laws in other branches of human endeavour where there is a highly used "core", outside of which there are successive zones of steadily increasing size with steadily decreasing usage.

Camcorder

A television camera, microphone, and recording tape integrated into one portable unit.

Candela (Cd)

The SI unit of luminous intensity. It is equivalent to the luminous intensity of a black body normal to the surface at specified conditions of temperature and pressure.

CAV

Constant Angular Velocity – the mode of rotation of discs such as gramophone (phonograph) records, floppy discs and hard discs. The driving motor runs at a constant speed, so that the much larger available area of an outer track holds only the same amount of data as an inner track.

CCD

Charge Coupled Device.

CCIR
Consultative Commission for International Radio Communication.

CCITT
Consultative Committee for International Telegraphs and Telephones.

CD
Compact disc.

CD-I
Compact Disc Interactive.

CD-R
Compact Disc Writable. A CD created without the need for certain intermediate processes normally used to prepare it. CD-R is used for creating Kodak Photo-CDs.

CD-ROM
Compact Disk Read Only Memory.

CD-ROM XA
Compact Disc Read Only Memory Extended Architecture. Its major feature is the interleaving of ADPCM audio data with graphical data.

CD-TV
Compact Disc – Television.

CD-V
Compact Disc Video.

Cel Animation
A method of animation in which motion is conveyed by adjustments to individual elements in successive frames.

CGA
Colour Graphics Adaptor.

CGM
Computer Graphics Metafile.

Charge coupled device
A semi-conductor element in which data is stored as an electrical charge which may be transferred to an adjacent, similar, element by a control pulse. In a CCD image sensor, a charge is generated when light is focused upon it. Sensors may be arranged in the form of a strip of CCD elements associated with an electronic transport system. After a given light exposure time, the charges are shifted by the transport system along to an output terminal where they represent a bit-by-bit serial representation of the light reflected from a strip of the image.

Chroma
>Synonym for Saturation.

Chrominance
>The difference between a colour and a specified reference colour of equal brightness, representing the hue and saturation values of that colour.

Chrominance Signal
>A signal representing the colour of a given point in an image.

Clip Art
>Files of useful drawings, logos, etc., which can be bought as a software package from which any object may be lifted into a user's design. For example when a diagram of a computer network is drawn, a clip-art representation of a microcomputer can be lifted out of the package and inserted in as many places as necessary on the diagram.

CLUT
>Colour Lookup Table.

CLV
>Constant Linear Velocity – a mode of rotation used for CDs. The motor speed is varied so that when the head is over an outer track the disc rotates more slowly, but considerably faster when the head is over an inner track. As a result each track can be filled with the maximum possible amount of data.

CMS
>Colour Management System.

CMYK
>Cyan Mauve Yellow Black(Key), the absorptive colours used in colour printing. A printed combination may be made to match a CRT radiated colour produced by RGB combination.

CNAPS
>Connective Network of Adaptive Processors.

Codec
>A "Coder-decoder" for compressing and decompressing pictures in a video conferencing service.

Colour Graphics Adapter
>A printed circuit board installed in early IBM or IBM-compatible PCs. It provides for 320 x 200 pixels in 4 colours.

Colour Lookup Table
>A table containing a limited number of locations, say 256 8-bit locations, each controlling a set of RGB values which select a far larger number of different colours, say 256 x 256 x 256 (24-bit) alternatives. The table of 8-bit locations provides a far larger number of choices than would be possible by using the 8-bit number for directly selecting different colours. The numbers in the table may be changed to, say, 134

x 223 x 120. The system provides for 2^8 colours displayed at one time out of any 2^{24} colours.

Colour Temperature
The colour of nominally white light, more accurately defined as the temperature of the source generating it. Thus a low intensity source such as a candle produces a yellowish light at a temperature of 1800 degrees Kelvin, while clear sunlight represents a temperature of 25,000 degrees Kelvin.

Computer Graphics Metafile
A method of encoding graphic elements so that graphics can be more easily exchanged between programs.

Convolution
The combining of two sets of pixel intensity levels into a single value. The combination is effected by overlaying a set of pixels in an image with a set of pixels in a mask and executing the convolution with an algorithm.

CRT
Cathode Ray Tube.

CYMK
The "primary" reflected colours – Cyan, Yellow, Magenta and Key (Black).

D/A (Digital Analogue) Convertor
An electronic circuit used, for example, to convert digitized intensity levels into smoothly varying analogue waveforms suitable for varying the intensity of a Cathode Ray Tube beam.

Three such convertors are used for colour CRTs to convert the three digitized signals representing Red, Green, and Blue into analogue intensity levels for the three beams of the tube. Speed problems have almost disappeared in recent years – 8-bit D/A convertors are available to be clocked at up to 450 MHz.

DCT
Discrete Cosine Transform. The processing operation performed on pixel blocks of an image, typically 8 x 8, in which the cosine terms of a Fourier transformation are retained and coded, the result being codes containing runs of consecutive zeros. This presents the opportunity for run length coding to achieve compression in such schemes as the JPEG scheme.

Descenders
The lower part of the characters "gpqy".

Desktop Publishing

The preparation of material ready for printing, or of the printed material itself, using inexpensive equipment and DTP software. DTP became possible in the period 1984 to 1986 with the advent of the Apple Macintosh microcomputer, and the Hewlett Packard LaserJet printer using Japanese Canon laser technology.

Digital Television

The benefits of digitisation in overcoming problems associated with noise and amplification, and the comparative ease with which processing may be carried out in digital systems are well known.

If PAL analogue broadcast television pictures were to be converted into digital format, the equivalent bit rate would be about 216 Mbps. To be transmitted through an existing 8 MHz TV channel, the signals must be compressed so that they run at a bit rate of about 16 Mbits per second.

If methods of processing the signal combined with currently available methods of compression were to be adopted, many more TV channels within the presently allocated bandwidth could be made available. See also High Definition Television.

Digital Video Interactive

A system developed by General Electric/RCA, subsequently further developed by Intel, to enable video data to run for one hour on a Digital Video Interactive (DVI) disk – the same size as a CD-ROM disk.

DIP

Document Image Processing.

Dithering

A method of halftone printing with a laser printer by sub-dividing a bit-mapped area into small blocks of pixels – say 4 x 4 blocks - and filling them with from 0 to 16 pixels in some pre-arranged pattern corresponding to the average brightness detected in corresponding areas of the original image. See also Halftone.

Document Image Processing

A technique for reducing the amount of paperwork and improving access to it in business organisations by photographing or scanning business documents, indexing them, and storing them in a computer. When the document is needed it is retrieved and viewed on a VDU of which there may be dozens or hundreds scattered around the organisation. If pictures or images are contained within the image of a business document they will be retrieved with it.

DTP

Desktop Publishing.

DVI

Digital Video Interactive.

EGA
> Enhanced Graphic Adaptor.

Electroluminescent display panel
> A possible replacement for a CRT display consisting of a flat panel display composed of a large number of small elements each comprising a sandwich of a phosphor layer and electrodes. The phosphor glows when a voltage is applied to the electrodes. The system requires a rather elaborate high-voltage driving circuit arrangement. EL panels have been used in portable micro-computers. Large screens up to 18" in width have been manufactured.

Electronic Library Image Service for Europe (ELISE)
> A programme operated by the IBM UK Scientific Centre, De Montfort University, Leicester, The Victoria & Albert Museum, and Bibliotheque Publique D'Information, Paris, with the intention of exchanging images via the ISDN.

ELISE
> Electronic Library Image Service for Europe.

Enhanced Graphics Adaptor
> An improved method of display introduced by IBM. EGA is normally 640 x 480 pixels with 16 colours.

Exhaustivity
> Depth of indexing.

Extended Definition Television (EDTV).
> See High Definition Television.

Fibreoptic transmission
> Fibreoptic communication is achieved by modulating a light source such as a Light Emitting Diode (LED), or for greater energy a laser, with digital electrical signals. The modulated light is propagated along a thin glass fibre and detected the other end by a photodiode which generates electrical signals when light falls on it. Laser-generated single-frequency data can travel very long distances with little attenuation.

Fourier analysis
> The breaking down of a complex waveform into the set of sinusoidal waveforms of which it is composed.

Fractal
> A property of many objects where small portions resemble larger portions as in ferns, snowflakes, coastlines, etc. Codes may be devised to eliminate redundant information, so images may be scaled-up or scaled-down, thereby providing very high compression ratios.

Frame grabber
A device for capturing a video frame and storing it on a computer. To capture colour a frame grabber converts the YUV to RGB values by sampling the colour sub-carrier. The best conversion is obtained by 4:4:4 sampling – i.e four samples of each component. 4:1:1, for example, would provide poor colour.

Fuzzy Logic
A method of representing smoothly variable functions in digital form. Fuzzy logic has an application in image matching where a match is deemed to occur when a query-picture approximately matches a picture in a database. Fuzzy logic enables a matching decision to be made even if the matching is inexact.

Gamma Correction
A correction factor applied to a cathode ray tube monitor to provide linearity between intensity level and phosphor brilliance.

Genlock
The means by which two video sources are synchronised so that, for instance, an image from one source and text from another may be viewed as a stationary composite single picture.

GIF
Graphics Interchange Format.

GKS Standard
The Graphics Kernel System Standard, now an ISO standard, which defines the "primitive" elements from which an image may be constructed – lines, arcs, polygons, etc. The elements may be described by a standard code called CGM (Computer Graphics Metafile).

Gouraud shading
A means of altering individual pixels to produce smooth changes in appearance.

Gradient
A gradient in an image is formed by the difference in the intensity levels of a string of pixels on either side of a continuity such as an edge.

Graphics Interchange Format (GIF)
A hardware-independent protocol devised by Compuserve Inc., for the interchange of graphics data. It is defined in blocks and sub-blocks.

Graphics Signal Processor (GSP)
A GSP consists of two separate processors – the Graphics Processor, which receives CPU commands from a special instruction set, and the Display Processor. Both have access to a special form of buffer memory – a display Video Random Access Memory (VRAM).

A GSP, given the appropriate command, can execute complex operations on large blocks of pixels and can address (typically) 128 Mbits of memory – adequate to hold high resolution representations of pages to be displayed or printed in colour.

Graphics User Interface (GUI)

The part of a computer which gives rise to the "look and feel" of the machine – namely the screen and the method of controlling it. The GUI was invented by Xerox and adopted by Apple with its WIMP arrangements – windows, icons, mouse and pop up menu. For the first time a computer could be controlled by pointing and selecting instead of typing exactly correct code commands.

Grey scale

See Halftone.

GSP

Graphics Signal Processor.

Halftone

An illustration broken up into dots for printed reproduction. The dots are created by photographing the illustration through a fine screen. For representing, say, 256 shades in a digital tonal scale form, each value in the scale would be represented by an 8-bit number.

HDTV

See High Definition Television.

High Definition Television (HDTV)

HDTV has applications in high quality text and image display for information systems, as well as for entertainment TV. It impacts semiconductors, display devices, and general consumer electronics and provides improved viewing approaching that of a cinema theatre. The number of lines is increased so that more detail becomes visible and the screen is made considerably wider.

A variation called Extended Definition Television (EDTV) – an improved but compatible version of the existing NTSC system – is a contender for adoption in the US.

Histogram

The representation of the number of occurrences of a pixel value in an image as the height of a column or the length of a row.

HSI

Hue-Saturation-Intensity.

HSV

An alternative to RGB as a way of specifying a colour. It is obtained by combining hue, saturation, and value (brightness) - properties which are more amenable for describing a colour in a way which relates to human perception.

Hue

A colour named from its subjective appearance and determined by the frequency of its radiated energy.

Huffman Code

A code in which the shortest code group is allocated to the symbol with the highest probability of occurrence, and the longest to the symbol with the lowest probability of occurrence. Thus in the English language, the letter "e" will be allocated the shortest code, and a letter such as "q" the longest.

Hypercard

An Apple software product launched in 1987. A form of database using a card-like display with the means of jumping from one card to another and for controlling external peripheral units.

Hypermedia

A synonym for multimedia.

Hypermedia Time-Based Structuring Language (HyTime)

An ANSI/ISO standard (ISO 10744) specifying how hypermedia document components may be represented using the Standard General Markup Language (SGML). It covers document structures, association of objects in documents with hyperlinks, and related matters.

Hypertext

A word coined by Ted Nelson in 1981 describing software which breaks up text into non-linear inter-connected chunks enabling access from different perspectives.

HyTime

Hypermedia Time-Based Structuring Language.

Icon

1. A pictorial representation of an object, for example a folder.
2. The miniature representation of a complete picture.

ICONCLASS

A thesaurus consisting of 17 volumes of hierarchically arranged codes associated with a textual description in English, designed for classifying the content and subject matter of fine art material.

IIF

Image Interchange Facility.

Ikon

See Icon.

IKS
Image Kernel System.

Illustrator
Proprietary name of software originated by Adobe Inc. who also designed Postcript and which is used in conjunction with it. It provides for enhanced typographic and artistic effects in DTP systems.

Image Interchange Facility (IIF)
A Standard (ISO 12087-3) under consideration by ISO and others for defining a format for exchanging structured image data, including exchange over international telecoms services.

Image Kernel System
A variation of PIK devised by Lowell University, Massachusetts, intended as a "portable image standard" – that is a "device independent" framework enabling images to be transferred between different types of machine.

Integrated Services Digital Network (ISDN)
A telecommunications network arranged between PTTs overlaying the conventional telephone network and providing a user with either two 64 Kbps channels, one normally used for digitized voice, or with 32 64 Kbps channels to be normally used for connecting a PBX. Extra narrow-band channels are included for control purposes.

Interface
1. The boundary between computer, and peripheral devices or functions. The word may be used to include details ranging from plug and socket pin connections to quite complex control software.
2. The boundary between the device presenting information and the human observing it.

IPSS
International Packet Switched Service.

IRE Levels
Standardised levels used in video cameras, originally agreed by the Institute of Radio Engineers. In NTSC video signals, 140 IRE corresponds to 1 volt peak-to-peak.

ISDN
Integrated Services Digital Network.

ISO
International Standards Organization.

IT
Information Technology.

Joint Photographic Experts Group (JPEG)

The name of the committee which wrote a compression Standard, also used to refer to the compression Standard for still images which the committee devised. It covers the compression of colour pictures up to 24 bit and grey-scale (halftone) pictures.

The compression method is based on Discrete Cosine Transformation followed by Run Length Coding, together with the development of special JPEG chips to implement an algorithm and obtain image compression/decompression.

JPEG

Joint Photographic Experts Group.

Kbps

Kilobits per second.

Laser

(Light Amplification by Stimulated Emission of Radiation). A laser consists of a cavity (The Fabry-Perot cavity) with partially reflecting mirrors at either end. In a semiconductor laser a layer of semiconducting material inserted into a p-n sandwich forms the waveguide cavity. Radiation occurs and the dimensions of the cavity reinforce radiation at a particular wavelength by resonant reflections between the mirrors.

The extraordinary benefits of a laser light beam for communication, industrial, or control purpose is that the light is radiated at a virtually single frequency, very short, wavelength with the power concentrated into an extremely narrow beam. The beam may be easily controlled from its electrical source and optically by using collimating optics followed by directing mirrors.

LCD

Liquid Crystal Display.

LCLV

Liquid Crystal Light Valve.

LED

Light Emitting Diode.

Luminance Signal

A signal representing the brightness value at a given point in an image.

Luminosity, Luminance

Synonyms for Brightness.

Mask

1. A technique used in image processing where a grid or mask containing intensity values is successively applied to adjacent areas of an image in order to produce a new combination of values in the area to alter its characteristics. See Convolution.

2. A bounded area of any shape or size which can be applied to an image in order to prevent that area from being painted or filled.

Mbps
> Megabits per second.

MHEG
> Multimedia and Hypermedia Information Coding Expert Group.

Microfiche
> See Microforms.

Microfilm
> See Microforms.

Microforms
> Micrographic Systems provide for the creation, processing, retrieval, and reproduction of small images for viewing. Microforms are photographs of images, often from printed pages, which have been reduced in size for compact storage. Special machines are available for page photography to produce microforms which usually operate on a step and repeat basis using either a flat bed or rotary method.
> Microfiche contain a number of film frames on a card while microfilm usually refers to images in film-strip form.

MIDI
> Musical Instruments Digital Interface.

MIT
> Massachusetts Institute of Technology.

Modulation Transfer Function
> An objective method of measuring and expressing the resolution of a display in terms of the response to a sinewave.

Moire Fringe Pattern
> A patterned effect formed by the intersection of sets of lines at particular angles, or by dots of different pitches.

MPC
> Multimedia Personal Computer.

MPEG
> Motion Picture Expert Group, also used to refer to a compression Standard for moving images devised by the Group.

Multimedia
> A computer-controlled system embodying at least two of the media text, images, pictures, sound, video, motion video, or graphics.

Multimedia and Hypermedia Information Coding Expert Group (MHEG).
> A group considering methods of standardising object and interlinking data in multimedia disc-based publications, and perhaps ultimately in home entertainment systems. The proposed Standard will deal with Input Objects (e.g.menus), Output Objects (e.g. graphics), Composite Objects embodying both, and Hyperobjects – linked input and output objects.

Multimedia Personal Computer (MPC)

A personal computer which includes a CD-ROM drive, an audio adaptor, Microsoft Windows with Multimedia Extensions and speakers or headphones. This is the MPC Marketing Council's definition so other collections of equipment embodying similar facilities may qualify for a similar definition.

Multiscan Monitor

A monitor capable of altering its scanning rate to accommodate a higher resolution display.

Munsell Colour System

A method devised by Albert Munsell for allocating three attributes to a colour – hue (e.g. red blue green), brightness, and chroma or saturation. Saturation describes the amount of white in a colour; a pale colour has low saturation, but a vivid colour, high saturation.

MUSE

Multiple Sub-Nyquist Sampling Encoding – a Japanese method of data-reduction used in HDTV.

Neural networks

A neural network usually consists of a number of nodes or "neurons" – small computer units whose outputs are the result of input signals modified by weights and threshold levels which can be changed as the result of feedback, enabling the network to "learn by example".

Neural network may be used for instance, to learn the data contained in parts of an image sufficiently well for them to be matched against parts of images in a database in order to find the best match.

NTSC

National Television System Committee. US television specification for a 525 line with two 30 frame interlaced fields, repeated at 60 frames per second. During transmission, colour data contained in a narrow segment of the frequency band occupied by the complete signal.

Object Linking and Embedding

A way of individually designating different parts of a document as objects so that they may be appropriately handled by the software.

ODA

Open and/or Office Document Architecture.

OLE

Object Linking and Embedding.

Open and/or Office Document Architecture

ISO 8613 uses the word "open" in the Standard. It describes the encoding of all parts of documents including text and graphics with a view to easing inter-system document exchanges.

PACS

Picture Archiving and Communication Systems. PACS are multimedia systems specifically designed to handle the high speed imaging and transmission of medical data.

PAL

Phase Alternate Line.

Pantone

A colour matching system embodying a large number of standard colours, each referred to by its own number.

Path

A shape produced when a series of points, inserted by the user on to a display, are automatically inter-connected.

PCM

Pulse Code Modulation.

Phase Alternate Line

European specification for a television system formed from two fields of interlaced lines of video and synchronising data to provide a frame containing 625 lines which is displayed 50 times per second. Colour data is contained in a narrow segment of the frequency band occupied by the complete TV signal.

PHIGS

Programmers Hierarchical Graphics System.

Phong Shading

An improved version of Gouraud shading capable of providing more accurate shadows.

Photo-CD

A system introduced by the Kodak Company to enable CD images to be reproduced from domestic 35mm film.

Photodiode

A type of photosensor used in image scanners in a similar manner to a CCD element. A photodiode is a semiconductor device in which the reverse current varies according to the incident light.

Photoelectric Scanning

The original form of image scanning in which light reflected from the image is picked up by a photoelectric cell.

Photon

A packet of electromagnetic light energy.

Photonics

The study and operation of information technology systems using photons instead of electrons.

Photosensor

A device which converts light energy into electrical energy.

Picture-query

A query containing picture content information such as a sketch, and/or colour and texture, to be matched against database pictures. A major alternative or addition to indexing by words.

PIK

Programmers Image Standard.

Pixel

Picture element; the small visible component of a displayed image. In the CRT of a digital computer system, data bits converted to analogue voltages are supplied to beam modulating electrode(s) in order to present a pixel on the screen. The pixel may be specified in 1 bit for black and white, or multi-bit to present a half-tone or colour pixel.

Plasma Panel

A panel divided into small glass cells containing a gas which glows when a voltage is applied. Plasma panels are a potential replacement for the cathode ray tube, being thin, flat, and strong, but they are still relatively expensive.

Postscript

A programming language devised by Adobe Systems which controls the beam of a laser printer to print almost any kind of symbol or illustration. Computer-created dot structures are converted into vectors (quantities having magnitude and direction).

Thus a rectangle would be formed by specifying the co-ordinates of its corners, the thickness of a connecting line, and using the instruction "move to". These data become commands saved in a Postscript file. The benefits are economies in data, versatility, and resolution limited only by the printer in use.

Precision

The extent to which an indexing system is able to retrieve only the relevant items in a database.

Programmers Hierarchical Graphics System (PHIGS)

An extension of GKS for describing 3D graphics by means of data arranged in a tree structure.

Programmers Image Standard (PIK)

Under consideration by ANSI as an image specification for use in medical, machine vision, satellite imaging and other areas.

PSTN
>Public Switched Telephone Network.

PTT
>Post, Telegraph, and Telephone. "PTT" is an acronym (originally for French words) for the national telecommunications authorities in Europe.

Pulse Code Modulation
>A method of digitising analogue signals.

Quadtree
>An operation consisting of the splitting of an image into quadrants and sub-quadrants for analysis purposes.

Quantization
>A division of a continuously variable signal into discrete levels so that each level may be transmitted as a digital code.

Quicktime
>An Apple file format for exchanging data between different machines, including "movie" data- i.e. time-sequenced data

RAMA
>Remote Access to Museum Archives. A telecommunication system to be used between European museums for access to their databases.

Raster
>The pattern of scanning lines on a CRT screen produced by a spot which traces out a line and then rapidly flies back to trace another adjacent line beneath the first, and so on until the whole screen is traced.

Ray-Tracing
>A semi-automatic process provided with certain kinds of imaging software which calculates the effect of imaginary rays of light on surfaces and then alters pixel values to improve realism and to provide a photographic quality.

RBG
>Red Blue Green – the primary colours.

Recall
>The extent to which an indexing system is able to retrieve all the relevant items in a database.

Redundancy
>The addition of information to a message which is more than is strictly necessary to convey the required information. Images often contain redundant information which, when removed, will alter their appearance very little, if at all.

Refresh

A single frame presented on a cathode ray tube rapidly decays. To provide an enduring image a succession of frames are rapidly displayed so that the eye perceives an apparently stationary image.

Rendering

A method of improving the realistic appearance of an image by adding light, shade and shadows to appropriate surfaces using a Ray-Tracing technique.

Resampling

Changing the shape or resolution of an image by discarding pixels or adding additional pixels by interpolation.

Resolution

The capability of an electronic display to reproduce data of a given minimum size so that its detail may be seen.

Resource Interchange File Format (RIFF)

An IBM/Microsoft multimedia file architecture for data exchange. It defines "chunks" of data and covers playback, recording, and exchange.

RGB

The values fed into the Red, Green and Blue guns of a cathode ray tube to provide the right colour by combination in a triad phosphor dot.

RIFF

Resource Interchange File Format.

Run Length Coding

An opportunity arises for compressing the data in a message when there are long strings of identical symbols. For example in images a large area of black could be transmitted by a short code indicating that the following n pixels are "black", instead of transmitting an individual data group for each black pixel.

Saturation

The amount of white light in a colour contributing to the vividness of the Hue. High saturation means a small amount of white.

Screen (printing)

The photograph ("bromide") of a continuous tone illustration, used by printers to make a printing plate, is taken through a piece of glass with closely spaced lines ruled on it. This "screen" produces lines of variable width corresponding to grey levels on the photograph which take up ink on the plate and produce a halftone reproduction. The screen is usually rotated through an angle – often 45 degrees – to avoid interference effects associated with vertical or horizontal lines in the original.

SCSI
> Small Computer System Interface.

SECAM
> Sequential Couleur a Memoire.

Server
> A station or node on a network that provides a communal resource such as managing the means of retrieving and despatching data simultaneously to a number of subscribers.

SGML
> Standard Generalized Markup Language.

Shadow mask tube
> Cathode ray tube for colour containing three electron guns converging on holes through which they are projected onto a phosphor screen containing closely spaced triad phosphor dots.

SIMD
> Single Instruction Multiple Data. A description applicable to a set of parallel processors where the same instruction is applied to all the processors via a common bus.

Skinning
> Applying a surface to cover a wire-frame defining the shape of an object during the process of forming computer models.

Small Computer System Interface (SCSI)
> A fast interface for rapidly exchanging data between disc and memory. A number of external discs or other peripheral devices may be "daisy-chained" into one SCSI interface.

SMDS
> Switched Multimegabit Data Service.

SMPTE Time Code
> A code used to identify a frame in a video sequence. The code was originated by the Society of Motion Picture and Television Engineers and consists of a series of two digit numbers representing hours, minutes, seconds, and number of frames. Any individual frame can be thereby identified.

Sobel operator
> A mask containing values which accentuate edges.

Soliton
> A wave which can travel enormous distances. The phenomenon seems to have been discovered in canals. There is a critical speed at which the displacement wave caused by a barge assumes a circular motion, rolls along the canal's bottom, and returns to the underside of the vessel where it is travelling in the same direction as the vessel.

The important modern equivalent is the discovery of a light wave travelling along a single mode fibre for enormous distances. The effect is due to an interaction between dispersion and the fibre's non-linear properties. In 1991 it was discovered that a soliton can be amplified to make it travel almost limitless distances.

Specificity

The degree of precision of an indexing term.

Staged storage

A method of storage in which the least used records are contained in the least accessible units in a set of storage units. Data is moved up a hierarchy of storage units from the least used storage level to the most used storage level as appropriate.

SuperJanet

A high speed network to interconnect a number of establishments in the United Kingdom, mainly universities, with a data rate of up to about 600 Mbits per second. SuperJanet will use the Asynchronous Transfer Mode (ATM) method of packet switching which is able to carry data in bursts or continuously equally well.

S-VHS

The format introduced by JVC using the same size cassettes as are used in VHS, but providing better resolution.

Switched Multimegabit Data Service

A service designed to supply bandwidth on demand to any user within a group of users.

Tagged Image File Format (TIFF)

A machine-independent standard proposed by Aldus with the support of other companies for the interchange of digital image data between imaging devices such as scanners, cameras, word processors, etc. It includes provision for compression of the kind standardised for Group 3 facsimile machines.

A TIFF image file consists of a header, tag directory, and tags. Tags include such items as Resolution, Length, Width, Colour specification, compression used, etc.

TELCLASS

A classification scheme used for the BBC's film and video tape library which takes account of verbal, schematic, actuality, simulation, technical, and formal attributes of the material contained in the library.

Threshold

The level at which the transition of black to white or white to black is set in a bi-level pixel system.

Thumbnail

A low resolution small size representation of a higher resolution image usually, but not always, contained in the same system. A rapid successive display of sets of thumbnails enables a user to rapidly home in to a wanted picture.

TIFF
Tagged Image File Format

Transform Coding
The conversion of data to a different form – as used, for example, when compressing an image by processing blocks of pixels to reduce redundancy. The new JPEG standard specifies transform coding. It works on the principle that a pattern of all-black or all-white pixels contain very little new information and may be rapidly processed. There is little redundancy in the rapid changes of detail in a chequer-board pattern which must therefore be processed more slowly.

Trichromatic Coefficients
The relative intensities of the primary colours required to combine to produce a specific colour.

Trinitron colour cathode ray tube
A tube resembling a shadow mask tube except that the holes in the mask are vertical slots and the triad phosphor dots on the screen are in the form of stripes.

TTL
Transistor-transistor logic. A logic circuit composed of directly inter-connected transistors designed rapidly to switch a high capacitance load.

Tweening
A method of creating frames in between the key frames which mark the beginning and end of a motion sequence in an animation.

Ultimedia
A name adopted by IBM for its range of multimedia products.

VCR
Video Cassette Recorder.

VDU
Visual Display Unit.

Vector
Many types of image may be broken down into component structures called vectors – lines, arcs, polygons, etc., described in terms of co-ordinates and dimensions. Such a representation is far more compact than a bit-map, and requires much less storage. Its advantages were recognised by Xerox and later Apple who used it in Lisa and in Macintosh's Quickdraw software. Vector software, particularly that designed for CAD/CAM use, provides fast action and storage economies. A form of vector representation has been adopted for the Postscript language.

VGA
Video Graphics Adaptor

VHS

Video Home System.

Video Cassette Recorder

A recorder which records and plays back video and audio signals.

Video Graphics Adaptor (VGA)

Graphic control system introduced by IBM to control a CRT display. Its specification became the *de facto* standard for a CRT resolution of 640 x 480 pixels and 16 colours.

Videophone

An "audiovisual" (sound plus vision) communication system where subscribers can see and talk to each other.

Videotex

The generic name covering systems for disseminating information electronically for display on terminals or modified TV receivers with easily understood control procedures. The original systems were called Teletext and Viewdata.

Virtual Reality

Virtual reality is a computer-generated environment within which the human user appears to reside and with which he or she interacts.

A typical system consists of computer and software, visor embodying head tracking device and LCD stereo colour display, joystick control, and feedback exo-skeletal glove. The system provides the necessary real-time graphics, sound for instructions and effects, motion and tracking data, and a connection point to a LAN enabling users to "meet" each other.

Vision robotics

Systems which attempt to model visual images. Information is contained in a TV-like representation of an image fed into the machine via its camera-eye. A set of stored rules will have been worked out in order to display an image reconstructed from information received by the "eye". At the present state of development the rules enable it to "know" something about very simple schemes – for instance the interior of a living room.

The machine examines edges contained in the electrical image - it might test for vertical edges consisting of a sequence of more than n elements followed by an abrupt change of contrast. When found, the sequence might be labelled "wall boundary". The machine might then explore long, not necessarily continuous, edges which join the wall boundary in order to construct the outline of the complete wall.

Its "recognition" of an object may prompt further actions according to the machine's capabilities.

Visualisation
A technique used to change abstract or complex data into graphical, often three dimensional, form. The significance of very large amounts of difficult to assimilate numerical data then becomes easier to understand.

Visual Thesaurus
A thesaurus in which a range of images are linked to thesaurus terms in such a way that the terms retrieve not only broader, narrower, and related terms, but also the images associated with them.

Vocoder
A device for the reproduction of speech using a very small number of bits per speech sample.

Voxel
Volume pixel. A pixel positioned in a 3D display according to defined X, Y and Z co-ordinates. The 3D effect is produced by the Z data which provides positional information about the location of a pixel on one of many "slices" through the object.

VRAM
Video Random Access Memory.

Warping
The changing of the shape of an image using mathematical operations which make it appear as if the image is printed on a flexible rubber sheet.

WIMP Interface
A program interface that uses windows (W), icons (I), a mouse (M), and pull-down menus (P). Windows and the Macintosh interface are both WIMPs.

WORM
Write Once Read Many.

WP
Word Processing.

WYSIWYG
What You See (on the screen) Is What You Get (on the printer).

XCMD command
A Hypercard command used to execute a resource. The resource may exist on an associated peripheral.

XGA
Extended Graphics Array.

Y signal

A signal transmitted in a television system to represent average brightness.

YUV

The luminance (Y) and chrominance (U,V) components of a colour TV signal.

Zatocode

A code invented by Calvin Mooers for punching holes to represent meanings in the limited number of holes available in edge-notched selector cards.

Zoom

A means of providing an apparent progressive enlargement of a selected area of a screen or window.

INDEX